Date Due

NOV 1 3 1980			
NOV 2 2 1980			
De 16 '80			
De 27 '80			
Ja 6 '81			
Jul 9 '81			
NOV 1 2 1981			
FEB 2 4 1987			
JUL 1 8 1987			
SEP 0 5 1995			

DESPERATE SIEGE
THE BATTLE OF HONG KONG

Also by Ted Ferguson

A WHITE MAN'S COUNTRY
KIT COLEMAN: QUEEN OF HEARTS

TED FERGUSON

DESPERATE SIEGE

THE BATTLE
OF HONG KONG

1980
DOUBLEDAY CANADA LIMITED   TORONTO, ONTARIO
DOUBLEDAY & COMPANY, INC.   GARDEN CITY, NEW YORK

Library of Congress Cataloging in Publication Data

Ferguson, Ted.
    Desperate siege.

    Bibliography
    Includes index.
    1.   Hongkong—Siege, 1941.   I.   Title.
D767.3.F43   940.54'25
ISBN 0-385-14694-9

Library of Congress Catalog Card Number: 78-20071

The maps in this book were prepared by Ann Ball.

To Don Bell, for being a friend

AUTHOR'S NOTE

The Hong Kong expedition was a shameful tragedy. Nearly two thousand Canadian soldiers, poorly trained and badly equipped, were sent to help defend an outpost that Winston Churchill had already written off as expendable. After only seventeen days' fighting, the British colony collapsed on Christmas Day 1941, and the survivors spent the remainder of the war in barbarous POW camps.

Today, over three decades later, the Hong Kong veterans have impaired physical health, recurring nightmares, and a high rate of alcoholism. In traveling across Canada to conduct interviews, I contacted many men who refused to talk about what happened. Others drank heavily during interviews and two men wept as they remembered how friends died.

More than I can possibly say in words, I would like to express my appreciation to those who submitted to extensive questioning in spite of painful memories. I would also like to thank the Canada Council Explorations' program and Alberta Culture for providing the research funds that enabled me not only to interview survivors throughout the country but to delve into the files at the Department of National Defense and Public Archives of Canada in Ottawa.

W. A. MacIntosh of National Defense was particularly helpful, giving me unrestricted access to fifty-odd files containing everything from battlefield strategy and postwar debriefings to personal diaries and letters. The Public Archives, on the other hand, released some files but denied a request for one thick file that, I can only surmise, contains material adding weight to the contention that the Canadian Government mishandled the Hong Kong debacle in the same manner that the United States Government botched the Bay of Pigs invasion.

Vital background data was provided by L. F. Murray of the Canadian War Museum; A. F. Hart of the Department of External Affairs; Philip Reed of the Imperial War Museum, London; J. L. Walford of the Public Records Office, London; A. H. Nelson of the British Museum, London; Carol Mathe of the Winnipeg Public Library; Monique Tessier of the Montreal City Library; Y. P. Yager of the British Columbia Maritime Museum; and Douglas Chueng of the Hong Kong Secretariat.

Two professional researchers, John Davies of Leeds, England, and Nancy Dwyer of Hong Kong, deserve special mention. I would also like to thank Fern McCracken, Mrs. Augusta Lawson, David Bergamini, Joyce Douglas, W. O. Mitchell, Tina James, Gerald Anglin, James H. Gray, Farley Mowat, Nellie Swarbrick, Marion Hagerman, D. E. Monroe, Donald Watt, Frank Howard, Jessie Swaikoski, William Allister, John Patrick Gillese, and Horst Schmid.

TED FERGUSON
Westlock, Alberta

The minute I got off the boat in Hong Kong, I realized that if the Japanese attacked, they'd wipe us out. "We've got no air force, no navy, no place to go," I told my pals. "The Japs can back us up to the sea and even the best goddamned swimmer in the Grenadiers couldn't make it all the way home to Canada." My pals laughed. "We won't have to worry, Wilf. It's them that will be running away."

Former Private WILF LYNCH
in a 1978 interview

DESPERATE SIEGE
THE BATTLE OF HONG KONG

CHAPTER ONE

Hong Kong, July 1, 1941

The damn British. They were so sure of themselves. A race born to govern, the very embodiment of all that was noble and cultured. John Fonseca could not accept that kind of thinking. He felt he was as good as any Englishman; yet the whites who controlled Hong Kong society smugly refused to regard him as an equal. He could eat in the same restaurants, wear the same Western-style clothing, and drive a British car, but he was forbidden to drink gimlets at the Hong Kong Club or buy a ticket for the St. Andrew's Ball.

It was not a question of financial worth. His father, a Portuguese merchant, had made a fortune introducing Grape Nuts Flakes and Gillette razor blades to China in the 1920s. Fonseca had been raised in a mansion and, in a milieu where a man's success was gauged by the number of servants he employed, his father had never had fewer than six. The Depression had destroyed the import business and the family had suffered the humiliation of having to live in a shabby flat their former servants would have disdained. But not for long. While working as a waiter at a posh hotel, the seventeen-year-old Fonseca had purchased a sweepstake ticket that brought a seven-thousand-dollar windfall. He had moved his family into a fine house, bought two cars, and hired three servants.

He was never poor again. With a solid bank account—and a new wardrobe reflecting prosperity—he had had the confidence to persuade the manager of a British import-export company to take him on as a purchasing agent.

The wages were good—and so was the "squeeze," the Oriental version of kickbacks. No one ever directly handed him cash. No promises were spoken, no secret meetings held. While dining at a client's home his wife would find a diamond ring in her soup bowl and silently put it in her purse. An expensive suit would be delivered to his office, along with a note saying the bill would be mailed later (it never was). Or a client stopped his son coming back from school and gave him a brown paper bag, stuffed with ten-pound notes, to take to his father. Almost every businessman he knew used "squeeze" to untangle bureaucratic knots or get merchandise moving faster. Fonseca neither approved nor disapproved: it was simply a fact of life that was as essential to survival in the commercial world as a head for figures and an instinct for a lucrative deal.

No, the English did not reject him because of money. He had plenty, and still any snotty bank clerk, earning one tenth his income, could stumble off the boat and, if he had a letter of introduction, hobnob with the Hong Kong Club elite. Obviously, it was his mother they objected to. His *Chinese* mother. Despite all that rubbish about fair play and justice, the British were racists. He had a British passport, his skin was white, and he had gone to an English school, but there were places in his own homeland where he could not set foot because his father had, in the English view, married a substandard species.

The bloody fools. His mother could trace her ancestry back seven generations. When the Anglos were huddling in caves, the Chinese were weaving silks, casting bronze statues, and writing in a language with two thousand characters. And what did the British bring to this magnificent culture? Opium. In exchange for tea and silk, English merchants brought ships to the China coast bearing opium grown in India. The Anglo greed spawned a country of drug addicts. So how could they feel so superior? So blessed certain that they had a divine right to say what was best for Asia?

Invincible, too. That was something else that troubled him. In 1937, the Imperial Japanese Army had begun butchering its way through China. Five major cities had fallen, including Canton, eighty miles across the bay from Hong Kong. Now several regiments of battle-hardened Japanese soldiers were within striking distance of the Crown colony, but the British were not worried. They arrogantly believed that no puny Orientals would dare start a war with the mighty English. The cocktail parties and dances went on as usual; the beaches and Happy Valley Race Track were crowded; the pipers had already been chosen to perform at the next St. Andrew's Ball.

Fonseca thought it was madness. There were only four infantry battalions stationed at Hong Kong, comprising roughly ten thousand men. The RAF had three obsolete Wildebeeste torpedo bombers and two Walrus amphibians at Kai Tak Airport, while the naval command consisted of three antiquated destroyers, a gunboat, and six motor torpedo boats. With that kind of military power, Hong Kong would be lucky to last a week against a Japanese assault.

Fonseca was aware that his concern was shared by a handful of retired British Army and Royal Navy officers. They had made an appeal for Whitehall to bolster the colony's fortifications and when no satisfactory response was forthcoming, an insurance company executive, A. W. Hughes, had formed the Hong Kong Volunteer Defence Corps in 1934. When he retired to England, the Volunteers came under the command of Major J. J. Paterson. Two thousand civilians—clerks, professors, engineers, men of every occupation—took turns training in an old warehouse and at a two-week summer camp in the countryside. Fonseca, five foot five and bone thin, joined the Volunteers in April 1939. To his amazement, he was a better physical specimen than many of the misfits who stumbled and sweated through weekly drill sessions. Some had never done anything more strenuous than refilling an office inkwell, while others handled their weapons as though they were poisonous snakes.

To make matters worse, their equipment was dreadful: World War I revolvers, rifles, and gas masks. Assigned to a machine-gun unit, Fonseca was given a 1915 Lewis that had been painted so often for inspection that the drum would not turn. Was this any way to get ready for a war? Had British Intelligence missed the rumors that the Japanese were using modern weapons?

Belonging to the Volunteers did nothing to alleviate Fonseca's anxiety. Indeed, it only served to heighten it.

The War Office was well aware of Hong Kong's military deficiencies. Aware, but unwilling to do much about them. For one thing, the outbreak of war with Germany in September 1939, had caught England woefully unprepared. Like the Hong Kong Volunteers, Britons joining the regular army that year had been amazed to find that submachine guns, percussion grenades, and rimless cartridges were almost nonexistent. Furthermore, the tanks were rusty museum pieces, the solar climate helmets had been made for the Boer War, and the RAF had no dive bombers to carry its leftover World War I explosives. By the autumn of 1940, British factories were cranking out munitions at an awesome pace, but most of the hardware was earmarked for the European and Middle Eastern fronts: Hitler's swift conquest of Holland, Belgium, and France and the beginning of the Blitz convinced the Chiefs of Staff that the greatest need was to stop the German advance, not to send weaponry and men to the Far East to await a conflict that was unlikely ever to happen.

Then, too, there was the knowledge that Hong Kong was

expendable. The colony was, after all, a 400-square-mile patch of little strategic importance. Its capture would be scarcely more than a psychological victory for the enemy.

Lord Hastings Ismay, a desk-bound general who became Prime Minister Winston Churchill's Chief of Staff in 1940, deplored the idea of dismissing the colony so callously. While working for the Intelligence Directorate of the War Office in 1933, he had assessed the Far East situation and concluded that an eventual war with Japan was a distinct possibility. He proposed the demilitarization of Hong Kong. Otherwise, he told a War Office conference, the colony and its military personnel would be "needlessly condemned to death." In his postwar memoirs Ismay revealed that his suggestion was received coldly and, in fact, "surprise was expressed that I should hold such defeatist views."

Hong Kong Governor Sir Geoffrey Northcote believed Ismay was a realist, not a defeatist. Writing to Whitehall in October 1940, Northcote urged the withdrawal of the British garrison "in order to avoid the slaughter of civilians and the destruction of property that would follow a Japanese attack."

Neither Ismay nor Northcote was heeded. With nearly all of the influential Britons in Hong Kong complacently saying the colony was an impregnable fortress, it was understandable that no one would listen to a couple of dissenters. Besides, Northcote was on his way out. Thirty-seven years of Colonial Office duty in Africa, mostly on the sun-baked Gold Coast, had ruined his health and, physically exhausted, he was soon to be replaced by a new man, Sir Mark Young.

The Hong Kong residents—and the War Office policy makers—preferred to accept the advice of Major General Edward Grasett, the Toronto-born commander of the British troops in China. Although he had been in the Far East only three years, Grasett was considered an expert on Japanese behavior. He told staff officers and civilians alike that

Japan was bluffing. "The Emperor knows he can best serve his own interests in the Orient by remaining friends with the English and the Americans," he said. "All those threats are merely empty posturing."

However, Grasett did feel that the Hong Kong garrison should be reinforced: the more muscle the colony showed, the warier the Japanese would be. The same month that Northcote expressed his concerns in a memorandum to Whitehall, Grasett put in a request for an extra infantry battalion. The request was denied; the troops were needed elsewhere. Just over a year later, Air Chief Marshal Sir Robert Brooke-Popham declared that Hong Kong could endure a siege for at least six months; yet he did think Grasett was right in recommending additional troops. Brooke-Popham, the newly appointed commander-in-chief in the Far East, sent a series of telegrams to the War Office which came to Churchill's attention. The Prime Minister had no illusions that Hong Kong was impregnable or capable of withstanding a prolonged siege. On January 7, 1941, Churchill wrote a memorandum in which he referred to the Brooke-Popham-Grasett proposal:

"This is all wrong. If Japan goes to war with us there is not the slightest chance of holding Hong Kong or relieving it. It is most unwise to increase the loss we shall suffer there. Instead of increasing the garrison it should be reduced to a symbolical scale. We must avoid frittering away our resources on untenable positions. Japan will think long before declaring war on the British Empire, and whether there are two or six battalions at Hong Kong will make no difference to her choice. I wish we had fewer troops there but to move any would be noticeable and dangerous."

A holder of the Military Cross for gallantry during the Great War, Grasett stubbornly continued to campaign for reinforcements even after he learned of Churchill's decision. When he retired from China Command in July 1941, he stopped off in Ottawa en route to England. There he held lengthy talks with Canada's Chief of General Staff, H. D. G. (Harry) Crerar. If Hong Kong was attacked, Grasett said, he was certain the addition of one or two battalions would render the garrison strong enough to withstand an extensive siege. He did not suggest to Crerar that Canada should supply the manpower, but, the following month, he did make that proposal to the British Chiefs of Staff. Grasett was so convincing that the Chiefs sent a message to Churchill, urging him to abandon his previous stand. To appease his advisers, he did. On September 19 the Dominions Office in London dispatched a Most Secret telegram to the Mackenzie King government, asking Canada to provide one or two battalions for the defense of Hong Kong. Ottawa moved with uncustomary speed and, by October, two battalions had been culled from a carefully prepared list.

None of the messages from London preceding the Canadians' departure for the Far East revealed any concern that there might be more than a few thousand Japanese soldiers entrenched near Hong Kong. There were, in fact, sixty thousand experienced combat soldiers massing on the Chinese border, sixteen miles north of the colony's commercial core. Nor did the messages disclose Churchill's earlier misgivings and his opinion that, in the event of war, Hong Kong would be sacrificed. As Canada had no intelligence-gathering organization of its own in the Far East (it relied on London for data of that nature), nearly two thousand Canadian soldiers were committed to the defense of an isolated British enclave without anyone in Ottawa fully realizing the enormity of the task awaiting them.

CHAPTER TWO

Jamaica, August 1941

The target was one hundred yards away. A Nazi flag flapped lightly over Hut 10 in the prisoner-of-war compound. The boys had wagered ten bucks on his escapade but it meant nothing to Private Dennis Murphy—he was out there, crawling toward the brightly lit internment camp because, more than anything, he was bored stiff.

Since coming to Jamaica in May 1940, the Winnipeg Grenadiers had been assigned to guarding the POW camp and, on occasion, boarding foreign vessels to search for contraband weapons. Four months of dull routine had been enlivened only by rum-drinking bouts in local bars where, if you tossed pennies on the floor, black kids danced and sang. You either made your own excitement, by breaking rules, or you could go stark raving mad.

Murphy, a rule-breaker from away back, had a .303 cradled in his arms. He hated the darn thing. It was forever jamming on the firing range and he could understand why, at Ypres in 1915, Canadian soldiers had thrown their Ross rifles aside and picked up the more efficient Lee-Enfields lying beside dead Britons. Well, unless it jammed again, the single-shot Ross would do nicely for tonight's job.

Murphy stopped crawling. It was a dark night and, although the underbrush outside the barbed-wire fence had been recently cut down, he was sure he was far enough from the camp lights to remain unseen. Smiling to himself, he sighted the rifle. He had not had such fun since he decided to quit a Saskatoon radio station and, knowing it would upset his boss, he introduced a religious program by naming some local merchants considered to be sinners.

He could see two guards, neither of whom he recognized. One was standing by the gate, half asleep, the other walked along the fence, checking for holes. The two hundred prisoners, mostly Nazi sympathizers rounded up in the Caribbean, were in their bunks. Several dozen enemy sailors were mixed in with them and, Murphy suspected, it was the captured seamen who cheered when the flag, a crudely painted black swastika on a piece of white flannel, had been hoisted up that morning. By Jesus, he would give them something to cheer about!

Murphy squeezed off his shot. He was a superb marksman and instinctively he knew he hit the flag dead center. Scrambling to his feet, Murphy sprinted for the trees.

"What the hell's going on?" a sentry shouted. "Who's out there?"

Running and laughing, Murphy escaped. The next time, he thought, I'll be shooting at real Germans and not a crummy flag. For the word was spreading along the barracks grapevine that the Grenadiers would soon be transferring overseas. And where else could they be going except to help stop the Krauts from invading England?

The two battalions chosen for the Hong Kong expedition were not among Canada's finest. The ranks of the Winnipeg Grenadiers and the Royal Rifles of Canada included men who had never thrown a grenade or fired a mortar and, in many cases, had yet to complete their basic training. Mobilized on September 1, 1939, the Grenadiers had protected prairie railway depots and factories before their transfer to Jamaica. The Royal Rifles, a Quebec-based outfit mobilized

July 8, 1940, had performed similar chores in Montreal and Quebec City prior to being posted to Newfoundland where, armed with rifles and Bren guns, they were under orders to fend off German air or submarine invasions.

When the British Government issued its troop request, the Canadian Chiefs of Staff asked Colonel John K. Lawson, Director of Military Training, to analyze the fighting prowess of twenty-six infantry battalions. Lawson divided the battalions into three categories: A(best-trained), B(second-best), and C(insufficiently trained and not recommended for operations). The Grenadiers and Rifles received a C rating.

Colonel W. S. Macklin, Director of Staff Duties, wanted to send an A and B battalion to Hong Kong but he was talked out of it by Major General C. F. Page, General Commanding Officer of 4th Division. Page persuaded Macklin and other military brass that the fittest troops should be shipped to England rather than wasting them on a guard-duty assignment.

In September and October 1941, the Grenadiers and Rifles were brought back to Canada. As neither battalion was at full strength, the Army scoured the nation and found 436 reinforcements, some of whom were sixteen- and seventeen-year-olds with less than six weeks' service. "We got the odds and sods," Captain Wilfred Queen-Hughes, a Grenadier transport officer, said in a 1958 magazine interview. "Literally the sweepings of the depots. Men no other command had wanted and rejected. My God, there was even a hunchback!"

To his chagrin, Colonel Lawson received notification that he was to command the very battalions he had advised against sending. Along with the appointment came a promotion to the rank of brigadier. Lawson's negative assessment of the units' combat readiness prompted General Crerar to schedule week-long weapon-practice sessions for both battalions. Due to a lack of ammunition, the men used empty

mortars and dummy grenades. Crerar either surmised that
the units had overcome the deficiencies Lawson cited or did
not have them in the first place. Whatever his reasoning, he
wrote this memo to Defcnse Minister J. L. Ralston:

"As these units are going to a distant and important
garrison where they will be detached from other Canadian
forces, a primary consideration is that they should be
efficient, well-trained battalions capable of upholding the
credit of the Dominion under any circumstances. The duties
that they carried out (in Jamaica and Newfoundland) were
not in many respects unlike the task that awaits the units to
be sent to Hong Kong. The experience they have will therefore be of no small value to them in their new role. Both
are units of proven efficiency."

By late October the two battalions were issued sub-
tropical clothing and, for security purposes, informed only
that they would be boarding a transport ship in Vancouver.
Hardly anyone figured on a Hong Kong destination; most of
the men thought they were probably going to India for another humdrum assignment.

Ottawa, October 23

Brigadier Lawson was in a terrible mood. Opening and
closing drawers, peering under chairs, poking around in closets, he moved from room to room of his home in the Sandy
Hill area, hunting for the missing ID tag. He did not want
to leave Canada without it. Hanging around his neck, the
tag had become his talisman during the Great War. He had
worn it on the shell-pocked battlefields of France through
four years of the glaring horror in which sixty thousand Canadians added their lives to the eight million death toll.
Now another war was coming. Despite Whitehall's assurances that the Japanese were reluctant to step on the British
lion's tail, Lawson believed just the opposite. Cocky from

their victories over Chiang Kai-shek's tattered army, the invaders were bound to think they could whip the British, too, for in their eyes the English seemed to be effete creatures whose strengths had been sapped by too many years of soft colonial living.

Lawson's wife, Augusta, an attractive, dark-haired woman, entered the living room as he was rifling the bookshelf. She was surprised to see him so agitated. Enlisting as a private in the 101st Edmonton Fusiliers, he had advanced through the ranks by steady, even-tempered devotion. He put in long hours wherever he was stationed—Calgary, Toronto, England, or India—and he often stayed up late in his study, reading military history. When something at the base upset him, he refused to brood or to take it out on her and their two small children. Instead, he would pack the family into the car and go off on a fishing trip. A lithe, quiet-speaking man of fifty-one, his sole vices, if they could be called that, were a regular predinner scotch and soda and his cherished briar pipe.

"It's not upstairs," Augusta told him. "I've looked everywhere. I'm afraid you'll have to go, dear. The train will be leaving without you."

Reluctantly Lawson ended the search. A superstitious person, he felt this was another bad omen. Augusta and her twin sister had recently lost identical strands of pearls on the same day. Now the ID was gone. As he left the house and headed for the train that would carry him to Vancouver, Lawson tried to shrug off the disturbing feeling that the Hong Kong assignment was going to be a calamity.

Saskatchewan, October 25

Sitting alone in the coach, Kay Christie watched for signs of life on the broad prairie. A tractor hauling hay, children playing in a rural schoolyard, cattle grazing in a coulee. Not exactly the most gripping scenes on earth, but at least they gave her something to think about besides the nagging worry over where she was going. Back at Toronto Military Hospital, Captain Hardy told her to make out a will, pick up a steel helmet, and board a Vancouver bound train the next day. "You'll be getting a foreign posting," he said, "but I can't say where. All I can tell you is it won't be England."

Kay had slept badly for the last two nights. She could cope with bombs and bullets if she kept busy, but lying around, an inanimate lump being carted off to an unknown destination, was unnerving. Yet she had no one to blame except herself: she had volunteered for overseas duty because she felt she could serve the nursing profession better in a battle zone than in a convalescent ward. And, for that matter, considerably better than she had before she entered the Royal Canadian Army Medical Corps.

Remembering those days as a private-duty nurse, Kay always smiled. "Baby-sitting rich old ladies" was how a friend described it. Her patients had been bedridden Rosedale matrons who were not even sick. They had just wanted full-time pampering. That, and someone to show off to. One wrinkled old dear had actually scampered happily around the bedroom displaying her dresses (forty-seven in all) and silk stockings (eighty-nine pairs) and her husband's shoes (twenty-eight pairs). "Get me soup, nurse." "Nurse, my pillow's on the floor." "Miss Christie, will you turn on the radio, please?" Kay had felt like a baby sitter, all right. Especially after learning that the doctor employing her was prescribing placebos for the patients because there was nothing physically wrong with them.

Anyway, that was all behind her. She was off to the wars, wherever they were, and moving closer to being the kind of nurse she wanted to be, the kind Aunt Doll had been.

Aunt Doll (her real name was Dorothy) had come from Ireland in 1911 to stay with Kay's family in Little Current, a Georgian Bay settlement. Tall, willowy, and unmarried, she had landed a nursing job at the local doctor's office. When typhoid fever and influenza epidemics swept through Ontario in 1918, killing thousands, Aunt Doll had ridden out on a horse-drawn cutter, enduring blizzards and subzero temperatures, to treat stricken families, sometimes sleeping in the same room with dying patients. She had never accepted a single penny from a poor family: she said it was her sworn duty to help people, not to build her bank account on their suffering.

Aunt Doll had remained in Little Current when the Christies moved to Sudbury in 1920. Kay's father had labored at the INCO plant for a while, then went to Toronto, where he settled into a warehouse superintendent's job at Sun Oil. As a child, Kay had resolved to model herself after Aunt Doll. Quitting school at sixteen, she had done clerical work for a brokerage company so that she could save enough money to study nursing. In 1930—now nineteen and a slender, vivacious, good-natured redhead—Kay had enrolled in the three-year course at Toronto Western Hospital.

What an exhausting experience that had been! Twelve hours a day, six and a half days a week, and, in lieu of salary, room and board at the nurses' residence. With such a punishing schedule, no wonder so many girls had fallen asleep in class. She remembered the afternoon in Room 108 when Professor Blotz was droning on and on about psychology. One hundred student nurses had slumped at wooden desks, facing him. Kay had drifted off, and so had fifty others. Realizing half his class was no longer with him, Blotz had thrown up his hands and stomped from the room. When Kay woke up, only a few heavy sleepers remained.

Whatever happened to the girls of 108? Most had probably married doctors, or patients, and were at home this very minute, deciding whether to have spaghetti or fish for dinner. That was definitely not for her. Like Aunt Doll, Kay was a strong-willed, independent soul who had no intention of giving up her career for domestic bondage.

Kay's thoughts were interrupted by the sound of the con-
ductor's voice. He was telling a passenger that some soldiers
had been disembarking at prairie stations and disappearing.
Kay wondered if the desertions had anything to do with the
mission she was on.

Vancouver, October 27

The *Awatea* was a good ship. Barely five years old, she
had been carrying freight and passengers for New Zealand's
Union Steamship Company until the British Government
commissioned her to transport the two Canadian battalions
across the Pacific. She was 545 feet over all, displaced 3,248
tons, and her 6 steam turbines gave her a respectable maximum speed of 28 knots. But the *Awatea* was made to ac-
commodate only 540 passengers.

The Grenadiers and Rifles discovered this drawback
shortly after their arrival in Vancouver. Marching from the
train yard to a Burrard Inlet pier where they boarded the
ship, the soldiers were dismayed at the sight of the cramped
living quarters. The bulk of the 1,975-man force was placed
on the *Awatea;* 109 officers and men boarded the *Prince
Robert*, a Royal Canadian Navy cruiser accompanying the
larger vessel. Within hours, tempers flared and between 40
and 50 soldiers jumped ship. Armed NCOs and officers con-
fronted the men in a dockside shed and, following a twenty-
minute argument, persuaded them to return.

All the same, the expedition lost fifty-one men. Eight or
nine vanished from the train, roughly twenty others did not
turn up at the embarkation point after furloughs, and the
rest slipped away from the dock while helping load supplies.
Their reasons varied. The most common complaints were
anger at being dispatched on what appeared to be a tedious
posting, an unwillingness to tolerate the *Awatea*'s discom-

forts, and, in the case of extremely young recruits, a sudden fear of leaving home to face an unknown destiny.

The loss of the 50 Grenadiers and one Rifle did not worry Lawson as much as the lack of mechanical transport. The Chiefs of Staff had promised him 212 vehicles, including 104 trucks, 57 Universal carriers, and 45 motorcycles, but no freighter had been provided to depart simultaneously with the *Awatea*. How could he transfer heavy supplies without trucks? How could his men patrol Hong Kong's hilly terrain adequately if they had no Universals? Lawson requested that at least 20 vehicles be loaded in the *Awatea's* two big holds. However, the Quartermaster General's Branch did not act quickly enough and the ship sailed without any motorized transport aboard. (All 212 vehicles were put aboard the American freighter *Don Jose* in Vancouver a week later and, failing to reach Hong Kong before the war started, wound up in the hands of United States forces defending the Philippines.)

The night before the *Awatea* weighed anchor on October 27, Canadian Military Headquarters in London cabled a Most Secret message to Ottawa containing the War Office's latest sentiments concerning the Far East situation. Tojo and his radical advisers had assumed control of the Japanese Government but, according to the War Office, the possibility of war was "unlikely at present." Moreover, the British Chiefs of Staff opined that, should Japan initiate further military expansion, it would "probably be northerly against Russia and not to the south against our forces."

The telegram stated that the Japanese had only three thousand soldiers within a twenty-mile radius of Hong Kong and, if they did attack the colony, the Chinese Army was ready to tear into their rear with ten divisions. As was intended, the message reassured the Canadian militia that it had no reason to be the least bit apprehensive about the Hong Kong venture.

The soldiers on board the *Awatea* found another aggravating fault besides the lack of space. The food was awful. Rifleman Sidney Skelton noted in his diary, "Things began to look bad the first night. Supper time came and the lads waited hours for it and it turned out to be a tripe and onions."

The meals got steadily worse. Instead of tripe, the British crewmen cooked up batch after batch of dried-out mutton, which the Canadians grudgingly ate sitting in their crowded compartments. The unpopular menu was brought to Lawson's attention when several hundred soldiers stood up during a mutton serving and, turning their plates face down, exclaimed in unison, "Baa! Baa! Baa!" The brigadier arranged to have a consignment of fresh beef picked up at Honolulu, a move that, in Grenadier Private Ed Bergen's opinion, "averted a certain mutiny."

The men had other grievances too. There were not enough glasses to go around, so they had to drink the canteen beer from empty jars, helmets, and large ashtrays. Also, the only women on the ship, Kay Christie and May Waters, a chubby, blonde army nurse from Winnipeg, were confined to the officers' section: what right did Lawson have to deny the boys access to feminine company?

On the fourth day out, the forty-odd seasick victims in sickbay were joined by a young Grenadier. He was vomiting and semicomatose. He told the senior medical officer, Dr. John Crawford, he had never suffered from any previous illness and he had never taken medicine or drugs. He died of hypoglycemia a few hours after admission. An officer going through the dead youth's kitbag found a number of syringes and sufficient insulin to last a severe diabetic six months. The soldier had kept his condition secret because he feared being dismissed from active service.

Other than that, the crossing was uneventful. A Fred Astaire–Ginger Rogers movie was shown; a band played "Old Soldiers Never Die" as the officers entered their mess for meals; the warm, calm weather prompted hundreds of soldiers to sleep on the open deck.

Once the *Awatea* left Hawaii, Lawson informed the men that they would be stationed in Hong Kong. His announcement was greeted by a chorus of groans: Hong Kong promised to be as dull as India, Jamaica, and Newfoundland. Yet both battalions displayed great vitality during shipboard drills. Their marksmanship improved slightly and they seemed to throw themselves wholeheartedly into the physical exercises held daily. While the over-all efficiency of the units displeased him, Lawson was delighted to find both battalions had excellent instructors. He was also happy about his top aides, Colonel Pat Hennessey, Lieutenant Colonel W. J. Home and Lieutenant Colonel J. L. R. Sutcliffe. All were dedicated army men with World War I combat experience. If the battalions had a few more months of training, he was sure they could be shaped into Class A or B material.

To prepare the men for their new assignment, Lawson, Dr. Crawford, and others gave lectures on Chinese religion, tropical sanitation, and the supposedly inferior Japanese Army. "The British have held Hong Kong for a hundred years," Lawson said. "Our job is to ensure that it remains part of the Empire."

None of the lectures even partially conditioned the soldiers for the terror and misery that lay ahead.

CHAPTER THREE

Hong Kong, November 16

An English-language daily, the *China Mail*, published an
Extra edition to herald the arrival of the Canadian reinforcements. Beneath a front-page headline—BIG CANADIAN
CONTINGENT DESCENDS UPON COLONY—the *Mail* said the ships
carrying the two battalions had "loomed through the mist"
and entered Hong Kong Harbor at 7:30 on a Sunday morning. While the new governor, Sir Mark Young, and the new
garrison commander, Major General Christopher Maltby,
welcomed the Canadians, three RAF planes flew overhead
and five MTBs zigzagged around the *Awatea* and the *Prince
Robert*. The decks of both ships were jammed with troops,
all in tropical uniforms, and every porthole seemed occupied.

The *Mail* quoted Lawson as saying his men were glad to
be in Hong Kong. He declared that although the composi-
tion of the units' equipment was an official secret, "There is
not a single horse in the Canadian Army today; the whole
army is mechanized."

At 10 A.M. the troops disembarked and, led by a Royal
Scots' pipe band, began the two-mile march up Nathan
Road, a wide commercial thoroughfare, to Sham Shui Po
barracks on the mainland. As word of the troops' arrival
swept the district, the small waterfront crowd thickened and

thousands of whites and Chinese soon lined the march route, cheering and applauding.

The *Mail* refrained from mentioning that the Hong Kongers' enthusiasm was mixed with relief. For weeks the rumor had been circulating that the Canadians coming to the colony were prairie Indians who had the potential to wreak almost as much havoc as the Japanese. It was feared that Englishwomen could not walk the streets at night without being raped and scalped. During the march many soldiers were puzzled to hear white women shouting gleefully, "They're not Indians! They're not Indians!"

There was no mention in the story either of the fact that the Canadians were astounded by Hong Kong itself. They had been told to expect poverty and overcrowding, but no one prepared them for its glittering assets. "The city looks beautiful," Grenadier Corporal Sam Kravinchuk scribbled in his diary after he got to the barracks. "Nicely landscaped. Lots of trees and fine houses. Very impressed. Colony under good economic standard. People don't suffer financially."

Kravinchuk revised his opinion of how widespread the high standard of living was once he saw the Chinese refugees crammed aboard sampans, existing twelve to a room in filthy rabbit warrens, and sleeping on sidewalks. The affluence he cited was, in fact, confined mostly to a few select areas.

When the British acquired Hong Kong island in 1842 by virtue of the Treaty of Nanking, it was a small town, inhabited by fishermen, coolies, pirates, and merchants, clustered in mat sheds and wooden huts at the base of a bald mountain that seemed to rise slightly off center. The island was only eleven miles long and five miles wide, but the early English settlers realized it had great potential as a trading port. Envisaging the future need for more space, the Crown gained possession of the adjacent Kowloon peninsula in 1860. Thirty-eight years later the British signed a ninety-nine-year lease for the New Territories, a mountainous stretch of mainland running from Kowloon city to the Chinese border. Under British leadership, the colony developed into a seaport that compared favorably with London, Rotterdam, and Sydney in tonnage shipped; it also became a vital banking and foreign exchange center.

The steadily growing affluence attracted thousands of Englishmen who, bringing wives and children, wanted more style and comfort than a two-bedroom flat in Victoria, the mushrooming city on Hong Kong island, could offer. So in the late nineteenth century, they began moving up the mountain slopes, building houses that looked down on Victoria, on the blue waters of one of the world's finest natural harbors, and on the flatlands where the city of Kowloon was rapidly expanding.

The houses on the Peak, as the district was officially named, ranged from cozy, smartly appointed bungalows to the ultimate in palatial splendor: lush gardens, tennis courts, and fish ponds surrounding thirty-room mansions. Almost every Englishman in Hong Kong in the 1880s, even the lowest of clerks, had at least three servants (a houseboy, a cook, a wash *amah*) and some Peakites had as many as fourteen. To reside on the Peak meant never having to do any housework or, for that matter, to do much walking either. Coolies carried the English everywhere in sedan chairs and, although it cut their income drastically, the coolies must have been delighted when the funicular Peak Tramway opened in 1888, reducing the number of trips they had to make up the steep, winding roads.

The Peak dwellers' mode of transportation often changed —camels, horses, motorcars, and buses all were used at one time or another—but their attitudes of invincibility and racial superiority remained solidly intact over the decades. Indeed, by 1941, the British living on the mountain slopes were perhaps more complacent than their forebears because they had been entrenched in the same way of life for so long.

Established in 1846, the stately four-story Hong Kong Club was still the most prestigious place for an Englishman to play billiards, dine, or catch a couple of winks in the reading room. The annual St. Andrew's Ball, the biggest event of the social season, continued to draw selected guests in black ties and elegant gowns to the Peninsula Hotel. Swimming and boating at Repulse Bay, golfing in the New Territories, and staging amateur plays remained favorite leisure activities.

Even after the Canadians arrived, there was very little talk of a Japanese invasion. Instead, Peak residents spoke of having their spaniels deticked at the Kowloon Dogs' Home, the imported air-conditioning units replacing ceiling fans in the more stylish mansions, the scrumptious Peking Duck the Hong Kong Hotel had on its ten-page menu. Bazaars and tea parties raised funds to help purchase RAF planes—but not for the defense of Hong Kong. The money was sent to England to aid in the fight against Germany.

Not all Englishmen lived on the Peak, of course—only the wealthier businessmen and top-level civil servants who ran the colony. Career-minded young executives and the sons and daughters of the elite occupied modern flats and villas midway up the slopes, on May, Robinson, and Conduit roads. Other Britons preferred to be near their businesses in Kowloon or close to the white sandy beaches where they could seek relief from the punishing summer humidity and not have to bear the dismal fog that covered the upper reaches of the Peak for four months of the year.

Most of the English obeyed a common commandment: Thou shalt do business with and, on occasion, have Chinese dinner guests but thou shalt not become romantically involved with an Oriental. Dating or marrying a nonwhite resulted in slammed doors and, if you were a civil servant, a dead-end career. According to the British view, the Chinese were either amusing or frustrating to deal with; they lacked honesty, discipline, proper social graces, and—quite frankly, old boy, they look quite different from us, what?

Rich Chinese were regarded no more highly than the store clerks and coolies were. In her 1944 book, *China to Me*, American journalist Emily Hahn said she knew an Oxford-educated lawyer who, because he was Chinese, was treated contemptuously by even the most slovenly and vulgar of the Hong Kong English. That attitude extended to other nonwhites. Incredibly, the vast majority of the 20,000 Britons could exist among 1,500,000 Chinese, 4,000 East Indians, 3,200 Portuguese, 2,200 Japanese, and 900 Eurasians without recognizing any single one of them as a social equal, worthy of marrying into their families. (Those figures include an estimated 1,000,000 refugees, wealthy and poor, who poured into the colony from war-ravaged China.)

Some daring souls defied the social norm and married Chinese, while others simply kept their love affairs secret. There was one area where the racial taboo actually contributed to a flourishing profession: prostitution. Eager to sample forbidden fruit, many pillars of English society visited bars, "escort bureaus," brothels, and certain elegant flats that they would never admit knowing about at the Club or at a Repulse Bay cabaña.

Kowloon, Late November

People were dying in the streets. One-ton government trucks crawled through the mainland city in the early-morning hours, picking up the bodies of dead refugees. Cause of death: malnutrition, old age, or, who knows, perhaps just the trauma of having to flee their homes in China and sleep on sidewalks, begging, stealing, and dreading slaughter if the Japanese followed them to Hong Kong.

Private George Merritt had thought the Depression was

bad, but, he conceded, this was far worse. You could not walk along a dark street at night in Kowloon without stepping on a prostrate Chinese, and you had no way of knowing if they were half starved and sleeping or dead.

How different it was from rural Manitoba. From the one-room school. From swimming bare-ass in Birch Creek; going five miles on the farm without meeting another person. Merritt, a handsome black-haired lad, had cut brush on municipal roads before joining the Grenadiers. At forty cents an hour, he figured he was just doing okay. Now, compared to the miserable buggers in the Hong Kong streets, he figured he had been living in absolute luxury back home.

The death-trucks reminded him, too, of how fragile a human life really was. You had to get all the pleasure you could because the whole thing was liable to end suddenly. Especially when there were Japanese soldiers on the border itching to get a shot at you.

For Merritt, the pleasure to be had in Hong Kong did not lie in visiting smoky gambling dens and Nathan Road curio shops or touring the colony in rickshaws, swilling beer. He liked to spend his time off the base in the company of a particular young Chinese girl. Short, slim, and glowingly pretty, she had been sold to him by her poverty-stricken parents for a bargain-basement ten dollars a month. That was less than he had paid for the meal he and his buddies had at the Peninsula Hotel. And her sexual favors were only part of the deal. The girl did his laundry, shined his boots, and shaved him. All in the comfort of her family home, while her mother cooked dinner.

The girl's parents would have been outraged had anyone suggested that their daughter was a whore. She was merely doing what so many Chinese girls had to do—making a civilized arrangement to ensure her family's survival. Whores were the painted ladies in bars and brothels, wretched creatures who never saw the sun and would surely perish from venereal disease.

On paper, prostitution did not exist in Hong Kong. The colonial government had outlawed the business ten years earlier. But the world's oldest profession is also the world's craftiest. It had gone underground and, enlisting the aid of corrupt policemen, resurfaced in a new guise. Exquisitely groomed call girls now plied their trade in expensive Victoria flats and "escort bureaus" had clients make their selections from glossy photographs. The girls with lesser-priced attractions frequented seedy waterfront bars and brothels, posing as dance hostesses.

The younger the girls, the more customers they had. Fifteen-, sixteen-, and seventeen-year-olds were in constant demand at one dollar a session and Merritt had heard of guys with bizarre tastes paying twelve dollars for ten- and eleven-year-old virgins. Brothel visits became payday rituals for Canadian and British soldiers. Wearing gaudy dresses slit to mid-thigh, the girls usually took customers into ugly cubicles that lined the walls of large, dimly lit rooms.

Naturally, Merritt preferred his arrangement. He actually grew fond of the girl but he never for a minute considered taking her to Canada when the Hong Kong tour finished. She was a lovely diversion, but what man would want to marry someone who sold her charms to a total stranger?

Kowloon, Early December

Private Ted Schultz was enjoying a beer with four other Grenadiers when a group of Rifles appeared at the top of the stairs. They just stood there, looking around the crowded dance hall, counting Grenadiers.

"Let's get the bastards!" someone shouted.

Schultz jumped up and, running to the stairs, punched the first Rifle he reached. The soldier fell backward, tumbling into six or seven Rifles halfway up the steps.

The brawl was on.

A dozen Grenadiers had arrived at the Sun-Sun Café early to establish a beachhead, and they had no intention of letting a solitary Rifle enter the place. For two weeks Grenadiers and Rifles had been mingling at the Sun-Sun, savoring the Chinese cuisine in the downstairs restaurant, then climbing the broad wooden staircase from the sidewalk to the second-floor dance hall. The beer was cheap and potent, young boys crawled under the tables to clean boots for a penny, and the Chinese girls loved to dance to the Glenn Miller records on the glowing, ceaseless Wurlitzer. The mirrored walls, the whirling ceiling fan, and the girls' flashy dresses lent the Sun-Sun an exotic atmosphere far different from Sham Shui Po's gloomy barracks.

Exotic or not, the atmosphere did nothing to erase the rivalry—and smoldering hostility—between the two Canadian battalions. Nightly arguments erupted over which outfit did what in World War I. The Grenadiers called the Rifles (even if they were English-speaking Ontario recruits) "frogs"; the Rifles called the Grenadiers (even if they were city dwellers) "grain-brains." Then, the previous night, two Rifles had grabbed a Grenadier and, tossing him outside, said the café was now the Rifles' private domain. "If any grain-brain shows his face here, we'll push it in."

Schultz sure as hell was not going to let them get away with that. He was a big man, over two hundred pounds of hard muscle. His wrists were so thick he could not find a watch strap to fit him. He was used to fighting too. A Saskatchewan farmer's son, he had moved to British Columbia in 1935 and gone to work in a Bridge River gold mine. Biting holes in hardrock eight hours a day with a pneumatic drill had toughened his body. On weekends he had stayed at a hotel in town, playing blackjack and boozing, and he would deck anyone who gave him any trouble. No matter how big and mean the Rifles were, Schultz was going to stand his ground.

After the first Rifle crashed down the stairs, his buddies

rushed to the top. Schultz and his friends went after them with fists and feet. The Rifles retreated and, congregating on the sidewalk, concluded they were outnumbered. While they went for reinforcements, more Grenadiers showed up. The dance hall was soon packed with soldiers, nervous girls, and an angry Chinese manager. "You fight, I phone army police," he threatened. Ignoring him, the soldiers ordered beer.

Fifteen minutes later the Rifles came back. Schultz could not determine how many men they had, nor could he say how many Grenadiers were in the hall. All he could see was a swarming mass of soldiers punching, kicking, pulling, and pushing. Chairs, bottles, tables, and anything else that was movable flew through the air. Mirrors shattered and fell, girls shrieked, a chair bounced off the overhead fan. Behind the bar, the manager was frantically phoning the Embassy Bar and other soldier hangouts, trying to locate patrolling MPs.

Somehow the Grenadiers succeeded in holding the Rifles back. The steps and the dance floor were littered with fallen soldiers, some moaning and recovering from blows, others unconscious. Miraculously, no one was seriously hurt.

The Rifles' tenacity amazed Schultz. They would retreat, regroup, then make another run at the Grenadier wall blocking the top of the stairs. The battle lasted, off and on, for an hour. Wherever the MPs were, the manager failed to find them, and if the Hong Kong police knew about the brawl, they did not want any part of it.

"We're losing ground," Schultz heard his friend Art Lyons shout. "Get the Wurlitzer!" With Schultz and three others pushing, the jukebox was moved to the stairway and heaved down at yet another group of advancing Rifles. The Rifles fled before the machine reached them, and this time they did not return.

After promising to pay for the damage, the Grenadiers drank victory beers. The Wurlitzer was hauled upstairs and plugged in: it still worked. Later that night two Rifles who had no knowledge of the fracas sauntered into the dance hall and, surveying the damage, asked what had happened. Too tired to fight, a Grenadier answered, "Earthquake. Didn't you notice it outside?"

The next morning Schultz awakened to see a grim-faced Japanese male leaning over his bed, holding a razor near his throat. Thinking the war must have started, he sprang upright and shoved the startled man against the wall. A couple of his barrack mates stopped Schultz from hitting him. The Jap's a barber, they said. He's shaving the soldiers for a nickel apiece and, as he has so little time before reveille, he's doing some guys while they are sleeping.

Suddenly aware of the lather on his face, Schultz laughed and motioned the barber to proceed. Four months later the barber was seen striding through a Japanese POW camp wearing an officer's uniform. Schultz and his buddies had innocently allowed themselves to be shaved by an undercover agent.

Not all of the Canadians were caught up in the swirl of Hong Kong's glittering nightlife. Grenadier Corporal Sam Kravinchuk, for instance, spent his off-hours in public libraries, reading Oriental history, while Corporal Lionel Speller, a Royal Canadian Signal Corps dispatch rider, often attended the nightly prayer meetings run by the Plymouth Brethren at the Duddell Street Gospel Hall. Still, the stories of the Canadians' wild conduct began multiplying soon after the contingent's arrival and Brigadier Lawson felt compelled to beef up the MP patrols. He did not, however, confine his men to the base. Like many a commanding officer before him, he realized the soldiers needed a break from their daily grind. For all the Canadians did in the three weeks prior to the invasion was dig trenches, man pillboxes, clean weapons, hold drills, and listen to more lectures on how the Japanese supposedly thought and acted.

Victoria, December 4

At eight o'clock on a cool Thursday evening, the regimental band adroitly switched from a Gilbert and Sullivan medley to the traditional number summoning officers to dinner, "The Roast Beef of Old England." The British officers left their cigars and cocktails in the anteroom and, talking loudly, entered the messhall. It was the 1st Middlesex Regiment's guest night and the featured visitor was none other than the man in charge of the Hong Kong garrison, Major General Maltby.

For such a festive occasion, the officers wore their best uniforms: waist-length scarlet jackets, tight blue overalls, and black Wellington boots. The floors and walls of the officers mess had been scrubbed clean and the long banquet table was bedecked with fresh flowers, cut glass, and polished silver. The highlight of the menu was, of course, the regimental favorite, roast beef and baked potatoes.

Maltby, a fifty-year-old who had served thirty years with the Indian Army and had received the Military Cross, appeared to be in a jovial frame of mind. Adhering to the customary officers mess ban on mentioning women or "talking shop," he spoke of the upcoming army boxing championships, the balmy weather, and whatever else passed for light, pleasant conversation. In reality, he was suppressing an intense feeling of foreboding, a dark suspicion that the Middlesex and, indeed, all of the men under his command were perched on the rim of a bubbling volcano.

The tall, sandy-haired Maltby had taken over from the departing Major General Grasett in July 1941, and in spite of the latter's assurances that two more battalions would render the colony indestructible, he was extremely apprehensive about the garrison's fighting ability. Like the Canadian units, the two British (the 1st Middlesex and the 2nd Royal Scots) and two East Indian battalions (2/14 Punjabis and 5/7 Rajputs) fell far short of Class A material. Their ranks were swelled with too many young recruits, too many middle-aged reservists called away from comfortable homes, and too few seasoned professionals. Malaria, venereal disease, and Hong Kong's fairyland atmosphere had softened the core of all the units.

But what could he do? The garrison's meager ammunition supply made it impossible to order rigorous training programs and the War Office stubbornly rejected all requests for additional men and equipment. Counting the Canadians, Maltby had twelve thousand men at his disposal. He trusted British intelligence reports claiming that the Japanese soldiers (now estimated to be five thousand) near the border were ill equipped and poorly trained: he repeated those claims to his troops in parade-ground lectures. All the same, he could not dispel his nagging doubts.

Those doubts had led him to have a private meeting with a highly placed executive of the colony's most powerful financial institution, the Hong Kong and Shanghai Bank. Voicing his worst fears, Maltby suggested that the two-thousand-man Hong Kong Volunteer Defence Corps be put on full-time mobilization. The banker was appalled. "Don't be ridiculous," he scoffed. "Most of our male employees are Volunteers. The bank would have to close. There is no war, sir, and there never will be. The Japanese have more sense than to attack a British colony."

(The Canadians discovered the same kind of haughty resistance among the English hierarchy. Lieutenant Colonel Home, the Rifles' commanding officer, said in his diary, "We seem to be on some peacetime festival rather than on the brink of war." And one of his aides, Major Jack Price, reported that when his men tried to dig slit trenches on the

Peak, irate residents chased them off because they might trample on flowerbeds.)

Even though most of the locals believed an invasion was out of the question, Maltby worked hard, staying up late every night, to put the colony on its best possible defensive footing. First of all, he asked his staff to compile a list of the quantity and locations of the anti-aircraft guns. It was a short list. Eight mammoth 9.2-inch guns formed the backbone of the heavy armament. The 9.2's had been manufactured in 1918, but, because their 380-pound shells could still pack a good wallop, Maltby had them moved to what he thought were the most vulnerable positions, three locales on the south shore of Hong Kong island. By sighting the 9.2's toward the south, Maltby presented physical evidence that he perceived that the main Japanese thrust would come from the sea and not from the badly organized troops in the north. The big, steel-plated guns were mounted on high ground—three at Mount Davis, three at Stanley Peninsula, and two at Cape D'Aguilar. Six eighteen-pounders and four two-pounders were shifted to beach-front positions and the remainder of the armaments, primarily howitzers, were placed throughout the colony on a mobile basis.

Altogether, Maltby had twenty-nine fixed guns and forty-two mobile guns, most of them obsolete and with scandalously low ammunition stores. In the way of lighter arms, the situation was equally distressing: each battalion, for instance, was given several three-inch mortars and seventy rounds of ammunition—hardly enough shells for more than ten minutes of rapid bombardment. Clearly, a battle for Hong Kong would quickly deteriorate into a last-ditch, street-by-street affair. When the artillery and mortars ran out of shells, the soldiers would have to rely on rifles, bayonets, grenades, machine guns, and, above all else, raw courage.

How long could the defenders hold out? One week? Two weeks? Three? And, if by some awesome feat, his troops repelled the enemy for months on end, how would the colonial government feed the massive civilian population once the existing food reserves were depleted? These and other questions troubled Maltby daily. Yet anyone observing the smiling, self-assured commander at the 1st Middlesex regimental dinner, raising his glass at the well-stocked table to toast the King, might be excused for construing, as the Peakites did, that the radiant British light would never, ever, dim in the Far East.

CHAPTER FOUR

Kowloon, December 7

On Sunday, December 7 (Saturday, December 6 in Canada) seven hundred members of the Royal Scots and 1st Middlesex battalions marched to the Church of England cathedral near the city center. Roman Catholics, Muslims, Jews, and atheists were known to have attended past church parades in order to avoid the potato-peeling and barrack-scrubbing chores thrust upon those who stayed behind. But this Sunday service had more meaning than others, and even the shirkers were moved by its emotional impact.

Twenty-six hours earlier, two huge Japanese convoys had been spotted in the Gulf of Siam and, although there was no evidence that any of the warships were heading for Hong Kong, the men were acutely aware that this could well be their last religious service before the sword fell.

The Royal Scots bagpipes and the Middlesex brass band enlivened the march to the stone cathedral. Inside, Major General Maltby read a passage from the Book of Matthew and when he finished the reading, the soldiers' voices boomed out the hymn, "Praise My Soul, the King of Heaven."

Elsewhere in the colony, a few hundred Canadian, British, and East Indian soldiers patrolled residential and commercial districts, occupied concrete pillboxes and slit

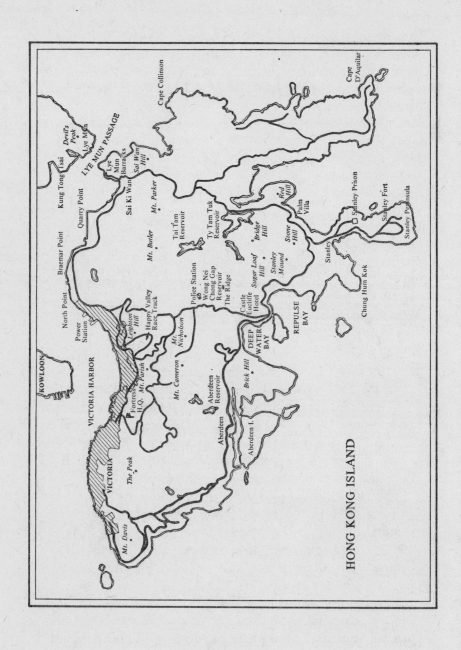

HONG KONG ISLAND

trenches in the outlying hills, and manned beach-front howitzers. To a man, they cast anxious glances at the cloudless
blue sky, watching for enemy aircraft. On Saturday the
China Mail had carried a page-one story reporting that President Roosevelt had cabled Emperor Hirohito, imploring
him to avoid a military confrontation. The soldiers specu-
lated that the Japanese convoys were probably bound for
Malaya, fourteen hundred miles south of Hong Kong, where
they planned to attack the British enclave of Singapore. If
Singapore was besieged, the soldiers realized, Hong Kong
would be next. The Volunteers commander, Colonel H. B.
Rose, responded to the news of the Japanese armada by ordering the full mobilization of his men. (The male employees flowed out of the Hong Kong and Shanghai Bank,
but a skeleton staff kept it operational.)

Still, the bulk of Hong Kong's white population behaved
as though the Japanese menace were a preposterous illusion.
The Happy Valley Race Track recorded its highest attend-
ance of the season on Saturday. Young couples drank punch
and did the foxtrot at a ladies'-club Music of the Roarin'
Twenties dance. And a rakish civil servant, Bunny
McWhirter, won second prize at a Saturday night costume
party when he turned up wearing a homemade Japanese
officer's uniform.

While the soldiers watched and waited Sunday morning,
the Japanese Army was moving. Heavy artillery and units of
storm troopers, specially trained for fighting in mountainous
regions, came overland from Canton to bolster the 38th Division's huge build-up opposite Fanling, a New Territories
village seven miles from the border. The sixty-thousand-man
Japanese strike force was under the command of Lieutenant
General Sakai Takashi, a tough, fifty-two-year-old Tokyo
factory worker's son who had spent six years directing China
campaigns.

The Japanese troop movements were spotted by a Punjabi
border patrol, and, part way through the Church of England

service, a British officer hurried to Maltby's pew to relay their report.

"The Punjabis say there are at least twenty thousand soldiers in the area," the officer whispered discreetly, "perhaps even more."

"They must be exaggerating," Maltby said. "Our intelligence people are certain there are only five thousand at the most."

Nevertheless, Maltby left the service and, summoning senior officers outside individually, informed them he had decided to activate the entire garrison. Twenty thousand, or five, the Japanese were obviously getting ready to attack. As the minister read the sermon to a steadily dwindling congregation, the officers rushed to their various units: by five o'clock that afternoon every soldier, volunteer, seaman, and airman was at his battle station.

The defense of Hong Kong against a northern invasion was divided into two stages: the initial battle for Kowloon and the rest of the mainland and, should that fail, a retreat to Hong Kong island, where all remaining troops would dig in for a siege. The Gin Drinkers' Line (named after a local bay) held the key to the colony's mainland defense. Approximately eleven miles long, the line was a series of slit trenches and pillboxes running across hilly, sparsely-populated terrain parallel to the Chinese border. Construction of the line had been abandoned in 1938 because there were insufficient troops in Hong Kong to man it effectively. When the Canadian contingent arrived, Maltby sent large work parties to complete it. There were still wide holes in the line and to give it depth would require two or three divisions. But Maltby reasoned that Gin Drinkers' had a good chance of standing up if the gaps between the pillboxes and trenches were patrolled at night and covered with machine guns and howitzers by day. He had not changed his mind about the main assault coming from the sea and, under those circumstances, he felt Gin Drinkers' was an adequate fortification.

All battalions had men on the line, but the Mainland Brigade was largely composed of Royal Scots, Punjabis, and Rajputs. Brigadier Cedric Wallis, a stodgy, slow-speaking Indian Army veteran, was in charge of the Gin Drinkers' Line, and Brigadier Lawson commanded the Island Brigade, comprised of Rifles, Grenadiers, and Middlesex. The Volunteers were split into two batches, one on the mainland, the other on the island.

At nightfall on Sunday the Canadians were on the beaches and in the hills on the south side of the island, the Grenadiers to the west, the Rifles to the east. Coiled barbed wire was strung along the beaches, and pillboxes overlooked every possible enemy landing site. British army vehicles rumbled through the streets of Victoria, and Canadian and British infantrymen waited on the slopes, ready to counterattack, isolate, and hopefully destroy any enemy invaders who penetrated the shoreline defenses. The Canadians had been told what to do if the Japanese swept in aboard landing barges and small ships. They had not been trained to fight a mobile, guerrilla-style action in the hills.

As it turned out, the massive sea assault never did materialize, and the Canadians found themselves engaged in a desperate battle against crack troops flowing across the narrow strait from Kowloon to hit them from behind.

The images stayed with Sergeant Major John Osborn. All through the *Awatea* voyage, the three weeks of tedious work on Gin Drinkers', even now when a war with Japan seemed imminent, he would lapse into quiet moments, worrying about his daughter.

The night before he left Winnipeg for Vancouver, five-year-old Patricia's dress had caught fire while she was playing near the wood and coal stove. His frantic wife had torn off the blazing clothing; they had rushed her from their sub-

urban frame bungalow to a downtown hospital; he had
given blood for an emergency transfusion in a white, antiseptic room. Then he had joined his battalion without knowing if Patricia had survived. No personal mail had arrived
from Canada, and here he was facing a menacing enemy,
still unable to push the images from his mind.

Some men might have gone AWOL and hidden out until
their child's fate was decided. Not Osborn. He was thoroughly Army, a career soldier who, thank goodness, had escaped pensioning off in spite of respiratory problems, a leg-
acy from a World War I gassing.

Osborn was, in fact, a model soldier. Highly disciplined
and a stickler for spit-and-polish, he had retained his military values at home. His five children stood at attention
every morning for an inspection to make sure they were
washed and neatly dressed. He was strict; back talk or de-
ceit to avoid a chore was liable to bring forth the large stick
kept behind the kitchen door. But he adored his kids and, in
turn, they loved and respected him. Singsongs around the
living room piano, country picnics, and trips to Judy Gar-
land movies helped keep the family a vibrant, happy unit.

The Army contributed to his family's sense of well-being.
Although it was not the greatest, the regular pay ensured
them that the rent would be paid and food would be on the
table. Osborn had known hard times: after growing to man-
hood on a Manitoba farm, he had endured many a frigid
winter's day on the ill-heated St. Mary's streetcar, riding to
central Winnipeg in search of work. Any work. Delivering
flyers door to door and laying ties on the railway were two
of the jobs he was glad to fill. Now, at forty-two, he was
deeply grateful to reap the material benefits of army life
and, at the same time, to have an occupation that suited his
temperament.

Osborn greatly admired Brigadier Lawson. Like him, the
brigadier had earned his rank through hard work, not
through an affluent family with Ottawa connections. And,

like Osborn, Lawson was all spit-and-polish. The brigadier's buttons always shone, his pants were perfectly creased, his boots clean and bright. And the brigadier insisted on being his own man. Three days after arriving in Hong Kong, Lawson toured the colony's fortifications and surmised that the local civilians—and the majority of the British military brass —were being utterly ridiculous in assuming that the addition of the two Canadian battalions provided all the strength that was needed. The brigadier persuaded Maltby to cable the War Office, recommending that Canada be asked to supply a third infantry battalion, a field regiment of engineers, and an ambulance corps. (The War Office invited the Dominions Office in London to request the additional Canadian units on December 6: the outbreak of war prompted cancellation of the request before it was sent.)

Osborn could do nothing about his daughter's fate except pray, but at least he did feel confident that his own future was in the best possible hands. If anyone in Hong Kong had the brains and moral fiber to guide the Canadians through the hell of pitched warfare, he knew it was Brigadier Lawson.

Victoria, December 7

For Private Dennis Murphy, the ex-Saskatoon radio announcer, that Sunday was as boring as any Sunday in Jamaica. With his platoon, he had left Sham Shui Po barracks and ridden the Star ferry to the island. Then he sat for three hours in a hillside pillbox, two hundred yards above the shoreline highway that circled the island.

Traffic was sparse: a fat Englishwoman on a bicycle, a truckload of live chickens, a bunch of ragged Chinese refugees carting their meager possessions on their backs. His hangover—a throbbing reminder of the Saturday night revelry at the Sun-Sun—finally cleared by midafternoon, and,

restless as usual, he wished he could join the young Englishmen in the white cricket outfits who sped by him in a bright
red Jaguar. Not that cricket had any special appeal for him;
he had never seen the game. But watching a lot of guys
bashing a ball had to be much more interesting than what
he was doing, staring at the blessed sky.

Around 8 P.M. Murphy was transferred to a southern
beach position. Three Grenadiers had come down with food
poisoning, and he was one of the replacements. While a sentry stood outside, Murphy organized a poker game in an
empty food-concession shack. Six soldiers crouched on the
floor, using a flashlight and hoping no one caught them
breaking the blackout rule. Murphy won twenty-four dollars. He would have done better, but, Jeez, it was hard to
cheat effectively when you could not see the cards very well.

It began to rain slightly before midnight. Scattered light
showers. Murphy heard voices outside and, switching off the
light, he opened the door. A tall, balding Englishman was
standing in the drizzle, wearing a bathing suit and sandals.

"I swim here every night except for the monsoon season,"
he was explaining indignantly to the sentry. "I don't understand why I cannot swim here tonight."

"The bay was mined today," the guard said patiently,
"and there's barbed wire further along the beach."

"Bloody nuisance!" the Englishman exclaimed, stomping
back toward his villa beyond the highway. "You'd think
there was a war on!"

Murphy closed the door, turned on the flashlight, and resumed playing.

Kowloon, December 7

At shortly after 11 P.M. on Sunday, Harold Bateson, the
night clerk at the Peninsula Hotel, telephoned a radio repair
shop in Kowloon. Two Japanese sisters who had been with

the hotel's cleaning staff for three years had failed to show up for their overnight shift. Bateson, a lanky, bespectacled Australian, knew the girls stayed with their uncle and his family in a flat behind the shop.

When the uncle answered, Bateson inquired if the girls were sick. "Yes, sick. Won't come work for long time," the man replied. Before he could be pressed for more details, the man hung up.

Well, that was no problem. Bateson could replace the sisters tomorrow: Kowloon was full of women desperate for jobs, although the hotel did insist upon references in order to weed out potential thieves. The uncle's attitude puzzled him, though. He had sounded hesitant, almost frightened, and was not at all convincing in claiming the girls were ill.

A little while later a Swiss businessman stopped at the desk and mentioned that when he had walked past the Matsubara Hotel, a mecca for local and visiting Japanese civilians, the lobby had been strangely deserted. Even the desk clerk seemed to be missing and, the businessman added, he had the distinct impression the hotel was closed.

Bateson wondered if the two incidents were related. Did the cleaning girls and the Matsubara lobby crowd know something he didn't? Was the word spreading through the Japanese community that Hong Kong's Sunday night tranquillity was, in reality, only a brief and beautiful prestorm lull?

CHAPTER FIVE

Victoria, December 8

At 4:45 A.M. on Monday (Hong Kong time), British intelligence officer Major Charles Boxer yawned, took a sip of tea, and twisted the knob on the short-wave radio set. A skilled linguist, he was assigned to the main Hong Kong military complex, Fortress Headquarters, to monitor newscasts on Japanese stations. The man he had relieved, Major "Monkey" Giles, was sleeping on a nearby cot in the small, silent office.

Boxer adjusted his earphones, skipped over a weak, indistinguishable signal, and brought the dial to rest on Radio Tokyo. The Japanese announcer was droning on about forthcoming programs, a Beethoven concert and the like, when another voice broke in. Abruptly Boxer was wide awake, a cold sweat coating his lean body. In a stern, ominous tone the second announcer stated:

"The Army and Navy divisions of Imperial Headquarters jointly announced at six o'clock this morning (Tokyo time), December 8, that the Imperial Army and Navy forces have begun hostilities against the American and British forces in the Pacific at dawn today." Boxer tore off the headset, and rushing to the cot, shook Giles excitedly. "Wake up, Monkey! The war's started! You don't want to miss it, do you?"

As Giles's eyes blinked open, Boxer grabbed the desk

phone and called Maltby's aide-de-camp, Second Lieutenant Ian MacGregor. Within fifteen minutes every high-level officer at Fortress Headquarters was awakened and given the stunning news; within two hours the Radio Tokyo announcement was common knowledge in the barracks, pillboxes, and trenches.

Shortly after 9 P.M. Sunday, December 7 (London time) Winston Churchill switched on the radio in the dining room at Chequers, his country retreat. The BBC newscast had already started and, keeping one ear cocked to hear the latest reports from the European and African fronts, the Prime Minister exchanged small talk with his weekend guests, U. S. Ambassador John Winant and Lend-Lease Co-ordinator Averell Harriman. The three men were relaxing after dinner and, as usual, Churchill was enjoying a cigar.

In a classic example of BBC understatement, the announcer ended his dry, undramatic account of the British Army's wins and losses in Libya with the terse comment that Japanese planes had bombed American ships in Hawaii. This was followed by a professor's five-minute commentary on flaws in the education system.

The announcement of the Pearl Harbor bombing was so matter-of-fact that Churchill, preoccupied with thoughts of the North African campaign, did not immediately absorb its implications. Winant and Harriman, however, both straightened in their chairs.

"Did I hear that right?" Harriman asked. "Have the Japanese attacked us?"

At that moment the butler, Sawyers, entered the room. "It's true, sir," he said. "We heard it ourselves outside. The Japanese have attacked the Americans."

Sawyers turned off the radio and the room fell momentarily silent. Churchill gazed at the carpet, considering his next move. On November 10 he had pledged at the annual

Guildhall meeting that England would leap into the fray "within the hour" if the Japanese declared war on the Americans. His promise of support followed President Roosevelt's clamping a stringent embargo on Japan, cutting off the flow of much-needed oil and raw materials. Roosevelt also asked Japan to withdraw from China and French Indochina, where it had seized control of the government in July 1940.

Churchill realized that the Hawaii attack was a prelude to a full-scale strike at British holdings in the Far East. Rising quickly from his chair, he walked to his study. Winant followed him and suggested that Churchill speak to Washington before making any drastic moves. After all, the bombing supposedly had occurred two and a half hours earlier and, if the BBC broadcast was accurate, surely someone would have informed him? A few minutes later Churchill had Roosevelt on a transatlantic telephone line.

"Mr. President, what's all this about Japan?"

"It's quite true," Roosevelt replied. "They have attacked us at Pearl Harbor. We're all in the same boat now."

When the two leaders finished talking, Churchill phoned London and set the machinery into motion for an official war declaration. Hanging up, he noticed that Winant, and Harriman who had joined them, were neither sad nor worried about their country being at war. They seemed almost relieved, as though they had been rescued from a prolonged agony.

Churchill himself experienced a similar sense of relief. The nerve-fraying tension of international negotiations— threats, promises, delays, suspicions—was finally over and, like the Chinese, he was pleased to have the Americans on his side. Together, the British and the Americans would restore peace and order to the Orient. "Being saturated and satiated with emotion and sensation," he recalled in the third volume of his memoirs, *The Grand Alliance*, "I went to bed and slept the sleep of the saved and the thankful."

At 7:57 A.M. (Hong Kong time) Monday, December 8—six hours after the Pearl Harbor catastrophe—a dark, thin smear appeared on the horizon over the New Territories. Peering into the bright blue sky 2/14 Punjabi Captain Harnan Singh remarked to a pillbox companion, "Those must be our reinforcements." But as the planes drew closer, Singh and every other soldier in the area was alarmed to see the dark blur take on the individual shapes of forty-eight Japanese aircraft. Air-raid sirens began wailing in Kowloon and Victoria, civilians ran for shelter, anti-aircraft guns boomed.

The planes were heading for Kai Tak Airport.

The Far East Combined Intelligence Bureau had assured Maltby that the tiny airbase at Kowloon Bay had an excellent chance of surviving enemy assaults. The Japanese pilots' notoriously bad eyesight, the bureau claimed, rendered them unable to conduct low-level bombing missions. Therefore, bombs would have to be released from such a height that they would likely miss their targets.

Maltby and the local RAF leader, Wing Commander James Sullivan, nevertheless had made representations to Whitehall for more anti-aircraft weapons and a squadron of modern fighters. The three Wildebeeste torpedo bombers had no torpedoes, the two Walrus amphibians were used for target towing, and the eight civilian planes at Kai Tak, including a Pan-American clipper, were unarmed. Sullivan and Maltby planned to build concrete hangars into the hillside but on the morning of December 8 the only thing protecting the obsolete planes sitting near the runway were four machine-gun placements.

When they were out of range of the Kowloon anti-aircraft guns, the Japanese planes dropped to five hundred feet to make their first low pass at the airfield. Thirty-six bombers and twelve Zeroes blasted the sitting-duck squadron and adjacent buildings with twenty-five-pound explosives and incendiary bullets as the machine guns opened fire in a hopeless effort to stop them. Within five minutes the enemy destroyed every plane on the ground.

Then they moved on to Sham Shui Po barracks, a collection of large brick huts covered with tarpaper and stucco. Fortunately, the Canadian troops had been evacuated to the mainland the previous day, but a handful of soldiers and the units' baggage remained on the base. Two Royal Canadian Signal Corps members were seriously injured in the brief but heavy bombardment that flattened or damaged many buildings. Before returning to Canton, the aircraft showered propaganda leaflets onto the streets of Kowloon. Written in Cantonese and English, the leaflets warned that the whole colony would be burned to ashes unless the foreign soldiers laid down their arms and surrendered.

From the stone terrace fronting her spacious flat midway up the Peak, Emily Hahn stared across the strait at the billows of dense black smoke over Kai Tak Airport and guessed that the smoke was probably all that remained of the pathetic RAF squadron. On the other side of the terrace an Englishman walked onto his veranda, puffing a pipe. "That's it," he said confidently. "The Japanese have committed suicide."

Emily was not so sure. She had traveled to Hong Kong to write a book on the Soong sisters (one sister was Chiang Kai-shek's wife, another the widow of the late Chinese strongman Dr. Sun Yat-sen) and, having finished the manuscript, she stayed on to be near Charles Boxer, the British intelligence officer. His wife was in Australia, and Emily, a radiant, St. Louis-born brunette, was so passionately in love with Boxer that she did not mind scandalizing Hong Kong society by unashamedly giving birth to their daughter, Carola.

Charles had phoned at 6 A.M., saying he had monitored a Radio Tokyo broadcast and Japan was at war with England. Emily fed the baby, packed two suitcases, and sat down to wait for her friend Hilda Selwyn-Clarke, the wife of the colony's medical director, to pick her up. She would be a guest at the Selwyn-Clarke's home on the Peak until Hong Kong's fate was settled and, watching Kai Tak burn, she feared that outcome might not be favorable. Japan could be committing suicide, all right, but it might be taking the Hong Kong colonials with it.

Charles had always said the white man's days in the Far East were numbered. "All this gaiety, all these cocktail parties, are like Rome before it fell." The locals had shrugged off his gloomy prognosis, but he understood the Oriental psyche better than any other European in the colony. Tall, graying, and very dashing, Major Charles Boxer was a Sandhurst graduate who had studied Oriental history and the Japanese language in Tokyo; he was so knowledgeable that he lectured at the Royal Asia Society and wrote historical articles for the literary magazine *T'ien Hsia*. The Peakites refused to have more than passing social relations with Chinese—the enormously rich Sir Robert Ho-tung was the only Chinese Emily knew of who lived on the Peak—and the few Japanese they encountered were gardeners, waiters, or Victoria businessmen. Charles, on the other hand, invited educated Chinese to parties and, in fact, two nights ago he had been at the border, having dinner with a prominent Japanese officer.

Anyway, it was here, the war that Charles dreaded; the war that everyone said would never begin. Too late now to return to the States and a script-writing job in Hollywood. And, by the looks of it, too late to board the passenger clipper for the hazardous night flight over Japanese territory to Chungking. Whether she liked it or not, she was trapped.

Emily went back inside the flat. Her wash amah, Ah Choy, was in the bedroom, folding clothing. "Are you scared, missy?" she asked nervously.

"No, not me. Are you?"

The amah started sobbing quietly. "Yes, yes. I very scared."

Emily walked to Carola's crib and looked down at the sleeping child. Whatever happens, she thought, I pray to God that Carola comes through it safe and sound.

New Territories, December 8

Early Monday morning, several hundred Japanese soldiers crossed the border on foot and in armored carriers. Spreading out and moving swiftly, carefully, the advance platoons followed the main highway and the nearby rail line south toward the village of Fanling. Two infantry battalions were close behind; so were two units of field artillery. To their surprise, the platoons penetrated four miles into British territory without spotting an enemy soldier. Frontier observation posts had been evacuated and the isolated farmhouses contained only terrified peasants.

The squat, muscular commander of the Hong Kong operation, Lieutenant General Sakai, was in a border hut, surrounded by his aides, studying a map on a trestle table, when the advance parties radioed word of the vanished enemy. "Tell them to keep going," Sakai ordered an aide. "The English must be there someplace. Where can they go?"

Where, indeed. The bombing of Kai Tak Airport coincided with the shifting of a large naval flotilla to a position several miles off shore blocking Hong Kong Harbor. As for the possibility of the Chinese Army coming up from the rear to open an overland escape route (as Chiang had promised in a November message to Governor Young), Sakai's forces had been thwarting scattered and weak Chinese attacks since August. The Chinese troops were pesty flies, not the ferocious tigers Chiang wanted the British and his own people to believe they were.

Sakai was under orders to capture Hong Kong in ten days. His superiors in Tokyo had retained the long-established deadline despite the arrival of the Canadian battalions. Speaking at a December 1 Imperial Conference, Army Chief of Staff General Sugiyama told Prime Minister Tojo and seven top-level army and navy officers that the Canadian contingent "will have no effect on our operations, since we have set up everything in such a way that an increase of this magnitude will be of no consequence." Sugiyama was so confident that Hong Kong would quickly topple that he had already handed Sakai his next project: the 38th Division would be fighting in the Dutch East Indies before Christmas.

A second message came from the forward platoons. The enemy was retreating toward the Gin Drinkers' Line, south of Fanling. Moreover, British demolition experts were blowing up bridges, roads, and fuel pumps between the village and the border. Sakai had expected strong resistance in the Fanling region, but, instead, the enemy was planning to make its stand elsewhere. No matter. The Gin Drinkers' Line was ragged and shaky and, with two battalions ripping into it, Sakai was convinced the 38th Division would soon have a clear path all the way to Hong Kong island.

At noon Monday, small groups of Royal Engineers were still in the hills north of the Gin Drinkers' Line, planting and detonating explosives. It was a futile job. Minutes after a bridge was blown, new materials were rushed up from the rear and Japanese sappers, well prepared to cope with delaying tactics, started laying down pontoon structures. The gaping pits the Engineers blasted in roads were rapidly filled in and, if a road bridge over a deep ravine was destroyed, the Japanese infantrymen forced Chinese guides to take them over little-used mountain trails.

Even though their actions obviously failed to appreciatively stall the enemy's advance, the Engineers courageously kept on working. Twice, Japanese platoons caught up with outnumbered demolition crews attaching explosives and opened fire, inflicting light casualties. Both times the Engineers detonated the charges before retreating. The close contact between the opposing forces created at least one grimly humorous episode. The Engineers were wiring a bridge when an enemy detachment rounded a road bend and, shooting and running, drove them off. A Japanese officer cut the time fuse and the soldiers strutted onto the bridge, laughing and congratulating themselves for having saved it. However, the Engineers had planted a second circuit, an electrical line leading to a plunger. The plunger was pushed and the Japanese, still smiling, went up with the bridge.

Two other incidents that Monday afternoon were far from amusing.

A Punjabi platoon, guarding a demolition crew, was in a deserted open-air market at the village of Tai Po. Crouched inside empty stalls and in the doorways of shacks vacated by fleeing villagers, the Muslim soldiers intently watched a narrow dirt road running from the adjacent hills to the market. For some inexplicable reason, the Japanese forward scouts had not probed the village and when the enemy soldiers came over the nearest hill, they were marching calmly in tight formation, pulling pack mules and artillery.

"I don't believe it," Major George Gray, commanding officer of the 2/14 Punjabis' C Company, whispered to an aide. "You'd think they were on a victory march through Trafalgar Square."

When the Japanese were 250 yards away, Gray yelled, "Fire!" The Punjabis' lightning barrage cut huge holes in the Japanese ranks. The survivors raced back over the hill without firing a shot, leaving fifty dead and wounded. The Punjabis wanted to pursue them with fixed bayonets, but Gray, under orders to withdraw to the Gin Drinkers' Line, refused to let them go.

The second incident involved another Punjabi outfit, a

platoon comprised of Afridi tribesmen from the sun-scorched plains of northern India. To them, personal ven-dettas, tribal wars, and banditry were accepted standards of living. The platoon was protecting an Engineers' bridge-demolition crew, when its tall, bearded leader, Jemadar (Captain) Sherin, sighted a Japanese detachment five hundred yards across a rocky field. The Japanese had taken women prisoners from a nearby village, intending to rape them later. The dozen Chinese peasants were now being used as a defensive shield: trembling and crying, they were being forced forward by soldiers holding bayonet-mounted rifles. Sherin called Gray on a field telephone to ask if he should fire or retreat.

"Do your job," Major Gray retorted. "Halt the enemy advance, blow up the bridge, and fall back to Gin Drinkers'."

Hanging up, Sherin told his men they would shoot when the Japanese got closer. His own words sickened him; even the fierce Afridi, who thought little of killing men in hand-to-hand combat, considered slaughtering helpless women a despicable practice. But they were soldiers now, conditioned to obeying orders, and, Sherin knew, the Japanese would undoubtedly kill the women once they had raped them. When the Japanese and their captives were within four hundred feet of the Punjabi position, Sherin issued his command. The Afridi bullets left no survivors.

CHAPTER SIX

Victoria, December 8

The Holy Terror was on the floor, striding from ward to ward, scrutinizing patients' charts, snapping at nurses, making herself generally unbearable. Kay Christie loathed her. But she had to do whatever the old witch demanded: H.T. was the senior nurse at Bowen Road Military Hospital and the two Canadian girls, Kay and May Waters, came under her supervision.

Some of those demands infuriated Kay. Like the rule about dress uniforms. The Canadians were not allowed to wear their pretty blue silk outfits and thin white veils outside the hospital grounds. No reason given. Just a verbal command. Well, Kay knew the reason. Jealousy, pure and simple. The British nurses, who got paid less than the Canadians, were stuck with drab gray uniforms. Furthermore, the old battle-ax resented the way the patients had taken to Kay, nicknaming her Torchy because of her thick red hair. The Holy Terror's hair was so thin you could see her scalp and, in contrast to the slender and cheerful Kay, she was stout and humorless.

Now H.T. was berating a young nurse in the ward across the corridor. Key tried to concentrate on the medical record she was reading at the desk, but the senior nurse's voice came through loud and clear. "You are as bad as the colonials," she said, referring to the Canadians. "You can't read a chart either. It says four o'clock, not five minutes past four. Medicine must be administered on time, my girl."

Lord, give me strength, Kay thought. I have enough problems without having a run-in with her today.

Kay's biggest problem was finding minor supplies. Bowen Road had the newest surgical equipment and sufficient medicine for treating very serious diseases, but for some reason it was terribly short on small items. Tongue depressors, for example. Kay had searched everywhere to come up with four during the mild flu epidemic that hospitalized dozens of Canadian soldiers in late November. In Toronto she would toss the depressors out after usage. Here she had to boil them so they could be used over and over again.

Luckily, there was a big store of quinine. Most of the patients had malaria, and the nurses fed them quinine, rolled them in wool blankets, and let the poor devils sweat it out. Working in the special malaria ward meant listening sympathetically to complaints about throbbing headaches and burning flesh. Kay could do little to ease the agony except administer liquids, and yet she felt far more useful at Bowen Road than she had baby-sitting the Rosedale matrons.

Glancing up from the desk, Kay came face to face with the Holy Terror. "You will have to stay on duty until nine o'clock tonight," the senior nurse said gruffly. "One of my girls is sick." Kay nodded, and H.T. moved away. Watching her proceed along the corridor, striding like a defiant, formidable tank, Kay thought of the fighting on the mainland. The British are missing a bet, she mused. If they painted a Union Jack on the Holy Terror and told her to walk to the border, the Japs would beg us to let them go back to Manchuria.

On Monday afternoon the Japanese fifth column struck. Recruits from the Canadian units on Hong Kong island had spent the morning commandeering civilian vehicles, and, by three o'clock, captain Harold Pierce of the Royal Canadian Signal Corps reported to Fortress Headquarters that eighty-five trucks and twenty-five cars had been rounded up. Bread vans, laundry trucks, Baby Austins, anything that could carry soldiers was claimed by the Army—including ten one-ton trucks used to transport "night soil" (as the colonial government called it) in metal containers from Sham Shui Po's flushless toilets.

Major General Maltby was concerned about intelligence reports revealing that trained saboteurs had infiltrated the local Japanese and Chinese communities; but the intelligence staff underestimated both their number and their potential for destruction. Chinese employees slipped into army depots and seriously damaged forty commandeered vehicles, smashing batteries and distributors. The tires of parked ambulances were slashed and Chinese drivers abandoned trucks in ditches, locking the doors and windows and taking the ignition keys. By Monday night the fifth columnists seemed everywhere, spreading false propaganda, tossing grenades, cutting telephone lines, setting fire to fuel and food stores, signaling offshore boats with flashlights and lanterns.

The snipers were the most persistent and most aggravating of all the fifth columnists. Working alone or in pairs, Japanese and Chinese agents took pot shots at army vehicles on the less populated streets and on rural roads. Fortress Headquarters increased the guards at fuel depots and other vital installations but, throughout the siege of Hong Kong, the unseen riflemen remained a constant peril to military vehicles.

The '36 Ford truck poked along the dark Victoria street, en route from a midtown supply depot to a Grenadier post in the hills. Seated in the cab next to the Chinese driver, Corporal Ed Bergen kept a wary eye on the rear-view mirror. The Japanese had jumped the frontier that morning but, for the moment, he had another worry: the rations in the back. Famished refugees liked to run up behind the slower supply trucks, cut holes in sacks, and scoop the spilled contents off the road. Sometimes, when he was loading food, he would throw a bunch of refugees a loaf of bread, but he was damned if he was going to let anyone steal from him.

The island was blacked out. Maltby's orders. Fortunately the driver knew the route, although he had to crawl at seven miles an hour to avoid hitting the odd pedestrian crossing in front of the dim slit-headlights. Limited visibility was not the driver's only problem. He was desperately in need of a bath. But, Bergen reflected, he should be the last person on earth to condemn somebody else's foul odor. Before enlisting, Bergen had loaded crates of ice-packed fish onto freights at the CNR yard in Winnipeg—fresh goldeye bound for gourmet restaurants in the States. After an eight-hour shift, Bergen had smelled so awful that nobody wanted to be near him. Which had had one notable advantage: he had always got a seat on the rush-hour streetcar. All he had had to do was stand beside some guy for a couple of seconds and the guy would vacate his seat.

To help him forget about the monotonous fish crates, Bergen had had two hobbies: joy-riding in haywire biplanes and going to cowboy movies. Whenever a flying circus visited Winnipeg, selling rides by the hour, he had been among the first in line. The same with Gene Autry pictures. He could have lived in a moviehouse, if they had let him, existing on popcorn and sleeping between screenings. Bergen was glad to be a bachelor; he could never afford such luxuries if he had a wife and kids to support on his skimpy salary.

The Army, of course, had promised to fill his days with more excitement than joy-riding or movies. So far, the promise had been unfulfilled. Bergen, a husky, friendly, twenty-year-old, was a quartermaster, an overwhelmingly unglamorous occupation thrust upon him because he had foolishly let it be known that he could type.

The Jamaican interlude and the Hong Kong venture had done precious little for him, except increase his knowledge of booze. Jamaican rum was dirt cheap and gave you a nice glow, but three quarts of the incredibly potent Hong Kong beer put most guys under the table.

"Better take the next right," Bergen said to the driver. "There's a side street that will bring us to the main road."

As he finished speaking, a bullet smashed through the windshield, barely missing his head. Bergen saw nothing but a few yards of deserted street and the dim shapes of two- and three-story buildings.

"Step on it," he said quickly. "Let's get out of here."

"We might hit someone."

"If we do, I'll say he was the sniper. Move this thing, for Christ's sake!"

The truck lunged forward, reaching fifty miles an hour in seconds. The frightened driver did not slow down until he was two blocks away. If the truck struck any pedestrians, they did not feel it. "Good thing the sniper took only one shot," the driver said. "He might have killed us."

Bergen relaxed. What a way to fight a war, he thought. An invisible enemy. Even Gene Autry would be frustrated.

Mainland, December 8–9

The pace of the Japanese advance pleased Sakai. Late that night his men were two miles north of the Gin Drinkers' Line, cleaning out small pockets of resistance. The Japanese strategy was imaginative. If a forward platoon ran into an enemy position that refused to yield on initial contact, it tried to swing around a flank to hit it from behind. If that maneuver failed to achieve fast success, the guerrilla-warfare specialists hurried in. These were battle-seasoned platoons, crack shots wearing rubber-soled shoes and quilted uniforms covered with grass and twigs. At night the Royal Scots and East Indian battalions, bolstered with a few Grenadiers and Volunteers, found the only way to deal with the camouflaged snipers was to fire a volley whenever they heard a strange noise in the dark. The defenders killed several Japanese, but they also wounded a Chinese farmer and killed his cow.

At dawn Tuesday, Major Gray radioed Fortress Headquarters that all but one of the demolitions had been completed. The lone exception was a bridge on the western highway to the Chinese border, Castle Peak Road, where a daring saboteur had dashed in under fire and cut the leads. However, Gray said, the same man tried to duplicate his action at another locale and was shot before he could do it.

The Japanese pressure on the scattered hold-out positions north of Gin Drinkers' heightened. Between sunrise and 2 P.M. Tuesday, camouflaged snipers picked off more soldiers and the attempts to pour troops around the flanks gained momentum. Fearful that they would be outflanked and surrounded, the straggler platoons reluctantly joined the main body of defenders at Gin Drinkers' on Tuesday afternoon. The fate of Kowloon and the New Territories now depended entirely upon how long the line could withstand assault once the snipers and forward platoons were replaced by the infantry battalions Sakai had trailing them.

Victoria, December 9

The Japanese air command in Canton did not have to guess about Hong Kong's susceptibility to air raids. Undercover agents had disclosed the whereabouts of all the antiaircraft guns and accurately pinpointed the strength, or lack of it, of the RAF squadron. Knowing that the biggest guns, the 9.2's, pointed out to sea—and with Kai Tak Airport in ruins—the Japanese air command realized that further bombing raids were bound to be highly successful.

Around two o'clock Tuesday afternoon, the Japanese launched the first of their daily air raids over Hong Kong island. Seventeen planes took part in the initial mission, battering Victoria and hillside troop encampments with bombs.

That raid brought the brutal shock of armed warfare to the English islanders. Bombs crumbled military and civilian buildings; low-swooping Zeroes strafed anything that moved on city streets. Meanwhile, platoons of Canadian soldiers took over posh villas on the Peak, forcing residents to move in with their neighbors. The air-raid-warning system, supposedly designed to alert the populace twenty minutes before planes arrived, seldom gave more than a five- or ten-minute warning during the siege.

From Tuesday on, the planes came at all hours, day and night; sometimes in large bomber formations, sometimes in small, compact fighter squadrons. The raids had two objectives: to cripple military installations and to demoralize the local civilians. In regard to the latter goal, the Canton air command was adopting the policies that Italian strategist Giulio Douhet set forth in his respected book, *Command of the Air.* Douhet stated that the fastest way to destroy the enemy's will to resist was to strike behind the lines, bombing civilian targets if necessary. The German High Command had thought highly of Douhet's theory and recommended it to the Japanese.

"Morale is more important in winning battles than weapons," Baron Wolfram von Richthofen, chief of the Condor Legion that devastated Guernica and a Douhet admirer, wrote in his diary. "Continuously repeated, concentrated air attacks have the most effect on the morale of the enemy."

Be that as it may, the raids failed to destroy the Hong Kongers' spirits. In fact, the bombings produced the same incredible result as the German Blitz on London: it made the people more determined to hold out. Two unsubstantiated rumors cemented their willpower—the rumor that Chiang Kai-shek's forces were mounting a massive offensive to smash through the Japanese lines, and the rumor that two of the Royal Navy's mightiest warships, the H.M.S. *Prince of Wales* and the H.M.S. *Repulse,* were in Pacific waters, hurrying to their rescue.

Kowloon, December 9

It had happened so suddenly, so inconceivably. Only a few weeks ago Ralph Ingram had been at the frontier, enjoying a friendly chat with the half-dozen Japanese sentries relaxing on chairs near a guard hut. His friends—also members of the Volunteers—had traded cigarettes with the Japanese and, relying on sign language, had expressed their passion for nicely shaped ladies and good food. The smiling guards had seemed harmless, just ordinary chaps yearning to go back to their homes and families.

Now Ingram himself was a sentry. Clutching a loaded rifle and wearing a khaki outfit, distinguishable from regular British uniforms by its red shoulder flashes, he was patrolling the smoldering remains of Kai Tak Airport. He had been there since Sunday morning when he heard a message on a local radio station asking Volunteers to report for duty. Going out the door of his flat, he told his father to expect him back for dinner. His father ate without him and, by all appearances, the thin, bespectacled twenty-eight-year-old would be lucky to have any more meals, at home or otherwise.

Whatever his fate, Ingram felt grateful that his wife, Maria, and his mother were safe. The colonial government, atypically taking heed of the darkening war clouds, had chartered a passenger liner in July 1941, to transport the families of Britons to Australia free of charge. Maria, a Canadian nurse he had met while holidaying in Banff, had

wanted to stay in Hong Kong. But she was four months
pregnant and the couple finally had agreed that the child
would be better off in Australia if war did develop. So the
women had sailed on the liner that, in its wake, left a bitter
controversy. The government was chastised for being too
soft and permitting hundreds of Englishwomen to remain
behind—simply because they did not think a war was coming and they refused to give up their villas and servants.
And the nonwhite community generally labeled the evacuation outright racism: only white women and children were
allowed on board and no ship was chartered for the families
of Portuguese or Eurasian civil servants holding British
passports.

Ingram did not take sides in either dispute. They were
none of his business. What did concern him was his personal
obligation to defend his birthplace. He was not a wealthy
man—he did not have a mansion stuffed with *objets d'art* to
protect—but his feeling for Hong Kong went beyond material things. It encompassed such intangibles as pride of
work. A senior accountant with the revenue branch, he felt
the colonial government was among the most efficient in the
world. The budget always balanced and, over the years,
there was hardly any borrowing. He shuddered to imagine
what might happen to all that meticulous planning if the
government fell. Everything he was, everything he had, he
owed to the existence of Hong Kong. He could no more
abandon the colony than he could chop off a part of his own
body.

Others felt differently. Late Tuesday night, Ingram saw
the Kai Tak searchlights guide two small passenger planes
out of the black sky and onto a hastily repaired runway. The
pilots were enticed from Chungking by exorbitant fees.
Minutes after twin-engine aircraft landed, expensive cars
began pulling up. Influential Hong Kongers, mostly rich
Chinese businessmen, hurried aboard carrying suitcases
packed with valuables. There was no panic, no wild rush of

terrified refugees from Kowloon who must have heard the planes coming in. In an orderly, prearranged pattern, the chauffeur-driven cars dropped their owners, then disappeared. Ingram assumed the big shots would be the last people to fly out of Hong Kong, for when the fifth columnists reported the planes' departure the enemy would make certain no one else duplicated the feat. He did not resent the fleeing VIPs. Each man had a different conscience and, in the final analysis, what the other chap did was unimportant. Keeping peace in your own mind was all that really mattered.

Victoria, December 9

Panting and sweating, a gray-haired, chubby man ran up the beach, his face white with shock. Watching him approach, Volunteer John Fonseca wondered if the burst of gunfire he had heard meant that a patrol had come across the fifth columnist who had been spotted sending flashlight signals to an offshore fishing boat earlier that night.

"What's going on?" he asked the man who also belonged to a Portuguese platoon.

"One of our men was shot. I'm getting a doctor."

Maybe the Japs had landed. Fonseca's platoon had been dispatched to the isolated moonlit beach to look for enemy landing craft or paratroopers. The thought that they might be here deepened his already well-developed sense of anxiety. The Brits had sent their women away on a special ship, but his mother was still in Hong Kong, and so was his fiancée, the daughter of a Chinese merchant known as the Rice King. Fonseca feared the Japanese would rape and kill the two women he loved.

"A Jap shoot him?" he asked.

"No," the man replied, stopping to catch his breath. "He was creeping along the beach. God knows why. He was challenged—he froze—but he didn't answer. We couldn't see him properly in the dark. We challenged him again. He still didn't answer. One of the boys . . . he fired his Tommy gun."

"How awful. Killed by his own men."

"He's not dead," the man said, leaving. "He may wish he was. He was shot below the waist. The poor bastard, he's castrated."

Around midnight Tuesday, Brigadier Lawson left Fortress Headquarters, a large concrete complex which burrowed sixty feet into a Victoria hillside, and sank into the back seat of a British staff car. He was tired. He had caught only three hours' sleep since dawn Monday when Maltby, summoning the senior officers to a hastily arranged meeting, had declared solemnly, "I'm afraid it's war." Strategy discussions and inspections of Canadian positions on the island had kept Lawson so busy that he often sucked vigorously on his pipe without realizing it was out.

"Where to, sir?" the driver asked.

"Wong Nei Chong Gap."

Lawson had established Brigade Headquarters at the Gap, near a road that cut north-south across the largely uninhabited hills in the middle of the island. Some British officers were living at the Peninsula Hotel in Kowloon, but Lawson preferred to sleep in a concrete bunker half buried in a rocky hillside. Grenadiers and Rifles were deployed on the ridges and in the valleys throughout the region and Lawson wanted to be with his men.

As the car moved toward the hills, the brigadier stared at a patch of red flames and black smoke licking the sky near Happy Valley Race Track. An air raid had scored a direct hit on a supply depot.

"If that's all those sonovaguns can do, we don't have to worry," the driver said cockily. "We had bigger Halloween bonfires in Saskatchewan."

Lawson said nothing. Maltby had admitted ruefully that

the demolition parties had failed to delay the enemy advance as much as had been anticipated. And, only a few minutes ago, a radio report from the mainland disclosed that Japanese infantrymen were now striking the Gin Drinkers' Line in large numbers. The Far East Combined Intelligence Bureau's assertion that the enemy shunned night fighting because they were so bad at it had been proven false by two successive nights of relentless action. Was the bureau also mistaken in assuming Hong Kong could ride out a long siege? Lawson wished he could share the driver's optimism, but the Hong Kong mission, poorly planned from the start, was looking bleaker with every passing hour.

New Territories, December 9

The valley was dark and deathly quiet. Canadian Signalman Walter Jenkins squinted at the old farmhouse up ahead, and, although he saw no sign of life, he did not doubt the officer's word that a Grenadier platoon was posted inside.

"Okay, Teddy boy," he said, dragging the thin cable up an irrigation ditch. "Let's get on with it."

Jenkins and his pal, Ted Kurluk, were laying an aboveground telephone line from a Gin Drinkers' pillbox to the outlying farmhouse in what to them seemed a pointless task. The farmhouse would be evacuated at dawn and nobody would bother to use the phone. But the officer had insisted, and the two men had begun their three-mile walk a few hours before midnight.

Halfway up the valley they began clowning, telling jokes, singing the lyrics of popular songs. Why not have a bit of fun? Time enough for the grimly serious stuff once they were in the thick of battle.

"You're built like an ox," Kurluk said when they were within two hundred yards of the farmhouse. "Too bad they didn't have you at the Sun-Sun. You could've cleaned the Rifles out all by yourself."

"Not a chance. I would've left the minute the fight started."

He would have had to. A shy, strapping two-hundred-pounder who feared no man, Jenkins was too respectful of other people's feelings to use his strength in a belligerent manner. He remembered doing so only once. When his eighth-grade teacher went out of the room, the class bully punched little Vera Adams on the arm; Jenkins, a six-foot-two, one-hundred-eighty-pound fourteen-year-old, lifted the bully and threw him over a desk.

Football was something else again. There you pitted your muscle and skill against guys who were just as strong as you were. Quitting school in tenth grade, Jenkins had played two games as tackle for the Winnipeg Blue Bombers, then had gone into the Royal Canadian Signal Corps. In Hong Kong, he had worked out regularly with a set of exercisers bought in a Kowloon sporting-goods shop, and before Pearl Harbor, he had planned to take up weight-lifting at the "Y."

"You don't go to the Sun-Sun much, do you?" Kurluk inquired.

"Nope. I don't drink, and I feel sorry for those girls. They're sad things. I can't understand why anybody would want to sleep with them."

"Human nature, Wally. Some guys are so lonely for female company they'll blow their paychecks on anything with long hair."

The two men were still chatting when they reached the farmhouse. A couple of Grenadiers emerged from the building, staring incredulously. "What are you characters doing?" one of them asked.

"Bringing you a telephone," Jenkins said. "So you can call your wife in Canada and tell her you're tied up at work tonight."

"I don't mean that. I mean, you were making a helluva racket out there. Don't you know where you are?"

"Sure," Jenkins grinned. "In the middle of nowhere."

He stopped smiling when the soldier explained that he and Kurluk had just clowned their way through a valley heavily populated with enemy snipers. The Japanese must not have heard their voices too clearly and in the dark dismissed them as two of their own men. For it stood to reason that no soldiers, regardless of how courageous they were, would dare to fool around so freely in the heart of enemy territory.

CHAPTER SEVEN

New Territories, December 10

In the 1860s a Chinese monk named Chou Li-fu walked south from Hankow, searching for a good place to build a shrine. He passed up fertile valleys and pleasant streams because they held no personal significance for him. About ten miles north of present-day Kowloon, he saw a flock of white doves fly up from a windy, barren hill and, as the dove was his favorite bird, he vowed to remain there forever. Li-fu spread his tattered quilt and a wooden neck rest on the ground and, taking seeds from a leather bag, planted the first of many vegetable gardens that would help sustain him. The soil was hard and he hauled water in the leather bag from a distant river to ensure the garden's survival. On one of his water trips he found a rarity for the mountainous region, a bamboo grove. This, he concluded, was another indication that he was destined to stay on the hill.

Over a ten-year period Li-fu carried bamboo from the grove and erected a big slant-roofed temple. Zigzag walkways and bells were added to ward off evil spirits. When Li-fu was an old man, a marauding bandit chieftain, the embodiment of a substantial evil spirit, discovered the shrine while he and his men were seeking new horizons to plunder.

"Take my life if you desire," the monk told him, "but kindly allow the temple to stand. There should be one place of peace in this district that even murderous bandits will not disturb."

Surprisingly, the bandit agreed. Li-fu and his shrine were spared and, thereafter, the area was known as the Hill of Eternal Peace. On December 10, 1941, no trace of the shrine remained. The Hill of Eternal Peace, now called Shing Mun Redoubt on military maps, was the scene of the battle that determined the fate of the Gin Drinkers' Line.

Sakai's orders were explicit. The 228th Regiment, under Colonel Doi Teihichi, was to apply pressure on the enemy stronghold at Shing Mun Redoubt, beginning after midnight Wednesday morning. Periodic nocturnal raids would unnerve the enemy and, at first light, a large force of fresh troops would storm the hill.

On Tuesday afternoon Colonel Doi and a small reconnaissance party had surveyed Shing Mun Valley with field glasses and concluded that the region was weakly defended: a Royal Scots platoon was nestled on the hilltop and a few hundred Punjabis and Rajputs occupied the low ground beside a reservoir that helped provide drinking water for Kowloon. The hill itself covered roughly twelve acres. Fire trenches and tunnels connected five concrete pillboxes, and a narrow ring of barbed wire enclosed the position. Doi correctly surmised that the British were not expecting an attack that far to the left of the Gin Drinkers' Line and if he launched an all-out assault, instead of the sporadic raids Sakai wanted, he could easily capture the hill.

A few minutes after midnight, Doi ordered his 3rd Battalion to attack the redoubt. Wearing rubber-soled shoes and camouflaged uniforms, the infantrymen surged over the rocky terrain in a giant wave. The Scots did not see them coming until they were almost on top of them. A frightening battle ensued. The first Japanese soldiers flung themselves on the barbed wire, and their comrades scrambled over them, plunging into the midst of the Scots. Bayonets pierced

Scottish soldiers; Japanese collapsed, clutching rifle wounds. Rolling in the dirt, men frantically tried to strangle one another. The pillbox machine guns were useless at close quarters, and Scots fought hand to hand against ferocious Japanese who considered dying in combat a great honor. With that one tremendous thrust, the Japanese drove the Scots off the hill and into the Punjabi and Rajput encampments below. Ignoring reports that the Scots had been outnumbered four to one, Lieutenant Colonel G. R. Kidd, commanding officer of the 2/14 Punjabis, radioed Brigadier Wallis requesting permission to stage a counterattack.

"We've got to get that hill back!" Kidd exclaimed. "It gives the Japs command of the whole valley."

"Forget it," Wallis said. "If you send your men up there, it will only weaken Gin Drinkers' somewhere else. We can't afford to lose another key position."

Doi watched the 3rd Battalion raise the flag on Shing Mun Redoubt. Then he sent platoons down into the valley to rain mortar shells on the East Indians near the reservoir. This was followed by a series of infantry forays, all of which the Punjabis and Rajputs repelled. Japanese troops had been pressing at other spots along the Gin Drinkers' Line since nightfall but, obeying Sakai's orders, none of the commanders had gone all out for a breakthrough. The fact that Doi had taken Shing Mun hill—and, in effect, started the British withdrawal from the mainland—did not win him plaudits at headquarters. Incensed that his order had been ignored, Sakai demanded that Doi and his men retreat from the hill immediately! Doi refused to budge, and it was not until Wednesday that Sakai relented and agreed he could stay there. By holding the hill in defiance of Sakai's retreat orders, Doi was striving to save face, even if his action brought an eventual court-martial. Sakai, on the other hand, was worried that other officers would emulate the Shing Mun Redoubt charge and mount unexpected, haphazard assaults that, misjudging enemy strength, could result in a tragic loss of men. Prior to allowing Doi to retain the hill, Sakai made every top-level officer in his command vow to obey orders to the letter.

As the fighting went on below the hill—and Doi was obediently employing raiding parties rather than launching a full-scale attack—Company D of the Winnipeg Grenadiers was alighting from a ferry in Kowloon. On foot and in trucks, the Canadians moved to the junction of the two main arteries from China, Castle Peak and Taipo roads, about three miles south of Shing Mun Redoubt. Learning of the Shing Mun situation, Maltby had dispatched the Canadians to the mainland during the night to provide cover should the evacuation of the Scots and East Indians be deemed necessary. The loss of Shing Mun hill, occurring so swiftly, so easily, indicated the Japanese had more night-fighting expertise and numerical power than previously indicated and Maltby was now facing the forbidding prospect that the Gin Drinkers' Line, less than two days into the war, was already on the verge of collapsing.

Gulf of Siam, December 10

Fourteen hundred miles to the south, the British Navy's newest-model dreadnought, the *Prince of Wales*, was shearing through the Gulf of Siam, beneath a gray, overcast sky. Churchill had personally sent the 35,000-ton vessel and her battle cruiser escort, the *Repulse*, to the Far East in November, overruling Admiralty protests that they were needed elsewhere. The Prime Minister envisioned the ships as hit-and-run raiders, which in his words, "appear and disappear, causing immediate reactions and perturbations on the other side."

Anxious to fulfill that role, Vice-Admiral Sir Thomas Phillips took the battleships and four destroyer escorts out of Singapore on December 8, and, two days later, they were off the north coast of Malaya, hoping to find and sink Japanese troop carriers landing soldiers at Kota Bharu. "We are out to look for trouble," Phillips stated confidently in a memo posted on the *Prince of Wales* bulletin boards.

He had every reason to be cocksure. The *Prince of Wales's* armament, including a battery of fourteen-inch cannons and thirty-two pom-pom guns, could fire sixty thousand projectiles a minute and her plating was so thick she was dubbed the H.M.S. Unsinkable. The twenty-five-thousand five-hundred-ton *Repulse,* totally rebuilt in the 1930s, boasted an impressive array of fifteen-inch and anti-aircraft weaponry.

The highly touted invincibility of the two ships made their destruction a prime objective of the Japanese air command. The Tokyo naval brass scoffed at the theory that aircraft could destroy battleships, unless they were sitting-duck targets like they were at Pearl Harbor. Determined to prove a point, 106 planes scoured the gray waters after a Singapore spy reported the British armada's sailing.

At 10:05 A.M. on Wednesday, December 10, a lone Japanese pilot sighted the six vessels and radioed word of his finding to other aircraft loaded with bombs and torpedoes. An hour later a nine-plane squadron broke through the clouds directly above the *Repulse.* The nine belonged to the Misty Legion which, handicapped by crudely developed bombsights, nonetheless won first prize at a Combined Fleet precision-bombing contest. From ten thousand feet the bombers dropped explosives with such awesome accuracy that the *Repulse* crew ran about wildly, battling fires and tossing debris overboard. Then five torpedo bombers arrived and, zooming in low from different directions, aimed at the *Prince of Wales.* Her guns blazing, the flagship zigzagged and three torpedoes missed. The other two blasted holes in her side, the first hitting the communications room, the second severely damaging the propellers.

The *Repulse* and the four destroyers formed a barricade

around the stricken battleship. All six ships pocked the sky
with shellfire, but by early afternoon, the growing number
of Japanese bombers, attacking in waves, sank both the
Prince of Wales and the *Repulse*. Vice-Admiral Phillips, in
the best naval tradition, refused to quit the bridge and went
down with his ship.

The sinking of the battleships—virtually the pride of the
British fleet—robbed England of its long-cherished title,
Mistress of the Seven Seas. In London, Churchill was appalled. Writing in his memoirs, the Prime Minister said he
was notified of the naval disaster by a telephone call from
the First Sea Lord. "In all the war, I never received a more
direct shock," he wrote. "As I turned and twisted in bed the
full horror of the news sank in on me. There were no British
or American capital ships in the Indian Ocean or the Pacific
except the American survivors of Pearl Harbor, who were
hastening back to California. Over this vast expanse of
waters Japan was supreme and we everywhere weak and
naked."

Intense as it was, Churchill's feeling of alarm did not
match that experienced by the citizens of Hong Kong. A
local broadcast telling of the dual sinking shattered the illusion that the two warships would smash the Japanese naval
blockade and rescue them. On the same newscast, however,
a Chungking report stated that Chiang Kai-shek was about
to launch a major offensive. "The Generalissimo is said to
have sixty thousand soldiers ready to participate in the relief
of Hong Kong," the announcer declared. Regrettably, those
sixty thousand soldiers did not exist, and Chiang's plan for a
breakthrough offensive was merely hollow talk calculated to
shore up the colony's will to resist.

New Territories, December 10

Sergeant Bob Manchester crouched in the trench, his
head buried in his arms, listening to the shells exploding in

the surrounding clearing. Which side would get him first? The Nips or his own men? As part of a Grenadier platoon transferred from the Castle Peak-Taipo junction to make contact with the Royal Scots at Shing Mun Valley, the husky thirty-six-year-old Winnipegger and his comrades came under Japanese artillery fire before they reached their goal. Adding to the quandary of being pinned down in broad daylight was the disturbing fact that the British gunners, far to the rear, were lobbing their shells too short. The platoon was getting pounded from both directions.

Manchester was frightened. His conception of war as a glamorous adventure vanished the moment the first shell blasted an enormous cavity in the ground, less than fifty feet from his lair. Growing up in River Heights, he considered Buck-Buck, Pom-Pom-Pullaway and Can-Can Cricket too tame for his liking. Not anymore. The same with his old job at the city welfare office, shuffling three hundred file folders, deciding who should get food vouchers. Never again would he say he wanted to do something much more exciting.

That is, if he ever got to say anything. The way the shells punched holes, spraying dirt and splintered rocks all over the place, it was extremely likely that there would be nothing left of the platoon by nightfall. Aside from the loss of his own life, Manchester regretted having the Grenadiers suffer such an inglorious beating, for the trapped platoon was the first Canadian infantry unit on any World War II battleground to engage in front-line combat.

All day Wednesday the Japanese infantry jabbed at the Gin Drinkers' Line. Most of the thrusts took place in Shing Mun Valley where the East Indians and Royal Scots formed a thin line south of the captured redoubt, tenuously linking Gin Drinkers' left and right flanks. Sakai surmised that if Doi demolished the line at that tender spot, the 228th Regiment could romp to Kowloon without further ado.

The defenders showed remarkable grit, particularly the Rajputs. Not content with driving off repeated Japanese attack waves, a company of Hindus and Muslims under Captain Bob Newton scrambled out of their trenches at one point and, yelling defiantly, chased the Japanese back up Shing Mun hill.

Doi failed to accomplish his breakthrough Wednesday, but Sakai was not fretting. He had seven more days to take Hong Kong, and, if need be, he could muster battalions from the 38th and three other divisions being held in reserve. Waiting near the border, the reserve forces bided their time by going on a raping spree: the Imperial Japanese Army passed an edict declaring all border villages brothel areas and Chinese females, regardless of age, were "free prostitutes" for a forty-eight-hour period.

Unbeknown to Sakai, the Shing Mun Valley defenders' resolve was strengthened by an ugly rumor. In the pillboxes and trenches, between Japanese artillery barrages and infantry jabs, the Rajputs and Punjabis discussed the story that the Scots had surrendered Shing Mun hill too soon.

Descriptions of courageous hand-to-hand combat were interspersed with tales of Scots, confused and scared, running into East Indian encampments carrying full ammunition belts. It was said that some Scots had turned up while the battle was raging. If the Scots had broken and fled—and at least one Fortress Headquarters dispatch said they did—it should be remembered that many senior officers were hospitalized, suffering from malaria. The disease had struck the Royal Scots harder than any other outfit, incapacitating more than a hundred officers and men. Then, too, there was the fact that the battalion had a large number of raw recruits, some of whom were recovering from malaria and still shaky.

But the East Indians did not accept the excuses and the Scots, officially known as the First Regiment of Foot, were sarcastically labeled the Fleet of Foot. (British journalist Tim Carew, in his 1960 book *The Fall of Hong Kong*, revealed that the Royal Scots' second-in-command, Major

Stanford Burn, tormented by the story that his men acted in a cowardly fashion, ultimately shot himself.) Whatever the truth about the battle of Shing Mun Redoubt, the Rajputs and Punjabis swore to erase the Scots' shameful conduct by fighting with extraordinary valor. Hearing the same rumor, many surviving Scots took an identical pledge and, in their next assignment, they fought so bravely that one of their officers was awarded the Military Cross.

While the fighting raged on the mainland, the islanders waited and worried. The majority of the Canadian troops huddled in pillboxes and trenches, enduring air raids and watching the smoke rise from devastated buildings in Victoria and Kowloon. The bombing proved to be more than some men could stand. Sitting in a pillbox on a hillside behind Victoria, Rifleman Sidney Skelton wrote in his diary, "Two of our boys have gone crazy in the head. The bombing has snapped their minds." Other soldiers were killed by strafing Zeroes or shot by fifth columnists. Yet the scene on the island was relatively peaceful compared to the violence and chaos that would occur when the enemy eventually crossed the strait.

New Territories, December 11

During the early hours of Thursday morning, the rotund, hawk-nosed Doi stood atop Shing Mun hill and gazed at the black sky. The moon rarely emerged from behind dense clouds and few stars illuminated the valley. It was an ideal night for infiltration. Summoning his aides, the colonel said he had decided to stop hitting the Rajput and Punjabi positions head-on. Instead, the attack would shift slightly to the west and focus on Golden Hill, the sparsely fortified position where the Royal Scots had regrouped and dug in. Camouflaged patrols would penetrate the lower slopes and direct mortar and small-arms fire at the enemy, who had

gone three days with little sleep. At sunrise, fresh troops
would strike Golden Hill in full force; those troops were forbidden to cease fighting until they had routed the Scots. The
East Indians could still alter their line and deny the Japanese a path to Kowloon, but Golden Hill overlooked Taipo
Road, the enemy's supply route. Even the stubborn Rajputs
and Punjabis could not hold on once their food and ammunition were cut off.

All night long, Japanese patrols pierced the Scots' defenses, playing havoc with already frayed nerves. A soldier
would drift off to sleep only to be rudely awakened half an
hour later by bursting mortar shells or a fusillade of rifle fire.
The Japanese did not care where they aimed, so long as it
was toward the top of the hill and their outbursts disturbed
the enemy's sleep. The forward Scots sentries got the worst
of it. Crawling up the slopes, Japanese riflemen unleashed a
sudden volley whenever they heard a telltale noise in the
darkness. Some sentries came face to face with Japanese
infiltrators and had to use their bayonets to stave them off.

When the sun rose around 5 A.M., splashing light through
the clouds and onto the hillside, the Japanese patrols retreated. In their place appeared thousands of well-rested infantrymen, shrieking *"Banzai!"* ("May you live ten thousand years") as they swept over and around Shing Mun
Redoubt and raced toward Golden Hill.

The sight of that large number of Japanese, led by sword-
wielding officers, was terrifying, yet the Scots stood their
ground. For two hours the two companies on Golden Hill
poured machine-gun and rifle bullets into the enemy front
line, inflicting hundreds of casualties. Each Japanese retreat
to the base of the hill was followed fifteen minutes later by
another frenzied dash. The four-to-one ratio eventually won
out and the Scots fell back. Over sixty men, among them
both company commanders, died before the Royal Scots
yielded the summit.

The vigorous resistance displayed at Golden Hill did a

great deal to restore the Royal Scots' tarnished reputation. Yet Captain David Pinkerton felt it was not enough. Stationed to the right of the hill, Pinkerton's company watched the successive Japanese attacks and the capture of the hill with anger and frustration. His men practically itched to jump into the fray but were under orders to stay in reserve. When the hill fell, Brigadier Wallis asked the Scots' commanding officer, Lieutenant Colonel Simon White to have the remaining Scots stage a counterattack. White talked him out of it. His men were too tired and too inexperienced to pull off such a feat, he said. Wallis passed on his comments to Maltby, saying, "It's useless to force a battalion commander to execute a plan if he has no confidence in it."

White's instructions for his company to stay put did not get to Pinkerton in time. And, if they had, it is doubtful whether he would have heeded them. He had concluded that the best way for the Scots to vanquish any lingering suspicion about their fighting prowess was to regain Golden Hill. As the tiny, distant figures of Japanese soldiers shifted about, setting up new defenses atop the hill, the stocky, mustachioed Pinkerton called his men together.

"We're going to get those bastards," he said enthusiastically. "That hill belongs to us."

The counterattack was a foolish endeavor. The enemy had more weapons and more men, and, having achieved a second major triumph in the valley, they felt like world-beaters. But Pinkerton's company, in an astonishing demonstration that sheer willpower can work miracles, stormed to the top, forcing the Japanese to flee. The fight was brief and bloody. Running in front of his men, tossing grenades and firing his revolver, Pinkerton escaped death time and again. A mortar explosion knocked him off his feet and a bayonet lunge cut his left arm. Still he raced on, shouting insults at the enemy and brandishing a bayonet when his revolver was empty. A bullet grazed Pinkerton's temple as he approached the summit; he stopped, had a soldier tie part of a shirt around his head to halt the bleeding, and then resumed his relentless gallop. Pinkerton's heroism inspired his men to fight even more fiercely than they thought they were capable of, and it surprised absolutely no one when he was later awarded the Military Cross.

Advised of the rout, Sakai censured the officers in charge of the Golden Hill mission. To be defeated by an inferior foe was, he said, to be humiliated, and the price of humiliation for a professional warrior was frequently hara-kiri. On the other hand, the reward for victory was eternal glory. His pep talk had its desired impact: the Japanese returned to Golden Hill and Pinkerton's company, its energy drained by the initial battle, was pushed back down the slopes. By 10 A.M., the Japanese held the hill once again.

Maltby knew that Gin Drinkers' Line was doomed. The capture of Shing Mun Redoubt gave the enemy a stronghold from which they could deliver persistent blows to other positions until they crumbled. With Golden Hill gone, the paper-thin line of Punjabis and Rajputs would undoubtedly be attacked with renewed fury. The East Indians' chances of standing firm more than a day or two had been reduced to almost zero by the enemy's newly gained ability to cripple the Taipo Road supply route. At noon on Thursday, Maltby informed Wallis that the mainland must be evacuated; otherwise, the Japanese could rip a hole in Gin Drinkers' and, flooding through it, sweep the left and right flanks, trapping and massacring the defenders. "The evacuation order was given on regrettably short notice but was unavoidable owing to the rapidity with which the situation deteriorated," Maltby stated in his official dispatch.

Under the cover of darkness the Rajputs and Punjabis were to travel east to Devil's Peak Peninsula, where the biggest warship in Hong Kong, a 1922-model destroyer, would pick them up; all other personnel were to march to Kowloon and take ferryboats and launches to the island. On the military maps, the mass withdrawal looked like a smooth, low-risk operation; with luck the Japanese would not know the whole force had pulled out until the next morning. But Dame Fortune granted the retreating troops only a portion of the luck they needed and, for hundreds of soldiers, the evacuation became a chaotic, near frantic scramble to avoid being butchered.

CHAPTER EIGHT

New Territories, December 11

He was alive after all. The shelling had lasted an hour, off and on, and, to Sergeant Bob Manchester's utter amazement, none of the Grenadiers were killed or seriously wounded. He had climbed out of the trench, dusted himself off, and, with an euphoria born of relief, joked with some of the boys. A few minutes later a Japanese spotter plane had swooped over the ravine to assess the Grenadiers' strength; doubtless, the pilot had told the gunners the platoon was too small to waste ammunition on for the shelling did not resume. The British artillery was silent too—except for occasional barrages that, mercifully, found the range at last and walloped Japanese entrenchments in the hills.

The platoon settled down to await further instructions from the rear. They were slow in coming. In the morning Manchester and his mates exchanged small-arms fire with enemy soldiers, who were so far away they resembled scurrying insects. Then, late that afternoon, the platoon was ordered back to the Castle Peak-Taipo junction. They were to rejoin Company D for a march to Kowloon.

"Why can't we have friggin' trucks?" a soldier complained. "I'll wear out my boots and then what'll I do?"

"What you always do in Alberta, you goddamned hillbilly," someone replied. "Go barefoot."

Manchester did not mind having to walk. He was happy just to be among the living.

When Company D marched into Kowloon that night, the city was in an uproar. Thousands of Chinese civilians had descended upon the waterfront and were pushing, shrieking, begging for space on the few available vessels. A handful of English civil servants, attempting to organize lineups and issue special channel-crossing permits, were swallowed by the swirling crowd and had to give up all hope of establishing order and decorum. White residents of Kowloon joined the melee and many bribed sampan owners to carry them over to the island. In the midst of the crowd, policemen shoved and clubbed their way forward; they believed they were fighting for their lives, for one of the conquering Imperial Japanese Army's priorities would be the execution of all police officers. A notorious criminal took advantage of the crush to settle an old score and knife a policeman to death. He was grabbed by two policemen, dragged into a lane, and shot. And a Chinese restaurateur, pushing frantically, inadvertently shoved his brother off the dock, drowning him.

The civilian population had not been formally told of the evacuation, but Fortress Headquarters could hardly keep it secret once the demolition crews went to work. Around dusk, the Engineers blew up the central power station, a large cement plant, and the tracks leading into the railway terminal. Then came the few buildings still standing at Kai Tak Airport and a fuel dump on the city's outskirts. British and foreign freighters anchored in Kowloon Harbor were scuttled by opening the cocks and letting water in. The Star ferries would be destroyed last.

Alerted by the explosions and witnessing the soldiers streaming to the waterfront, the civilians panicked. But not all of them: thousands stayed behind to loot the city. Smashing windows to gain entry, thieves carted away every-

In October 1941 the Royal Rifles left Valcartier, Quebec, and headed for their embarkation point: Vancouver. (National Photography Collection, Public Archives: Z-3643-2 and Z-3645-1)

The Winnipeg Grenadiers entrained at Winnipeg en route to the troopship *Awatea*, in Vancouver. (National Photography Collection, Public Archives Canada Z-3647-11 and Z-3645-32-3)

Aboard the *Awatea*, from left to right, Major C. A. Lyndon, Brigadier John K. Lawson, Colonel Pat Hennessey, and Captain H. S. A. Bush. Bush was the only survivor. (National Photography Collection, Public Archives Canada Z-3646-33-1)

The crowded ship, which the British Government commissioned to transport the two Canadian battalions across the Pacific, sailed out of Burrard Inlet on October 27. (National Photography Collection, Public Archives Canada Z-3649-52-4)

On November 16, the Hong Kong paper *China Mail* printed an Extra edition with a banner headline to herald the arrival of reinforcements: "Big Canadian Contingent Descends Upon Colony." The troops disembarked and marched two miles to the Sham Shui Po barracks on the mainland. (National Photography Collection, Public Archives Canada C 49742)

A typical street scene in the Chinese quarter on Hong Kong island, Victoria.
(National Photography Collection, Public Archives Canada PR-587)

A view of the waterfront in Victoria. (National Photography Collection, Public Archives Canada PR-586)

Victoria Harbor, looking northward to Kowloon on the mainland. (National Photography Collection, Public Archives Canada PR-603)

Sir Mark Young, left, arrived in Hong Kong to become governor of the colony only two months before the Canadian commanding officer, Brigadier John Lawson, right. On Christmas Day the governor's message was: "Hold fast for King and Empire" and he vehemently opposed the decision to surrender to the Japanese that day. (National Photography Collection, Public Archives Canada C 49740)

thing from teakettles to car tires. The unoccupied homes of affluent Britons were stripped bare. Food and clothing were the most desirable items; one ragged Chinese coolie was seen running from a British journalist's house wearing a black bowler and pin-striped jacket and hugging a sack of flour. The deserted barracks at Sham Shui Po were picked clean, as though attacked by vultures. Doors, windows, bunks, electrical wiring, garbage cans—anything that could be moved was taken, leaving only the naked shells of the buildings.

By the time the Grenadiers marched through the condemned city, the ferry captains had sailed to Victoria, their boats filled with Royal Scots, white civilians, and Chinese coolies. The Japanese were close on the Canadians' heels. Fifth columnists had somehow informed them that the withdrawal was taking place, and the enemy was coming up fast at the rear, intending to trap the retreating soldiers at the waterfront.

Company D Captain Allan Bowman peered across the mile-wide strait and, noting the boats' stationary lights, concluded that they were not returning to Kowloon. Bowman contacted Grenadier transport officer Captain Wilfred Queen-Hughes on the island and explained the company's plight. Queen-Hughes took matters into his own hands. Proceeding to the wharf, he boarded a ferry and asked the captain to make the crossing. When the captain refused, saying that the Japanese were too close, Queen-Hughes drew his revolver and pointed it at the man's head. More frightened of the officer's gun than he was of the yet unseen Japanese, the captain complied. As the gangplank went down at the city of Kowloon pier, Company D advanced through the throng like a giant wedge. They were not alone on the boat. Chinese civilians clambering on board included four members of a funeral cortège and a black hearse. The Grenadiers' relief at having gotten off the mainland safely was tempered with a feeling of pending doom engendered by the presence of the hearse and mourners. The Chinese usually treated death as a cause for rejoicing, and funeral processions featured multicolored costumes and brass bands. These Chinese, eerily gloomy, were jokingly referred to as the Four Horsemen of the Apocalypse. But no one was really laughing.

Victoria, December 11

James Bertram was at the Ministry of Information on Thursday morning when his friend Hilda Selwyn-Clarke dropped in briefly on her way to the Red Cross office next door. Bertram, a New Zealand-born Rhodes Scholar who had served as the press attaché at the British Embassy, was writing a propaganda-riddled news release claiming that the Japanese were being wiped out in the New Territories.

"Better scrap that one," the attractive redhead advised him. "Rumor has it Gin Drinkers' is in trouble and the Japanese will soon be entering Kowloon."

Bertram mouthed a silent curse. That spelled the end of the hand-picked propaganda team that was, at that very moment, gathering somewhere else in the building. The ministry, although still awaiting an official green light from higher up, had been training singers, actors, and orators for a week, molding a team that would employ street-theater techniques and loudspeakers to boost the Chinese population's morale. With the Japanese in Kowloon, the war would be too close to bother about such tactics.

"There's still Fatty Liao's guerrillas," Hilda said. "Do you want me to get in touch with him?"

He certainly did. Liao, an obese colonel in the Chinese 8th Route Army, was a deft guerrilla fighter who had persistently implored the British to disperse arms to three thousand carefully selected Chinese on the mainland. Owing to its long-standing distrust of the natives, the colonial government had protested that the guerrillas might be persuaded by fifth columnists to turn the weapons on the British.

Tearing the propaganda story from his typewriter, Bertram asked Hilda to write a letter to Maltby, stressing the importance of the arms scheme. As Hilda and her husband knew Maltby socially, he thought the letter would lend weight to Liao's proposal. That afternoon Bertram delivered the letter to Fortress Headquarters. Maltby was too preoccupied with the mainland situation and, in his place, he sent Major Boxer to meet with Liao and Bertram late Thursday afternoon.

Liao said that he had men stationed on two tiny islands near the mainland who could distribute arms on immediate notice. After listening to Liao's argument, Boxer phoned a senior officer and stated that he favored the plan. If the guerrillas failed to halt the Japanese advance, Boxer said, they would hide in and around Kowloon, conducting hit-and-run raids and acts of sabotage.

The officer rejected the idea. "I'm sorry, old fellow, but we simply don't have the guns to spare," he said. "Like everything else, the guerrilla plan has been left too late."

When the disappointed Liao departed, saying he wanted to get his men off the islands, Bertram asked Boxer what he should do next.

"Get yourself a gun and man a barricade," was the retort. "The mainland is going to fall."

Dressed in corduroy slacks and a gray tweed overcoat, Bertram spent a quiet night behind a Bren gun on the waterfront. The following day he was handed a Volunteers' uniform and taken on a bus to Stanley Peninsula. Bertram and eight other Volunteers were to guard a pair of six-inch naval guns on a windy bluff overlooking the sea. His companions included a portly China Light and Power Company executive who could not button his jacket, a corporal who made his own stripes out of a shirttail, and a local character known for his feisty letters to the editor of the *China Mail* which he signed "Atheist." The gunners were, if possible, an even less impressive lot: Chinese students from Hong Kong University. They arrived on the bus with Bertram and appeared to be only slightly more knowledgeable than he was when it came to operating the guns.

With armed Victoria policemen patrolling the docks to discourage deserters (more than half the crewmen had already fled), the ferries ran all night, transporting civilians and army stragglers. The last of the military vehicles arrived around midnight and the final demolition party, after blowing up a radio communication center at Kai Tak, escaped in the RAF launch.

Six Royal Scots who had been separated from their company were aboard one of the ferries. A Grenadier officer, observing the stragglers disembark amid a throng of Chinese, noticed they were having difficulty walking. Going to them, he discovered the six were drunk. They had broken into a private home and emptied the liquor cabinet. The Grenadier took the six to the Scots' barracks and recommended to a second lieutenant that they be severely punished. After the Canadian left, the officer asked the men if any of them had been at Golden Hill.

"Yes, sir," was the slurred reply. "We was there. All of us. Horrible it was. Real horrible."

"In that case," the second lieutenant said, "I think you have been punished enough. Go to bed and get some sleep."

Kowloon, December 12

At 3 A.M. Friday, a lost Punjabi platoon advanced cautiously through downtown Kowloon. The deserted streets were littered with broken window glass and discarded merchandise from looted shops and offices that proved too bulky to carry away. Every few blocks a sniper popped up on a dark roof or in a doorway, but the fifth columnists were no match for the Punjabi sharpshooters: nine were killed while the Punjabis suffered three minor wounds.

The platoon had been fighting a rear-guard action against Japanese soldiers, protecting the Rajputs and Punjabi companies heading for their rendezvous with the destroyer at Devil's Peak. Somewhere on the unmarked mountain trails the platoon had taken a wrong turn and the senior officer, Lieutenant Nigel Forsyth, decided its only chance of escaping lay in reaching the ferry docks at Kowloon.

The Punjabis entered the city only a few minutes ahead of the Japanese. Their progress slowed by the snipers, the East Indians were two miles from the wharf when the Japanese patrols caught up and began attacking from the rear. Complicating matters further, some of the dark figures looming out of doorways turned out to be soldiers cut off from their units; the Punjabis could not be sure who was a fifth columnist and who was not until a sniper opened fire.

Despite the hazards the platoon made it to the dock. The majority of the Scots and Grenadiers had long departed and a mixed bag of stragglers—mostly Volunteers, artillerymen, policemen, and Engineers—were helping load civilians and their hastily packed luggage onto ferryboats. In the kind of gesture that typified the Punjabis' fighting record at Hong Kong, the platoon refused to board a ferry. Forsyth set up machine-gun nests behind cargo containers and other makeshift fortifications on the wharf and vowed that the Punjabis would not leave until the last passenger sailed on the last ferry. A Japanese patrol materialized minutes after the Punjabis settled in on the wharf. Greeted by a torrent of gunfire, the patrol fled. But it soon returned. Enemy soldiers kept creeping within firing range, trading bullets with the East Indians, then withdrawing. Copying the technique employed in the New Territories, the Japanese were saving their main assault until daylight.

While the ferries lumbered back and forth, the odd

straggler sneaked through the enemy lines and joined the huge crowd on the docks. A Scottish military policeman related a story that even under such tense circumstances evoked smiles. Having lost contact with his company, he was proceeding along Salisbury Road when he saw a group of soldiers lounging on a corner, smoking and chatting. In the darkness he could not tell whether they were Scots or Grenadiers. All the same, he felt obliged to warn them that the Japanese were in the city.

"Get a move on!" he shouted. "What do you think this is —a Sunday outing? The Japs are all over the place!"

The startled soldiers quickly dispersed, and when they started shooting at him he realized they were Japanese.

At first light the enemy descended upon the waterfront in a massive swarm. The civilians on the pier, screaming, jostling, and yelling that the end was near, raced in every direction. Some leapt in the water, others ran directly into the Japanese line of fire and died. Hundreds sprinted past Japanese soldiers and hid in vacant buildings. Firing as they moved, the Punjabis backed up. When the last civilian was off the pier, the East Indians joined two hundred Chinese cowering aboard the remaining ferry. As the gangplank went up, two wounded men on the wharf got to their feet and hurled themselves in the water. One, an army medical orderly wounded in the neck, swam to the island; the other, a Punjabi signalman who could not swim, paddled across in a life preserver.

The Punjabis aboard the ferry gathered in the stern, rifles and revolvers blazing. The Japanese blanketed the pier and several enemy soldiers, attempting to jump onto the departing boat, missed and fell into the water. The East Indians shot them as they thrashed about. Forsyth, wielding a chattering Tommy gun, did not tell his men to cease firing until the boat was well out of the sights of the Japanese infantrymen.

Rising early Friday morning, hotel clerk Harold Bateson pulled back the curtain covering the bedroom window of his second-story flat and scanned the street below. The noise of gunfire from the harbor and troop movements in his district had kept him awake most of the night. He noticed that the shops and office buildings lining the street had not been looted and, a block to the west, he noticed something else— two Japanese soldiers sitting on the sidewalk, their backs against a wall.

Still wearing his striped pajamas, Bateson went into the living room. His houseboy, Wu Li-jen, was at the window, staring out apprehensively. Bateson looked down and saw another thoroughfare that, strangely enough, had also escaped looting. A platoon of Japanese soldiers stood smartly in column formation in front of a graystone insurance building, ready to march at a moment's call. Four officers huddled together fifty yards up the street, studying a map spread on the hood of a car disabled by fifth columnists.

Bateson retrieved the lengthy letter he had written to his parents in Australia and handed it to Li-jen. "You keep this until the fighting is over. Give it to the British. No matter how many years, you keep it."

The houseboy nodded and pocketed the letter. Bateson then walked into the bathroom, shaved, and changed into the white shirt and natty double-breasted suit Li-jen had pressed and hung on the door. As he explained in the letter, he was turning himself over to the Japanese. It was a calm, rational act. Standing behind the reception desk at the Peninsula Hotel, he had spent many nights pondering what he should do in the event of a Japanese invasion. Like his father, a Melbourne realtor who had led anti-war demonstrations in 1914, Bateson was a staunch pacifist. He had joined the Volunteers because his friends had and because he did not really believe war would come. Two years of working in Japan had given him a great respect for the moralistic, highly principled Japanese. For one thing, they were much more honest than the Chinese. He had once left a camera on a Tokyo bus and a student had gone out of his way to find its owner. The Chinese had practiced "squeeze" for so many centuries that they had lost all understanding of what honesty meant.

The leaflets the Japanese dropped over Hong Kong after every daylight air raid contained an ever-increasing variety of propaganda messages. "Squash our common oppressors and throw off the yoke of British imperialism," the East Indians were urged. "Sabotage the enemy and make Hong Kong part of a new all-Asian empire," read the plea to the Chinese. And, for the whites, the Japanese devised a leaflet promising that "anyone presenting this paper to a Japanese soldier will be treated like a brother and can exist in peace." Bateson carried a copy of that leaflet in his jacket pocket. He did not trust the message implicitly—"exist in peace" probably meant internment in a POW camp—but he had decided that captivity was preferable to armed conflict, regardless of how harsh the camp conditions might be.

When he finished dressing, he returned to the living room and placed his leather-bound shaving kit in the suitcase he had packed Thursday night.

"You go to your family," he told Li-jen, giving him a handful of pound notes. "This money won't be any good now, but maybe it will be after the war."

Three minutes later Bateson was on the street, approaching the Japanese officers, his suitcase in one hand, the leaflet in the other. Startled by his sudden appearance, one of the officers drew his sword. In halting Japanese, Bateson explained that he was surrendering. The officer nodded, accepted the leaflet, and told him to stand on the sidewalk, a few feet away.

For ten minutes Bateson waited; the officers argued over the map; the column of soldiers eyed him curiously; Li-jen watched from the flat. Finally agreeing on where they were going, the officers folded the map and, ignoring Bateson, strode to the front of the column. The soldiers turned and, trailed by the officers, marched in the opposite direction. Two soldiers had been ordered to stay behind and deal with the prisoner. Bateson lifted his suitcase and walked to meet them. He was ten feet away when they raised their rifles and fired, killing him instantly. The soldiers rummaged the suitcase before leaving; the only item they bothered taking was the shaving kit.

Harold Bateson's body still lay in the street when Li-jen slipped out of the flat. The young houseboy was almost trembling with fear. If he was caught with the letter the Japanese might shoot him, but he could not bring himself to leave it behind. Bateson had been a kind, generous person who had let him take leftover food to his family and had bought a new radio for Li-jen's tiny room off the kitchen. Li-jen felt he owed it to the dead man to fulfill his final wish; he would, however, throw the letter away if the Japanese came too close to him.

Li-jen's parents lived in a squatters' shack, a two-room shelter made of packing crates and mud on the outskirts of Kowloon, about two miles from Bateson's flat. He made his way carefully along the near-empty streets, hugging doorways and watching for soldiers. Now and then Chinese faces peered anxiously from windows and, every block or so, he spotted coolies darting from building to building. The only traffic he saw consisted of a truck convoy, bearing Japanese troops, crossing a road two blocks ahead of him. The only sounds he heard were the distant thumps of artillery fire and occasional gun bursts; he assumed that the Japanese big guns were shelling the island and the small-arms fire indicated the Japanese were shooting civilians.

Turning a corner, Li-jen bumped into a Japanese soldier leaving a clothing store that had been wrecked by looters.

"Food!" the soldier demanded in Cantonese, aiming at Li-jen's stomach with a bayoneted rifle. "You tell me! Where food?"

His hand shaking, the houseboy pointed over his shoulder. "Very close," he lied. "A warehouse. Plenty of tinned food."

The soldier shoved him aside and hurried off. Japanese soldiers often went into combat zones with small bags of rice and little else; their generals theorized that they would fight harder if food was among the spoils of war.

Li-jen encountered no more soldiers until he was half a block from his parents' home. Three Japanese were in front of the only structure on the street that was not a flimsy squatters' shack, a low, dingy cement building that was once a power station. A dozen refugees lived inside. The soldiers had dragged two women outside and, at bayonet point, were forcing them to undress. Li-jen ducked into a lane entrance and watched, horrified. He knew the women slightly. One was a middle-aged widow who sold cheap jewelry in the market, the other a girl his own age betrothed to a soldier fighting in China. Two of the soldiers raped the girl, then the third raped the widow. A truck carrying more soldiers rumbled into view. The three soldiers got on, pushing the terror-stricken women ahead of them. The soldiers on the truck, hooting and laughing, passed the women back and forth as the vehicle departed.

Li-jen ran to his parents' house.

"I'm so pleased you are alive," his father said, closing the door behind them. "The Japanese are shooting people for no reason. Sometimes they go in a house and shoot everyone. It will get worse. The main army has not come from the border yet."

Li-jen's mother came from the back room; she had been hiding since she saw the three soldiers on the street. A wash amah for an English family for twelve years, she had been fired when her hands became crippled by arthritis. Li-jen's wages had been his family's sole source of income; his father was an unemployed laborer.

"Why didn't you take something from Mr. Bateson's?" his father said after Li-jen told him about the killing. "We could sell the radio he gave you."

"I was scared the Japanese would think I was a looter. They are looting themselves but last night they were shooting Chinese who did it."

As he spoke, Li-jen placed Bateson's letter on a shelf. From what he had witnessed that day, he doubted the Japanese would ever be driven from Kowloon. They were much too vicious and evil to be destroyed by the kindly, mild-mannered English.

Li-jen and his father survived the war, working as servants for Chinese businessmen who collaborated with the occupation force. In 1946 Li-jen took the letter to British authorities in Hong Kong and explained the circumstances of Bateson's death. The letter and a portion of his statement were eventually turned over to Bateson's father in Melbourne.

Devil's Peak, December 12

It took the last of Maltby's troops on the mainland, the Rajputs and Punjabis, nine hours to complete their ten mile trek from Shing Mun Valley to Devil's Peak. With all pack mules and trucks shipped to the island, the East Indians had to carry their machine guns, mortars, and rations over twisting mountain passes. Time and again the Chinese guides, confused at having to find the route at night, led the men in the wrong direction. Finally, at seven o'clock on that balmy Friday morning, the exhausted soldiers stopped to rest on a hillside a mile north of the rendezvous site. The trailing Japanese had lost touch with them but a reconnaissance plane, scanning Devil's Peak at 7:30, discovered their new position. Half an hour later, a dive-bomber squadron struck the hillside, inflicting heavy casualties, and soon after the planes disappeared, Japanese infantrymen raked the East Indians with intensive mortar and rifle fire. Characteristically, the Rajputs and Punjabis dug in their heels and refused to budge.

At Fortress Headquarters, Maltby was delaying the East Indians' evacuation, hoping that these indefatigable fighters would somehow stop the Japanese tide. With the New Territories and Kowloon now in enemy hands, the Rajputs and Punjabis held the last strategic line on the mainland, barring access to Lye Mun Passage. Less than half a mile wide, Lye Mun was the narrowest body of water lying between the mainland and the island. If the East Indians withdrew, the enemy could conceivably storm across Lye Mun in junks and jerry-built rafts.

Early Friday morning, Maltby bolstered the peninsula directly across from the East Indians' position with several infantry platoons and an artillery battery. He realized the peninsula was still inadequately defended, yet he did not think the Lye Mun threat justified drastically reducing the number of troops concentrated in the south, waiting for an enemy task force to come sweeping in from the sea.

CHAPTER NINE

Devil's Peak, December 12–13

The East Indians had to retreat. By Friday night the intensity of the Japanese air and land assaults had lengthened the casualty list to such an extent that Maltby feared both battalions would be annihilated unless they withdrew from the mainland. The evacuation was to be conducted in two stages. The Rajputs would fall back gradually, staving off the hard-pressing Japanese infantry while the Punjabis rushed to the Devil's Peak peninsula to board a flotilla of motor launches. The last warship in Hong Kong (the other two destroyers had gone to Singapore on December 7), the H.M.S. *Thracian,* would be used to bring the Rajputs across.

The first snag developed when Maltby's senior officers went to the docks in Victoria to supervise the operation. Most of the Chinese launch crews had deserted and many boats had been damaged by artillery fire. Civilian volunteers and Canadian and British soldiers with maritime experience —one fellow said he was the Class "A" dinghy champion of Montreal—came forward to help Hong Kong's small Royal Navy contingent man the launches. Mechanics succeeded in getting three of the damaged boats going and, around 9 P.M., eleven launches began crisscrossing Lye Mun Passage, ferrying Punjabis.

Unable to pinpoint their whereabouts in the dark, the

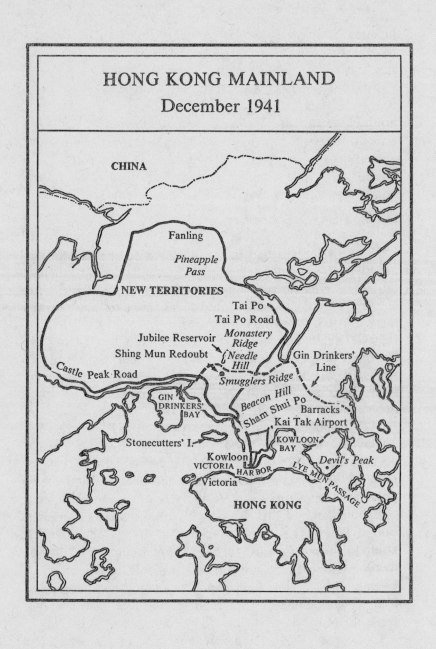

HONG KONG MAINLAND
December 1941

CHINA

Fanling

Pineapple Pass

NEW TERRITORIES

Tai Po
Tai Po Road

Jubilee Reservoir
Shing Mun Redoubt

Monastery Ridge

Needle Hill

Gin Drinkers' Line

Castle Peak Road

Smugglers Ridge

GIN DRINKERS' BAY

Beacon Hill

Sham Shui Po

Barracks

Kai Tak Airport

Stonecutters' I.

KOWLOON BAY

Kowloon

VICTORIA

Devil's Peak

HARBOR

LYE MUN PASSAGE

Victoria

HONG KONG

Japanese did not attack the retreating troops. The Rajputs were less fortunate. At 4 A.M. Saturday, after the last Punjabi was taken to the island, the tide went out and the *Thracian* was forced to anchor several hundred yards from the rendezvous point, a pier on the tip of Devil's Peak peninsula. Fighting a rear-guard action all the way, the Rajputs arrived at the dock in sections. Some men rode to the antiquated destroyer in shallow-bottomed sampans; others waded and swam out, holding their rifles. Fortress Headquarters wanted to complete the evacuation before daybreak, but the Rajputs' slow progress presented another worry—that Japanese aircraft would take advantage of the daylight to sink the *Thracian*. She was, after all, sitting in the open, and the British had hardly any anti-aircraft guns on the northeast corner of the island.

Fortunately, no planes appeared. But as the final remnants of the Rajput battalion made their way to the destroyer, Japanese soldiers rushed onto the pier, chopping the water with mortar shells and rifle bullets. Several East Indians died within a couple of feet of the gangway. Her four-inch guns pumping, the *Thracian* hauled anchor and, at 9:20 A.M., she put in at Aberdeen, the naval base on the west side of the island.

A short while later, upon entering their barracks to catch up on desperately needed sleep, the Rajputs learned that a Japanese delegation was in Victoria, demanding an unconditional surrender.

"I don't care what Fortress Headquarters says," Captain Bob Newton declared, flinging himself on a cot. "I'm not going to surrender. Those clods have killed too many of our men."

Victoria, December 13

The Japanese delegation arrived shortly after nine o'clock Saturday morning. Three high-level officers, a civilian interpreter, and two female hostages rode across from Kowloon in a launch flying a white flag and bearing a white banner inscribed PEACE MISSION on the bow. Sakai was confident that the mainland defeat had broken the defenders' morale sufficiently and he would be handed the island four days ahead of the Tokyo deadline. In a letter to Governor Young, the Japanese commander stated that a massive air and artillery barrage was planned unless the colony capitulated forthwith.

Steel-helmeted British soldiers, standing erectly in columns, lined the Victoria pier and cordoned off adjacent streets. The Japanese and British officers saluted one another, and Colonel Tokuchi Tada, the short, elegant-mannered officer in charge of the mission, approached the senior British officer, Major Boxer. "I have a letter for your Governor," he said. "We wish you to surrender. I will wait for a reply."

As Boxer departed in a staff car, Tada walked over to Gwen Dew, a pretty thirty-four-year-old Detroit *News* correspondent who was standing on the wharf, clutching a camera. "Would you like our picture?" he asked. She said she would and the Japanese delegation gathered for a group shot in front of the boat. "You may want some information for your caption," Tada volunteered. "I have a wife and three children in Tokyo. Both these officers are unmarried, poor souls."

The hostages then disembarked. Tada explained that one was a pregnant Russian woman, and she was allowed to leave for a hospital. The other, the wife of a British civil servant, would be kept to ensure the delegation's safe passage.

The Englishwoman left her two dachshunds with a British soldier and reluctantly returned to the boat.

Fifteen minutes later Boxer was back from Government House. Young had issued a one-word reply, he said, and the word was "No."

"It will be a pity if we have to level this beautiful city," the interpreter remarked, turning to leave.

Sakai's reaction was different. "I am amazed the governor has so much courage," he wrote in his daily journal. Young, in fact, had even more nerve than the Japanese commander now imagined. The scion of an aristocratic family, the fifty-five-year-old career civil servant had excelled on the sporting fields of Eton and Cambridge, notably as a bruising rugby player. He was a tough, proud individual who, serving as the governor of Tanganyika in 1939, skirted the desk and coolly disarmed an insane planter threatening to shoot him.

Twenty minutes after Young rejected the surrender ultimatum, Sakai told a staff meeting that he wanted a merciless two-day blitz, striking civilian and military targets alike. The bombardments would, he said, all but destroy the defenders' willpower, thus paving the way for an invasion on Monday.

With the East Indians now on the island, Maltby reorganized his troops' defensive posture. The Royal Rifles and Rajputs were assigned the eastern sector and the Grenadiers, Middlesex, and Punjabis the west. The Volunteers were scattered across the island and a large contingent of Middlesex was placed under direct command of Fortress Headquarters. Brigadier Wallis was in charge of East Brigade, Brigadier Lawson commanded West Brigade.

The new arrangement displeased Lawson. Although the two Canadian units stood cheek by jowl in some of their positions facing the south coast, the Rifles now took orders from British officers they barely knew. Canadian military historian C. P. Stacey remarked in his 1955 book, *Six Years of War*, that "the Canadians would have been more effectively employed fighting together under their own brigadier." Lawson held the same view, and he expressed his displeasure in a Most Secret telegram to Ottawa. However, he was a career soldier, accustomed to obeying orders, and at 2 P.M. on Saturday, following a tour of his new command, he went to Fortress Headquarters for lunch and a conference on how the West Brigade could improve its battle preparations.

Lye Mun Peninsula, December 13

On Saturday afternoon Dr. John Crawford, the head of the Canadian medical team, received a telephone call from a field ambulance officer, Captain Martin Banfill.

"I do think I should find myself a decent job," Banfill said lightly. "I'm enjoying this holiday, but all this lying about is bad for a person's character."

"What's wrong with the job you've got?" Crawford inquired.

"Nothing to do. The Japanese asked everyone to leave and, of course, they didn't want to cause a fuss, so they went."

The Quebec-born Banfill ran the first-aid post on the peninsula to the east of Victoria, facing Lye Mun Passage and the Japanese-held mainland. His staff was an odd mixture: trained army doctors and orderlies working alongside a female Eurasian art student, a half-dozen female St. John's Ambulance aides, two dignified lady volunteers from the Peak, a male Russian doctor, and thirty Chinese helpers. The post served the Rifles, Volunteers, and Rajputs at Lye Mun Barracks and an ack-ack battery.

Surprised to hear the barracks had been evacuated that morning, Crawford drove to the first-aid post, a big brick building formerly used as a Salesian Fathers' school. He did not have to speculate on what had prompted the sudden troop exodus. The Japanese had moved artillery up Devil's Peak and, in wake of Young's rejection, pasted the first-aid station and nearby barracks, damaging several buildings.

"I've lost my Chinese driver," Banfill told Crawford over coffee in the deserted barracks mess. "He's in Victoria, or heaven. A shell landed behind me and when I turned around he wasn't there. He either ran away or disintegrated."

The soldiers had withdrawn to a hillside half a mile south that offered more protection and still gave them unobstructed view of Lye Mun Passage. Many of Banfill's Chinese assistants had fled during the shelling but most of the medical staff remained, waiting for reassignment.

"Well, you can't stay here," Crawford said. "The Japanese are liable to resume shelling any minute. We'll look at the real estate to the south and see if we can find you a suitable place."

The two men drove up and down mountain roads until they located a vacant two-story building close to the hill taken over by the Lye Mun soldiers. The first-aid unit's pullback Saturday afternoon left the tip of the peninsula completely unoccupied, although it was covered by machine-gun and artillery placements to the west, east, and south. Obviously, Banfill and his corps were still in a highly dangerous situation. Should the Japanese knock out the machine guns and artillery, they could land on the tip and sweep inland in a matter of minutes.

Kowloon, December 13

Sometime Saturday the enemy artillery barrage was joined by a hefty nine-inch gun hidden on a Japanese-owned golf course in Kowloon. The gun had been smuggled over the border in pieces and reassembled during the sum-

mer in 1941 in a large shed marked PRIVATE: KEEP OUT, two
hundred yards beyond the eighteenth hole. When General
Sakai ordered the two-day blitz, the corrugated-tin roof was
stripped off and a truck convoy delivered ammunition.

That was only one example of the ingenious methods used
by the Japanese artillery battalion. Soldiers had trained for
months on how to drag a heavy gun to a hilltop and set it up
with the utmost speed. Guns were also located behind hills
and sound-ranging equipment employed to pinpoint the
source of enemy counterfire. Because the Japanese artillery
never fired at night unless supporting an infantry attack, the
possibility of locating guns by their flashes was greatly reduced. The gunners' accuracy rate was exceptional (though
one in every seven shells did not explode) and, unwilling to
tire their own men, the Japanese maintained the ammunition
supply by forced Chinese labor. Any coolie showing signs of
slacking off was taken aside and shot.

Captured Japanese strategy papers—and the testimony of
the Hong Kong invasion leaders at their subsequent war-
crimes trial—failed to reveal the precise amount of artillery
used in the battle. It is known that the Japanese armory included nine-inch, four-inch, seventy-five-millimeter and
two-pound guns and a raft of fifteen-centimeter howitzers.
And a Japanese officer said during a conversation with two
Grenadier officers after the colony fell that two hundred
guns were used, but this figure was never confirmed.

Whatever the extent of the armaments, the Japanese artillery battalion pounded the gun placements along the island's north shore with stunning success. One of the 9.2's at
Mount Davis on the northwest shore received a direct hit
Saturday and the next morning the enemy wiped out the
rest of the anti-aircraft battery stationed there. Three other
anti-aircraft weapons and a host of machine-gun nests elsewhere on the north coast were similarly demolished. Fires
caused by the systematic shelling raged throughout Victoria.
Soldiers helped the overworked local fire brigade, and some

of the more stubborn blazes took up to twelve hours to quell. Aided by dive bombers, the Japanese gunners reached farther inland from time to time, blitzing the white residential districts. The mansions on the Peak were a prime target.

The Peak, December 14

Emily Hahn hated the shelling worst of all. The Japanese planes dropped their lethal cargoes and sped on; if you survived the initial blast, you would be all right. The artillery hammered at the same spot over and over until it collapsed. Emily, her baby, and a dozen other strays—mostly doctors and their families who had lost their homes to shells—huddled in the cellar of the Selwyn-Clarke villa, listening to the explosions and praying the Japanese did not have their hiding place on their target list. Fifth columnists had reported which Peak villas were occupied by soldiers and which by prominent citizens; the Peak Tramway down the street was under constant fire and, by shifting slightly, the guns could destroy the home of Hong Kong's medical director, thus dealing the colony a sharp psychological blow.

All weekend Emily and her newly acquired friends remained in the cellar. Between shellings, they hurried upstairs to prepare meals, round up children who insisted upon slipping outdoors to play, and listen to the BBC overseas newscast. "The gallant fortress of Hong Kong is holding up well against the enemy assault," the announcer proclaimed. So, fortunately, was the Selwyn-Clarke house. The foundation shook, windows broke, a jade figurine fell off a table, but the shells never did come close enough to do serious damage. Emily's joy at having survived the two-day blitz was mixed with anxiety over her lover's safety. She had not seen or heard from Charles Boxer since the mainland fell and she was deeply worried that he might be a victim of the shelling.

Aberdeen, December 14

Steve Kashton was daydreaming. Slumped over a machine gun in a four-foot-deep hole, the Grenadier private was thinking about his childhood on his parents' homestead at Oakburn, Manitoba. The three-mile walks along winding roads to school; his brothers and sisters arguing over whose turn it was to haul water from the well to the house; the expeditions into the bush, bundled in scarves and earmuffs, to make sure the horses were okay after a February blizzard. How incredibly beautiful the prairies were compared to this godforsaken land, this lonely mountain slope with its dry soil, granite, and stunted shrubbery, that he had been guarding all week.

Was Hong Kong worth dying for? Would the ownership of a tiny island make any difference to the final outcome of the war? Kashton brushed aside his doubts. He had quit his job driving an ice wagon in Winnipeg and enlisted because he knew that if the Germans were not stopped overseas, they would be in Canada next. Maybe Hong Kong was a hell-hole—a mess of sleazy bars, starving refugees, and desolate hills—but if the Japanese were handed the island on a platter, they would get the idea that Canadians were pushovers and invade British Columbia. Hong Kong *was* worth dying for because what he was really doing was sticking up for his own homeland.

Kashton glanced at his watch. Almost five; time to pick up some grub. Climbing out of the hole, he started toward the slit trenches farther up the mountain where the rest of his section was posted. He had gone only twenty-five feet when he heard the faint drone of an aircraft engine. Shading his eyes with his hand, the twenty-two-year-old bachelor looked up at the hot sky and saw a white seaplane traveling low over the mountains, heading his way. He had been warned that the Japanese might try to drop paratroops behind Victoria but the plane, small and unarmed, was apparently on a reconnaissance flight, hunting for troop encampments.

Running back and jumping into the hole, Kashton swung the tripod-mounted machine gun around to face the aircraft. Any second he expected the pilot to see him and fly up to a higher altitude. But the plane kept on coming. When it was a quarter of a mile off, Kashton began shooting. He emptied a twenty-eight-shot magazine with no success: the plane passed overhead, then turned and, still not spotting him, the pilot brought it back, racing for the open sea. Inserting a second magazine, Kashton squeezed out another twenty-eight bullets. Abruptly the plane burst into flames and, trailing black smoke, crashed into the water.

Kashton was jubilant. Imagine, destroying an enemy plane with a machine gun! The brass would be delighted. He would be mentioned in dispatches, toasted at the regimental mess, maybe even awarded a medal. As Kashton was congratulating himself, a Grenadier captain galloped down the slope.

"Private Kashton!" he yelled. "What's the matter with you? You bloody fool!"

For one awful moment Kashton thought he had downed a British aircraft by mistake. Then he remembered the crimson circles on the wings.

"You know we're short of ammunition," the captain fumed, looking as though he wanted to strike him. "You wasted two magazines on that bloody plane. I'm going to have you court-martialed for this."

The captain was killed in action five days later and Kashton never did face court-martial proceedings. Nor did he receive a regimental toast or a medal either and, to this day, he wishes someone in the Army would acknowledge the fact that using fifty-six bullets to wipe out an enemy aircraft was not a foolish, wasteful act.

Victoria, December 14

Early Sunday morning the haunting voice of Vera Lynn drifted through the city streets and into the shell-battered gun emplacements rimming the north shore. She was singing, "We'll Meet Again." The Japanese had installed a loudspeaker on a Kowloon wharf and, turning the volume up, launched a propaganda campaign, combining recorded popular music with messages read by a Japanese officer in flawless English.

The soldiers loved the music. Besides Miss Lynn, they hummed and sang along with Deanna Durbin, Gracie Fields, Al Jolson, and Bing Crosby. Jolson's "Swanee" was a big favorite. Hundreds of voices belted out the familiar chorus and, for the amusement of their companions, many wags changed the lyrics to obscene versions proclaiming that what they really loved had nothing to do with the American Southland.

The spoken messages dripped with sentimentality.

"Christmas is coming, boys. Your mothers, your wives, your children will be gathered around the tree. They will miss you. And, during the Christmas dinner, all eyes will go to your chair. Your *empty* chair. Those eyes will be wet, boys. Wet with tears. When the Imperial Japanese Army comes to the island, throw away your weapons and tell our soldiers you want peace. You will be put aboard a neutral ship and sent home for Christmas."

The soldiers laughed and jeered. They considered the propaganda sessions so entertaining that whenever a bombardment ceased, they looked forward to hearing them again. Some actually expressed disappointment when a British artillery shell eventually demolished the loudspeaker and the Japanese decided not to replace it.

Private Tony Grimston's father had once worked as a footman for an English aristocrat. His mother had been a cook on the same country estate. And the young man had caught glimpses of the high and mighty while employed as a bellboy at the stately Empress Hotel in Victoria, British Columbia. He had, in fact, observed the highest and mightiest of them all, the King and Queen of England. On duty in the Empress lobby in 1939, he had watched the royal couple alight from an elevator and, surrounded by red-coated Mounties and gaping onlookers, enter the dining room to attend a banquet. The King wore a dark naval uniform, the Queen sparkling jewels and a beautiful gown.

Now Grimston himself was immersed in an elegant life, thanks to the Royal Canadian Signal Corps. Ordered to locate and temporarily occupy suitable quarters for a radio communications center, his platoon had, with great relish, selected a luxurious villa near the summit. The place had its drawbacks—no swimming pool and the liquor cabinet was bare—but the soft beds, fine cutlery, tasteful furnishings, and lovely garden compensated for those lamentable flaws.

Grimston would have given anything to let his father know how he was doing. A World War I veteran, Frank Grimston had often leaned across the kitchen table in the old house on Boyd Street and said he did not want his son to experience the horrors he had seen in France. When England declared war on Germany, he had shaken his head sadly. "I guess you'll have to go, Tony, but I won't like it."

Thus far, the lanky, easygoing youth had been spared the kinds of dreadful things that converted his dad into a pacifist, although he had come perilously close. On December 8, Grimston had been in a mainland ravine, having a cup of tea with an East Indian platoon, when an aircraft squadron had flown toward them. "That's a comforting sight," he said. "It's good to know the British have that many planes." Then the planes had passed overhead and he had seen the rising suns on their wings. Standing in the open, he had made a splendid target but none of the pilots had bothered: they were saving their bullets and bombs for Kai Tak and Sham Shui Po.

Two days later Grimston had been at the Gin Drinkers' Line, one of three Canadian signalmen on loan to the Rajputs. His task had involved sitting in a dry ditch, transmitting coded radio messages to Fortress Headquarters. The Rajputs had stood between him and the Japanese but, by the sound of the small-arms fire, the enemy was closing in and he was likely to be in the midst of a battle. Before the Japanese arrived, Grimston had been ordered to retreat. He had "borrowed" a '28 Chevy from a farmyard and driven to Kowloon. From there he had traveled to the island on a crowded tugboat.

Now this. The lap of luxury. The shells falling on the Peak were too far off to alarm Grimston and his companions, but they had had a scare Saturday night, when a sentry heard a noise in the garden and guessed the villa was being stalked by a fifth columnist. "Identify yourself or I'll shoot," he had shouted into the dense shrubbery. No answer. The sentry had uttered a second warning and then fired. For days afterward the guard would endure the taunts of his buddies: he cheated them out of a delicious dinner, they said, by missing the rooster his shot flushed from the shrubbery.

As much as he liked the place, Grimston knew he had to leave the villa. His orders were to keep changing his position so that the enemy could not get a fix on his radio. Other than the shelling and the fifth-columnist snipers, though, he felt there was nothing to sweat about. The Japanese would never set foot on the island. As the Kaiser discovered in World War I, when the Brits and Canucks got together, they were an unbeatable combination.

Kowloon Bay, December 14

"Thracian sinks ships." With that terse entry in his diary, Brigadier Lawson recorded the only cheerful news the beleaguered islanders received all weekend. Late Sunday night the British destroyer slipped out of her berth at Aberdeen and, cruising without lights, proceeded to Kowloon Bay, intending to make a hit-and-run raid on the Devil's Peak artillery position.

One mile short of her goal, she ran aground. Offshore rocks pierced her bottom, flooding the forward compartment, but the *Thracian* quickly pulled free. Lieutenant Commander Pears was about to order the ship back to port when he noticed two river steamers lying at anchor in a tiny cove, both jammed with Japanese soldiers waiting for dawn and an attempted landing on the island. The *Thracian's* four-inch guns barked and, within seconds, the closest steamer was blown to pieces. The second boat started moving, but, lacking speed, she was easily transformed into a flaming wreck one hundred yards from the first. Pumping water, the *Thracian* limped home to garner Maltby's praise for lifting the colony's spirits. In retaliation Japanese aircraft bombed the destroyer at Aberdeen the next day, inflicting enough damage to eliminate the possibility of any more surprise raids. But the Navy still had one card left to play.

CHAPTER TEN

Kowloon, December 15

Losing the two steamers spoiled General Sakai's plans. But only temporarily. Instead of a dawn attack the Japanese would have to spend Monday building rafts and collecting small boats for a crossing at Lye Mun that night. Bringing his senior officers together at 8 A.M. in the vacant dining room at the Peninsula Hotel, Sakai outlined his strategy. Shelling was to continue—not only Monday but every day until the island capitulated. Since the war had begun one week earlier, there had been twenty-seven air raids, usually consisting of seven-plane bomber squadrons striking a specified target. These raids proved less effective than the shelling, but, Sakai said, they would continue too. In addition to destroying the north-shore defenses and Peak villas, the bombardments were to demoralize the civilian population by destroying landmarks in Victoria's congested business district, notably the Hong Kong Hotel, the Hong Kong and Shanghai Bank, and the well-known Gloucester clock tower. (All three subsequently suffered light damage; the clock stopped after it was strafed by a Zero.)

A strong advance party would try to gain a foothold on the island. If it succeeded, the 229th Regiment would land en masse in the same region, Lye Mun. In the meantime the 228th and 230th Regiments would go ashore farther west at the shell-shattered North Point and Braemar Point coastal defenses, directly opposite the city of Kowloon. While sweeping over the northern part of the island, the three regiments would send units south to assail Canadian and British battalions entrenched in the hills or facing the sea. Closing the meeting, Sakai reminded his infantry commander, Major General Ito Takeo, that he had acquired a magnificent stallion and he was hopeful that he could ride it during a triumphant march through Victoria before the end of the week.

Victoria, December 15

Unbeknown to the general, a large segment of the Chinese populace was helping him achieve his goal. Believing an invasion was imminent, Chinese deserted military transport, gun placements, and vital hospital jobs by the hundreds on Monday morning. Compounding the problem caused by depleted manpower resources were the scare rumors regarding food supplies. Owners boarded up stores to discourage looters and, protecting their goods further, spread false stories claiming Hong Kong's wealthier residents were hoarding what little rice and vegetables remained. Panicking refugees raided the kitchens of private homes, sometimes maiming or killing the occupants. Governor Young put a halt to the hysteria before it got completely out of hand. An official declaration compelled all persons selling essential provisions to open their stores daily from 8 A.M until sundown. Many wary owners kept their shops boarded and conducted business through big peepholes in front doors; no customers were allowed inside.

Young also created communal kitchens, where the government ladled out free soup and rice. The dawn-to-dusk lineups wound through streets strewn with debris from the shelling, and in some places, refugees stood on rubble piles so high that the roads were impassable for vehicles. The panic was quelled, and yet a growing fear persisted that the food would soon run out. Untold thousands of Chinese, prominent citizens and poor refugees, undermined the colony's morale by purchasing outlawed Japanese flags and pro-Imperial Japanese Army posters from clandestine factories. Kowloon had been festooned with welcoming flags and posters the day Sakai entered the city, and Chinese islanders advised their friends to stop supporting the British: the conquering Japanese would, they reasoned, be sure to feed anyone who treated their presence like a heavenly blessing.

On top of this, gangs of armed hoodlums had begun to roam the island. Refugees sleeping on sidewalks were robbed of their meager possessions. Whites walking to and from civil defense jobs were taken into shell-ruined buildings and stripped of anything valuable, including their garments. Merchants were forced to pay fat fees to belligerent youths posing as "protection union" organizers. And when the shelling was particularly heavy, the gangs went into public air-raid shelters to rob the occupants at gunpoint.

Young imposed a strict curfew Monday. From that day on, police would arrest anyone walking on the street after 7:30 P.M. and prior to 6:30 A.M. unless they had a special permit. Refugees were urged not to move around at night lest they be mistaken for thieves. During the daylight hours all Chinese coolies were to walk with their hands at their sides. Young stated that people with their hands in their pockets or behind their backs could be suspected of carrying weapons and he was concerned that a nervous policeman might shoot someone in error.

The governor's directive curbed the gang activity substantially. So did the joint warning issued by the leaders of secret criminal societies. Asked by the police to help maintain law and order, the crime mandarins circulated the word that youths belonging to armed gangs would be put to death. The societies' motives had nothing to do with acting for the good of the community. They wanted to stamp out the gangs before they became too powerful and threatened to move into their own lucrative fields—prostitution, gambling, and opium.

The curfew had a beneficial side effect: the fifth columnists found it harder to prowl around at night. All the same, snipers and saboteurs remained a perpetual menace. The Chinese press printed front-page editorials imploring readers to tell police about friends or neighbors preaching defeatist talk, and a popular local figure, Admiral Chan Chak, called upon the Chinese to lend the English their full support.

On Monday morning, the police conducted a mass round-up of suspected fifth columnists. The most startling arrest was that of Chim Lim-pak, a prosperous merchant known for his reactionary political beliefs. Lim was rumored to have been plotting a *coup d'état:* he and a small army of followers were allegedly preparing to seize key government buildings and hold them until the Japanese landed. Whether or not the take-over plot existed, the widespread dissension spawned by apprehension over the food supply, the robber gangs, and the persistent activity of snipers and saboteurs meant that the defenders were almost as hard-pressed to contend with an elusive enemy within their gates as they were with the highly visible Japanese.

The Monday edition of the *South China Morning Post* carried a Government House communiqué reassuring the white populace that fresh troops would eventually relieve the colony. "There is every reason for confidence," the statement said. "Reserves of food, guns and ammunition are ample for a protracted defense on a siege scale. The garrison is in good spirits and the staunchness of the civilian population is marked. The simple task before everyone of us now is to hold firm."

On the same page the paper ran a cable that Churchill addressed to "Governor Young and the defenders of Hong Kong" shortly after the mainland collapsed. It read:

"We are all watching day by day and hour by hour your stubborn defense of the port and fortress of Hong Kong. You guard a link between the Far East and Europe long famous in world civilization. We are sure that the defense of Hong Kong against barbarous and unprovoked attack will add a glorious page to British annals. All our hearts are with you and your ordeal. Every day of your resistance brings nearer our certain final victory."

Understandably, the inspirational nature of his message ordained that Churchill omit any hint of his true feeling that Hong Kong could be neither held nor relieved in time. And a Most Secret telegram dispatched Monday from Canadian Military Headquarters, London, to National Defense Headquarters, Ottawa, stated that—disregarding the fact that the mainland had fallen weeks ahead of schedule—Whitehall retained the opinion that the colony was an inviolable fortress. The message said:

"Decision has been taken that Hong Kong should be held and if relief should prove impossible garrison is to inflict maximum damage on Japanese. Present garrison is of strength considered proper to hold island only and should be capable of prolonged resistance."

The promise of fresh troops and Churchill's message were, of course, of tremendous psychological value and, to ensure the newspaper the widest possible readership, civil defense volunteers pitched in to help deliver it throughout the island.

Lye Mun Peninsula, December 15–16

Around midnight Monday, a Japanese landing party set out from Kowloon Bay, using a junk, homemade rafts, sampans, and inflatable rubber boats. The 300 soldiers participating in the Lye Mun mission were carefully chosen by their regimental commanders, not for their fighting prowess but their blatant lack of it. These were the expendables, the low-grade soldiers whose poor marksmanship, limited physical strength, or general all-round ineptitude made them undesirable members of the crack 38th Division. If this congregation of misfits could establish a beachhead, Sakai knew the 7,500 superb specimens he intended to send in the follow-up wave could practically stroll across the island. If the mission failed, the general would at least have a better idea of the enemy strength on the peninsula. The Devil's Peak observation post reported that Lye Mun barracks appeared to be deserted and one third of the surrounding coastal batteries seemed devastated by the three-day barrage. The question was: how formidable were the surviving defenses?

Unfortunately for the landing party, the defenders expected them.

Late Monday afternoon, the Japanese were observed gathering boats in Kowloon Bay and, anticipating a night attack, Brigadier Wallis transferred three Volunteer platoons to bolster the Rifle and Rajput fortifications near Lye Mun barracks. The Volunteers brought two searchlights. After sunset the sand-bagged trenches and pillboxes fell eerily silent: the Volunteers and regular soldiers strained their ears, listening for the sound of movement. The gentle chugging of the junk's small motor was heard by a Rifles platoon and a machine-gunner gave the prearranged signal, firing a round across the black water. Immediately the searchlights blinked on and, sweeping the narrow passage, pounced upon the landing party.

The Japanese were clay pigeons. Volunteers manning six-inch howitzers lambasted the junk, and it burst into flames and sank. The Canadians and East Indians sliced through the troops on the smaller boats with machine-gun and rifle fire. Dead and wounded Japanese tumbled overboard. Paddling feverishly, the raiders tried to escape the beams; just as feverishly, some shot at the gunfire flashes on the shore. Witnessing the debacle, the Devil's Peak artillery post jumped into the fight, hurling shells at the searchlights. One light was hit and destroyed; the other stayed on the raiders until they reversed their rafts and boats and scurried back to the mainland. Many of the Japanese drowned; many others swam to shore.

At 2:45 A.M. the regrouped landing party took another stab at reaching the island. This time the soldiers steered their rafts and boats toward a destination a quarter of a mile west of the peninsula tip. The searchlight found them again and four craft were sunk before the Japanese turned and fled. Caught up in the action, the north-shore gunners did not pause to wonder why the Devil's Peak artillery, banging away furiously during the first short, heated battle, virtually ignored the searchlight station the second time. The reason had to do with a trim, thin-lipped Japanese officer and his devotion to the ideals of the ancient samurai warriors.

Like other Japanese soldiers, Lieutenant Minoru Okada's views on military conduct stemmed from the Bushido Code. Adopted by samurai warriors in the seventeenth and eighteenth centuries, Bushido (The Way of the Warrior) emphasized unquestioning loyalty to one's superiors and manly self-sacrifice for personal honor. As their feudal brethren had maintained, the soldiers of 1941 believed that to die in combat was a supremely honorable act: life after death would bring eternal contact with their families and relatives, living and deceased. Moreover, a warrior must kill with honor, be ruthless when confronting a base, inferior foe, and develop an appreciation for the beauty exhibited in poetry and paintings. To surrender was cowardly; to commit hara-kiri was admirable.

Japanese soldiers, sailors, and airmen pledged themselves to fight honorably for Emperor Hirohito and their homeland, but Okada's dedication to Bushido principles had existed long before he became an army officer. A thirty-two-year-old Nagasaki teacher and writer, he lived a Spartan existence—an austere apartment, no car or expensive clothing, simple eating habits—and practiced the martial arts. Okada published two novels romanticizing samurai heroes, and, in 1954, he wrote a third book, *Bofu no ato ni* (*After the Violent Storm*), describing his own samurai-like war exploits.

Okada was a superb athlete. He excelled at sprinting, high-jumping, and volleyball, and he had been a member of the 1936 Olympic Games team at Berlin. His forte was not track or volleyball, however: it was swimming.

The failure of the first landing party prompted Okada to ask a senior officer, Major Hara, if he could personally remove the remaining searchlight. The Devil's Peak artillery would destroy it, all right, and the British would probably replace it immediately. But, he suggested, the mainland soldiers would be greatly inspired if one of them actually got on the island and blew it up. The major agreed that Okada should make the courageous swim while the second attack was under way. But only if he took some men with him.

Okada and four volunteers were stroking through the bitterly cold water when the north-shore guns blasted the second landing party. All wore only thin undergarments, and all had waterproofed bundles of grenades, wire cutters, and dry clothing strapped to their backs. The half-mile swim brought them to a lonely beach. Crawling ashore, the five men donned Chinese coolie outfits, then cut a hole in the coiled barbed wire blocking their way. Okada kept a cautious eye on a pillbox two hundred yards to his right. Although he saw no one, he sensed it was occupied.

Scrambling through the barbed wire, the men moved to the base of a small cliff and, discovering a foot path, dashed to the top. By this time the second landing attempt had fizzled and the searchlight was blacked out. Unfamiliar with the terrain, Okada had trouble finding precisely where the light was located. At one point the five Japanese almost walked into the side of a parked military vehicle. A young Volunteer lay on the back seat, resting and apparently awake. If he had opened his eyes at the wrong moment, he would have seen five Orientals staring through the windows, ready to leap inside and throttle him. He did not, and Okada left him in peace.

At 4 A.M. Okada came across the searchlight. It was on an embankment, encircled by a high wall of sandbags, and, as best he could tell, a dozen Volunteers lounged around it, awaiting a possible third call to action. Okada breathed a sigh of relief. If he had failed to find the light before sunrise, the five men would have entered the closest community and tried to pass themselves off as Chinese refugees. They might fool the English, but not the Chinese, and the odds against being reported were very slim.

Creeping up on the light station, the infiltrators took grenades from their pockets and, yanking the pins in unison, flung them over the sandbags. Their collective aim was not as good as their collective swimming ability: the grenades exploded everywhere except at the light. The Volunteers fired rifles into the dark night; they saw only blurred figures but a shot hit home, killing one of the Japanese. Okada was considering a suicidal run at the light, a grenade in each hand, when one of his companions' grenades landed on a cache of explosives. The deafening blast destroyed the searchlight and Okada raced away, the other three Japanese at his heels.

He did not expect to leave the island. The enemy would, he thought, be all over the area once their presence was known. The enemy *was* all over, but the four men ran past an empty pillbox and dove off an embankment into the channel. "The searchlight was of little significance," Okada wrote in his war book. "What mattered was the deed. We showed that the enemy could not keep Japanese soldiers off the island. They were too fat, too decadent. Their destruction was inevitable."

Although the landing party was repelled twice, Sakai did not feel the mission was a total loss. The abortive raids yielded valuable information regarding the location and power of the Lye Mun guns. By the looks of it, the enemy definitely possessed limited fire power and another day-long bombardment should crumble their defenses. Sakai and infantry commander Takeo agreed that the north-shore installations should be subjected to ceaseless artillery shelling on Tuesday. At the same time heavy bombers would pound Lye Mun and enemy entrenchments elsewhere. A surrender ultimatum which the English were bound to accept would be delivered Wednesday morning. In the unlikely event that they did not capitulate, the 228th, 229th, and 230th Regiments were to stage a three-pronged invasion on Thursday night.

Victoria, December 16

On Tuesday afternoon Lieutenant Gordon Grey visited his flat for the last time. A doctor with the Royal Canadian Army Medical Corps, he was moving into Bowen Road Hospital permanently: the casualties were mounting so rapidly that he did not have time to sleep and eat properly, let alone walk a mile to his flat to do so. Opening a dresser drawer, Grey saw the bright red tin containing the Christmas fruitcake his mother had given him in Toronto. He now had grave doubts that he would be around to enjoy it on Christmas Day.

The hospital, a three-story red-brick building halfway up the Peak, flew a Red Cross flag but the Japanese insisted on trying to bomb and shell it into ruins. The hospital had taken no direct hit as yet, but, just in case, the top floor had been closed off and the patients were now crowded into hallways and wards on the lower two floors. It was a very old building—big ceiling fans, a wooden veranda, typhoon shutters on the windows, and no elevators. The absence of elevators was, perhaps, the building's biggest drawback.

Many patients were too sick or invalided to be moved down the stairway to the basement during the heavier bombardments: the nurses placed some under beds and arranged mattresses on top of those who were unconscious or incapable of getting to their feet.

Sleep was a luxury—twenty minutes here, thirty minutes there. In four days of shelling and bombing the medical staff had logged fewer than seven hours each on basement-floor mattresses. Worse than the exhaustion, hasty meals, and the necessity of making fast medical decisions was the steadily thickening atmosphere of despair. The twenty-eight-year-old physician overheard patients talking about their comrades' unfamiliarity with their weapons, the dwindling ammunition supplies, and the Japanese artillerymen's methodical liquidation of the north-shore defenses. By Tuesday, fifty per cent of the northern pillboxes had been destroyed. "If a shell or bomb doesn't get us, the Japs will kill us right here in our beds," said one Canadian soldier, gloomily expressing a dread that Grey himself silently felt.

The predominantly British nursing staff did their best to curb the spreading pessimism. Reinforcements are coming, they said. If not the Chinese, then British planes and ships for Churchill will not stand by idly and let British citizens be sacrificed to Japanese butchers. The Canadian girl, Kay Christie, was the cheeriest of the lot. She was a rare creature, an efficient, tireless nurse whose manner of speaking to patients somehow lessened their pain, their frustration, their anxiety. Her energy and devotion reminded Grey of Marite, the auburn-haired nurse he had married in August. At that very moment Marite was probably bustling around a Toronto hospital ward, administering medicine and comforting words.

Thinking of home, Grey lifted the cake from the drawer and placed it in his suitcase. God willing, he would share it with the staff on December 25. In that small way all of them

would have something tangible to remind them of what
Christmas Day was like in calmer times.

Hong Kong depended upon rainfall for its water supply.
Culverts between six and eight feet deep encircled the
higher mountains, catching the torrential rains and guiding
the water down to large reservoirs in the valleys. With the
capture of the important Shing Mun Valley reservoir, the
Japanese reduced the colony's holdings to four reservoirs—
Aberdeen, Tai Tam, Ty Tam Tuk, and Wong Nei Chong.
On Tuesday, Governor Young announced that, owing to the
fine, summery weather, the government was assuming a pre-
cautionary stance and rationing water. Young was not relying on the citizens' self-discipline. Unless they were needed
for fire-fighting or other emergencies, all water mains were
turned off except between 6 and 9 A.M. and 3:30 and 6:30
P.M. Meanwhile, civil defense workers, temporarily relieved
of first-aid, air-raid warden, and fire-control duties, helped
government employees scour the island to find and reacti-
vate old wells. For all their digging and shoring up of caved-
in walls, the amount of water drawn from the reopened
wells was minimal compared to the colony's enormous re-
quirements.

Taking steps to conserve water was but one restrictive
measure Young initiated that Tuesday. The sale of gasoline
to private car owners was halted and the handful of civilian
trucks not commandeered by the military needed permits to
buy fuel at twelve pumps manned by Transport Service personnel. Vehicular traffic on Victoria streets shrank to a
trickle. Public transportation dwindled too. The Japanese
succeeded in crippling the Peak Tramway, nearly all of the
buses were requisitioned for military use, and the streetcars
which had operated from sunrise to sunset since December
8, now stopped altogether. Even rickshaw drivers, normally
willing to do anything for a shilling, deemed the risk too
great and only an intrepid few stayed on the job.

Nonetheless, it was business as usual for some Hong Kongers.

While the heavily bombarded waterfront was avoided by most pedestrians, several hundred Chinese men and women walked to work in other districts as though nothing untoward was happening. A conscientious tailor climbed the Peak to deliver a silk suit; a sporting-goods salesman met a store manager for lunch and discussed basketballs; a civil servant chastised his secretary for arriving twenty minutes late at the office. These people seemed oblivious to the bursting shells, although that may have been a defense mechanism: pretend the noise did not exist and the war just might fade away. On some streets, however, the war was impossible to ignore. The shelling leveled entire blocks and, in numerous instances, firemen were hard pressed to contain treacherous flames. Several houses at mid-level and atop the Peak were blown to bits, including the unoccupied villa of the United States consul general. In an effort to stop shell vibrations from shattering glass, homeowners and shopkeepers glued strips of paper on their windows.

Piles of garbage began appearing amid the rubble. Lacking trucks and drivers, the colony's refuse-collection department no longer functioned and, despite the government's imploring people to bury or burn food waste, the garbage was dumped on sidewalks and bombed-out building sites. Adding to the horrifying threat of a cholera outbreak was the fact that the trucks normally used to collect night soil from houses without indoor plumbing were also halted. Excrement containers were carried outside and emptied on rubble-strewn lots. Young had no difficulty enforcing the water- and gasoline-rationing laws, but he could not make some Chinese, particularly the uneducated refugees, understand that the proliferation of garbage and night soil constituted an alarming health hazard.

CHAPTER ELEVEN

Victoria, December 17

Fifth columnists continued to plague the colony.

Five cars sitting in a military garage were set afire and gutted early Wednesday morning. Snipers killed a Chinese driver and a British soldier on a night ammunition run; a bus transporting troops from Aberdeen to the north shore was raked by small-arms fire, shattering windows and wounding four men. Three new developments worried the defenders. Snipers had started taking shots at anyone standing near the windows at Bowen Road Hospital, spies listened to telephone conversations, using stolen equipment, and many Chinese drivers were "borrowing" military vehicles to earn exorbitant fees carrying the valuable household possessions of rich families to hiding places in poorer neighborhoods.

The driver dilemma was easily resolved. Because the Army could ill afford to dismiss the few drivers it had left, Fortress Headquarters decreed that a Chinese person could not take a military vehicle past a checkpoint unless accompanied by a white NCO or soldier. Captured fifth columnists often met a harsher fate. A suspicious Chinese male apprehended in the Happy Valley compound around 3 A.M. Wednesday (the race track was now a military car pool and storage site) was turned over to the police: he was questioned and, five hours later, executed. Other undercover agents died in gunfire exchange with soldiers and, according to Rifleman Leo Leblanc, a Rajput sentry calmly knifed an unarmed Chinese to death when the man did not have a satisfactory explanation for why he was sneaking around a pillbox at night.

In spite of the restrictions placed on their movements by the curfew, the fifth columnists managed to keep in regular contact with the mainland Japanese. The most common method of communication was coded lantern signals from rooftops and hillsides facing north. Unable to obtain exact figures, the spies made wild guesses at the casualty numbers, basing their suppositions on shell damage and the hectic hospital conditions, especially at Bowen Road. (The agents apparently did not realize that Bowen Road was already busy with malaria victims prior to December 8.) In his 1958 book, *Asian Conquest*, American journalist Richard Summerlee reported that fifth columnists eager to show how efficient they were overestimated casualties: "One fellow stated 500 soldiers were dead and 800 wounded. A second fellow determined to prove his knowledge of the island's status was superior to his friend's said the casualties were 1,500 dead and 2,000 wounded." Actually, the casualty toll was quite low: as of midnight Wednesday, 55 dead, 95 wounded, and 65 missing. While no accurate figures were recorded, the civilian rate was roughly the same. Reading the fifth columnists' messages and surveying the ravaged coastal fortifications, Sakai had good reason to assume the islanders must be ready to quit.

At 11 A.M. Wednesday the "Peace Mission" boat, a white flag flapping, chugged across the harbor to Victoria. Colonel Tokuchi Tada, three senior officers, and a dark-suited interpreter were on board; there were no hostages this time. Standing on the wharf were a small group of British officers and two columns of rigidly erect soldiers. Major Boxer led the British contingent.

To Emily Hahn's delight, the handsome intelligence officer had telephoned the Selwyn-Clarke villa to say, no, he had not been killed by a shell; he had failed to call her for four days because he was totally immersed in military plotting. The truth was, although he had no time to talk to Emily, he thought of her often. During a strategy conference, as someone else was speaking, his mind would drift onto vivid memories of their love affair: he would force himself to shake off his fears for Emily's safety and to focus wholeheartedly on his demanding workload. Over the phone, he urged Emily to move somewhere else. The Repulse Bay resort area, perhaps. The Selwyn-Clarke house was situated between two enemy batteries and, the way the Japanese were pounding the Peak, they were bound to hit it sooner or later. Emily balked. She was helping out part time at a Peak-side hospital, the War Memorial, and she felt it was her duty to stay put. Boxer realized it was useless to argue. She was strong and stubborn.

As a matter of fact, so was practically everyone else he was associated with these days. There were still top-drawer officers on Maltby's staff, for instance, who laughed off suggestions that the Japanese would invade the island. "Preposterous notion, old boy. The Japs haven't the manpower or the skill. Why, one of our soldiers is worth three of theirs." To say the least, Boxer did not admire their obstinacy. But he did admire that of Sir Mark Young. The governor was telling people he would tackle the Japanese hand to hand if need be. Watching the Japanese boat pull up to the wharf, Boxer felt certain that Young would reject the latest ultimatum.

He was right. Tada informed Boxer that he was delivering a letter signed by Sakai and the naval commander, Vice-Admiral Masaichi Niimi, stating that Hong Kong was to surrender unconditionally. Boxer put the letter in his briefcase and asked Tada to return at 2:30 P.M. for a reply. As the boat departed, Boxer proceeded to Government House in a staff car. At 2:30 the Japanese delegation crossed the harbor again. Boxer was on the wharf and, with a terse explanation, he handed Tada the letter Young had written:

"The Governor and the Commander-in-Chief, Hong Kong, declines most absolutely to enter into any negotiations for the surrender of Hong Kong and he takes this opportunity of saying he is not prepared to receive any further communications on this subject."

Tada and his aides were visibly surprised by the rejection. But not as much as Sakai. Summerlee described the general's reaction in *Asian Conquest:*

"He was utterly flabbergasted. Why would the English invite more punishment? Were they all masochists? Did they not perceive that his troops greatly out-numbered theirs? His astonishment was devoured by his concern for his future. The pre-war time-table called for Hong Kong's capture in 10 days. The battle was presently in its 10th day. Would he 'lose face' in Tokyo?"

Wednesday night Tokyo took the pressure off Sakai. He was advised that because of the islanders' unexpected obdurate attitude he had until January 1 to effect their fall. The general was happy again. He was positive he did not need much more time. Thursday's attack would, in Summerlee's words, "drive a stake through the enemy's heart."

Naturally, Maltby saw the ultimatum in a different light. He agreed with Young that the islanders should fight until the last drop of resistance was drained, but a Most Secret message he sent to London revealed that he did not suspect the Japanese thought Hong Kong was on its knees. Indeed, two of the three possible reasons he listed for the enemy's issuing the ultimatum actually hinted of weak spots in the Japanese armor.

"The (Japanese) envoys seemed genuinely surprised and disconcerted when the proposals were summarily rejected," he wrote. "The second delegation coming within four days of the first suggested that either (a) they disliked the prospect of attacking across the water, (b) that the Chinese threat in their rear was taking effect, or (c) that it was an attempt to undermine our morale by fostering thoughts of peace and quiet."

Regardless of how Sakai and Maltby viewed the ultimatum, the British press treated the governor like a hero because he spurned it. "Young's reply to the Japanese should be read in every public place and school throughout the Empire," said the *Times* of London. "It breathes a spirit that needs no comment or elaboration." The considerably less refined *Daily Mirror* summed up Young's rejection in a three-word front-page headline, GO TO HELL. Only a handful of papers deviated from praise and bravado to stress that the colony was likely to collapse. A *Daily Express* editorial said Hong Kong "has neither the strategic value nor the fighting chance of Tobruk. We must be prepared for its fall."

In Canada, the newspaper coverage was similar. Front-page stories emphasized the colony's determination and gallantry and quoted Brigadier Lawson as saying, "We are ready for anything that might occur." More than the British press did, the Canadian papers played up the hope of a Chinese Army breakthrough. Analyzing the mainland retreat, a Canadian Press news agency story said: "This withdrawal was seen as a scheme to permit the Japanese to plunge into the extremity of Kowloon peninsula, where they might be vulnerable to Chinese armies operating at their rear." Other stories told of "savage" large-scale Chinese attacks at Tamshu, twenty-eight miles north of the New Territories border. In reality, the "savage" attacks were paltry guerrilla raids or acts of sabotage against the Canton-Kowloon railway. The Japanese had a special detachment, the Araki, guarding the rear and, of all the troops taking part in the Hong Kong invasion, they had the least amount of work to do.

The Hong Kong coverage by the Canadian news media consoled Margaret Osborn somewhat. The stout, dark-haired Winnipeg housewife was tormented by misgivings about her husband John's well-being, and reports claiming the Chinese Army was engaged in a rescue mission kept her hopes up. Her hands remained sore from that dreadful night she burned them pulling the blazing dress off five-year-old Patricia. Nevertheless, she would gladly suffer the discomfort to write John a letter if she was told that, by some miracle, it would get through.

There was so much to tell him. Patricia was off the critical list. The blood transfusion had saved her life and she would be spending Christmas with her four brothers and sisters. Margaret felt like crying whenever she thought of John and realized how anguished he must be, not knowing Patricia's fate.

There were other changes too. Neighborhood women were taking factory jobs, assembling tanks and trucks. Posters everywhere exhorted Canadians to collect rags, scrap metal, and bones for the war effort. Nylons were becoming scarce and Prime Minister Mackenzie King said he was getting ready to ration gasoline and sugar. The local moviehouses were swamped by patriotic war films. Fred Astaire and Rita Hayworth in *You'll Never Get Rich* ("Laugh-Bombing Comedy Smash of Army Camp Life"); Errol Flynn in *Dive Bomber* ("Filling the Sky with Glory and the Screen with Thrills"); Abbott and Costello in *Keep 'Em Flying* ("They're in the Air Force and They're Just Air-Plain Nuts!").

So many things to say. If only she could send a letter.

Aberdeen, December 17

Sergeant Bill Laidlaw felt certain he had walked at least a thousand miles since he had landed in Hong Kong, and late Wednesday night, he was on shanks' mare again, taking three other Grenadiers from an Aberdeen pillbox to a supply depot. It was six miles each way on a road curving through moonlit hills. The irony of his predicament was abundantly clear to the twenty-nine-year-old Winnipegger. For seven years he had worked at Eaton's mail-order division, collecting debts. His territory had covered four provinces but he had seldom ventured out from behind his desk: he had done it all by letter.

Given his sedentary lifestyle—and his newly developed dislike for walking—it was understandable that Laidlaw, rounding a bend and spotting the gleaming black Buick, thought the gods had bestowed a gift upon him. The car was backed into a hillside cavity that was so small the front half stuck out.

"That must be a mirage," one of the soldiers said. "Who the hell would park a car in the middle of nowhere?"

Someone explained who would: a high-ranking naval officer who had bought the car two months ago and was leery of having it shelled at the dockyards.

"Why don't we borrow it?" a soldier suggested. "Just to haul the rations back to the pillbox. I think I can start it."

Laidlaw assented. The soldier hot-wired the ignition, and with the foot-weary sergeant at the wheel, the car eased out of the cave. Adhering to the blackout restrictions, he drove without lights. Half a mile down the road, Laidlaw accelerated; the soldiers laughed and kidded him about entering the Indy 500.

"Don't worry," the sergeant assured them. "I won't hit anything. There's no traffic in this area at night."

Two miles farther, the Buick shot around a curve and, before Laidlaw could brake, crashed into a bulky object in the center of the road. The four Grenadiers crawled out of the Buick, stunned and shaky but uninjured. British soldiers swarmed everywhere; they had been moving a Bofors gun and Laidlaw hit it head-on. The gun was intact, but the car was wrecked beyond repair. Laidlaw and his three companions pushed the Buick into a ditch. The Canadians whispered comments to the effect that they did not want the British to know the car was not theirs.

"We'll have to ask the supply sergeant for another vehicle," Laidlaw told a Cockney soldier. "He won't like it. We have the stupidest regulations in the Canadian Army. Only one new car to each platoon. Is it the same with you fellows?"

After the incredulous Cockney private disclosed that, no, the British Army did not have the same regulation, the Grenadiers left the crash scene, walking and swearing never again to borrow another man's car.

About the same time Private Dennis Murphy was also making a vow. As long as he lived—be it nine hours, nine months, or ninety years—he would never gamble with another Chinese.

Seeking new sheep to shear (his Grenadier buddies refused to play poker with him anymore), the ex-radio announcer made an excuse to slip away and to visit a Volunteer artillery position farther along the beach. In the back of a requisitioned bread van, using a flashlight, Murphy introduced a half-dozen Chinese males to the marvels of poker. The offspring of prominent families, the young gunners spoke English with distinct British accents, and Murphy observed they referred to all lower-class Chinese disdainfully, as if they belonged to an entirely different species.

Murphy had been warned. A Volunteer named Collins, a full-bearded professor-type, told him the Chinese were the greatest gamblers on earth. "They'll bet on anything. Tomorrow's weather, the color of the next car coming down the street, how many pineapples are for sale on a market stall. Whatever you do, don't gamble with the Chinese."

Murphy shrugged off the admonition. He had seen the endless mah jong and backgammon games on Victoria street corners and heard tales of colossal wins and losses in the gambling dens of Macao, a Portuguese enclave forty miles to the south. Because the Chinese were gambling addicts, he figured he could talk the young gunners into a few hands and clean them out. All he had to do was insist on playing poker, a game they knew nothing about. As it happened, poker was similar to mah jong and the gunners, getting the knack right away, took $170 from Murphy in two nights. Around 11 P.M. Wednesday, down another $81, he returned to his pillbox to find an angry sergeant waiting outside.

"You lying bastard, Murphy. You weren't chasing a sniper, were you? You were gambling again."

"That's the last time, believe me. I'm broke. They skinned me."

"It's the last time, all right. If I wasn't your friend, I'd have you on the carpet for this. Instead, I'm transferring you to Wong Nei Chong Gap. Let them put up with you from now on."

Murphy smiled to himself. He had some poker-playing friends at the Gap and, with a bit of luck, he might be able to run his emergency money—a twenty-dollar bill secreted in the toe of his boot—into a killing that would make the $251 lost to the gunners a mere pittance.

CHAPTER TWELVE

Lye Mun Peninsula, December 18

The weather turned miserable Thursday.

Heavy rain lashed the island all day, slowing military traffic and causing soldiers to huddle in pillboxes, complaining of chilled bodies and damp clothing. By 8 P.M. the rain dwindled to occasional showers but the sky remained overcast and it was an unusually dark night. Japanese artillery fire had hit the Anglo-Persian oil refinery and, pushed by strong winds, black smoke from burning tanks covered the north coast. The foul weather and dense smoke cut visibility in many locales to a few feet.

Sakai and infantry commander Takeo considered the adverse conditions a blessing. How could the enemy repel what they could not see? At ten o'clock, thirty-five hundred Japanese soldiers set out in sampans, junks, rubber boats, and anything else that floated, bound for three different north-shore destinations. A second assault force consisting of roughly four thousand men was to follow two hours later.

Fully aware of the invasion schedule, a group of fifth columnists boldly seized a Lye Mun peninsula installation at precisely 10 P.M. Dressed in coolie clothing, the band entered Fort Sai Wan, an old walled redoubt atop a steep hill, in a truck supposedly delivering ammunition. When they were inside the gate, the fifth columnists drew knives and,

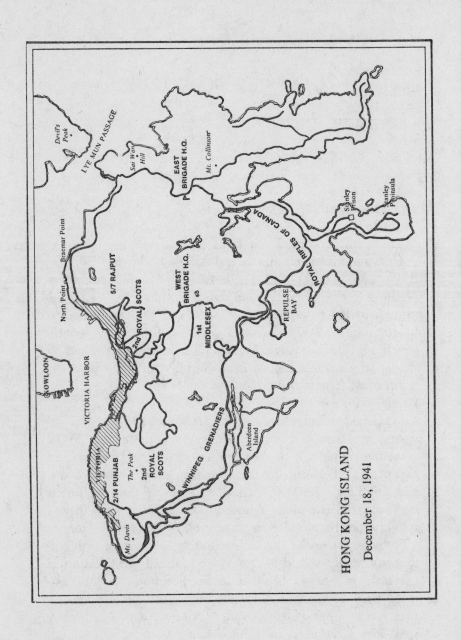

HONG KONG ISLAND
December 18, 1941

in a fast, well-rehearsed attack, cut down almost the whole Volunteer platoon. Those who escaped the long blades saw several intruders shed their coolie outfits to reveal Japanese army uniforms; other "coolies" put on armbands bearing Japanese insignia.

Rifles Major W. A. Bishop, an aggressive, sturdily built native of Sawyerville, Quebec, met fleeing Volunteers on a hillside. A Rifle contingent was camped near the captured fort, and Bishop was on his way to personally investigate reports of strange noises at Sai Wan. He had one soldier with him, Rifleman Gray.

"What are you doing here?" Bishop asked a Volunteer corporal.

"Coming to join you, sir. The enemy chased us out."

"You should've stayed and chased *them* out."

"What with? We have no rifles."

Bishop was astonished. "Are you telling me that you are manning a fort without arms and there's a war going on?"

"Yes, sir. We had Lewis guns, but the attack was so unexpected that we had no chance to use them."

Their conversation was terminated by the sound of gunfire. The fifth columnists were spraying the Rifles' encampment with the Lewis machine guns. Bishop hurried back to his command post and contacted Brigadier Wallis on a field phone.

"The Japanese are in Sai Wan," the major said. "I'd like you to drop some artillery on them."

"Ridiculous," Wallis retorted. "The enemy cannot possibly be there. There are Canadians in the fort."

Controlling his temper, Bishop replied: "I am in command of the Canadians in this region, Brigadier, and I assure you there is not, and never has been, a single Canadian at Sai Wan. It was manned by Volunteers and they've been turfed out."

"And I am advising you, Major, that Fortress Headquarters has it down on paper that friendly troops occupy the fort," Wallis said angrily. "We cannot shell it."

"Well, they sure as blazes aren't acting in a friendly manner!" Bishop said, hanging up.

Fortress Headquarters' refusal to believe that fifth columnists had seized a vital installation was logical in view of the prevailing contention that the island's defenses were inviolable. Even when reports of Japanese landings reached Maltby's command post, they were summarily rejected.

Captain John Hance, a Volunteer at the North Point power station, telephoned Fortress Headquarters shortly after ten o'clock to report that Japanese soldiers were infiltrating the mixed industrial-residential area. The North Point searchlight, usually capable of throwing its beam all the way to Kowloon, could not penetrate the thick smoke and consequently, Hance said, the enemy was coming ashore in vast numbers. Colonel Noonan, a respected adviser on Maltby's staff, discredited the account. "Go back to sleep," he told Hance. "I'll attend to your report in the morning." A second call five minutes later elicited a similar response from an unidentified officer. "Impossible," he said. "The Japs would never cross the harbor in the rain. The water's too choppy. They'd get seasick."

In some places the invaders ran into stiff opposition the moment they stepped ashore and, despite their numerical advantage, they were temporarily pinned down. In other spots the Japanese rushed inland to establish holdings in key positions.

Five Royal Engineers under Captain Caesar Otway were operating a newly arrived searchlight on Lye Mun peninsula when the Japanese crossed the channel. Discovering that the visibility was not as poor at Lye Mun as it was farther west, the enemy set off smoke flares to facilitate a landing. When the smoke lifted, the invaders found themselves directly in the path of the searchlight. Three times Otway and his men fended off charges by platoons of grenade-tossing Japanese. The sappers had only a machine gun, four rifles, and a revolver. During the third attack three sappers died and a grenade destroyed the machine gun. While Otway was pondering what to do next, the Japanese dragged a field gun off a raft and began hurling shells at the light. Every second shell damaged the surrounding concrete abutment and threatened to take out the light itself. "We haven't a chance," Otway announced. "We've got to get out of here."

Otway's aide, Corporal Harold Pelham, turned to leave and saw a lone Japanese soldier ten yards in front of him. Both men hesitated momentarily; apparently neither was accustomed to having such a close look at the enemy. In unison the two men raised their rifles and fired. The Japanese fell, clutching his stomach. Pelham was wounded in the hand. Dropping his weapon, he scrambled over a pile of sandbags and sprinted to the nearest cliff. Bullets whistled around him as he leaped into the water below. Otway and the other surviving Engineer followed him, but he lost track of them in the darkness.

For two and a half hours Pelham swam back and forth along the coast, hunting for a safe place to go ashore. Japanese boats passed within touching distance and he had to duck under water continually to avoid detection. Time and again Pelham approached land only to hear Japanese voices. Exhausted, chilled to the marrow and in pain, he finally swam to shore and climbed, inch by inch, an exceptionally high cliff. Reaching the summit, Pelham lay on the wet ground, shivering. Moments later he heard a movement and cautiously raised his head just as the ghostly forms of two soldiers emerged from the blackness and smoke. Were they Japanese or British?

> *"I'se the b'y that builds the boat,*
> *And I'se the b'y that sails her.*
> *I'se the b'y that catches the fish*
> *And takes 'em home to Lizer."*

Two drunken Grenadiers, singing and brandishing a near-empty rye bottle! Pelham was so relieved he laughed.

"What's the trouble, buddy?" one of the Canadians inquired, bending over the sapper.

"Nothing a good drink won't cure," the corporal replied. The Grenadier handed him the bottle and explained that their truck was out of gas. "Luckily, we brought our own fuel. A couple of swigs and you can go for miles." The Grenadiers helped Pelham to his feet and pointed him in the direction of a Royal Scots encampment, where he was to learn that the other two sappers were also safe. Before leaving the Canadians, the corporal thanked them for the drink. "It was better than a cake with candles," he said. "Today's my twenty-fourth birthday."

After taking the searchlight, the Japanese advanced on Lye Mun barracks. A Rifles platoon entered the evacuated compound, searching for stragglers, and ran into enemy troops hurrying up from the beach. Following a short, blistering battle the Rifles were overrun.

With his extraordinary disregard for personal safety, Major Bishop grabbed a Tommy gun and left the Rifles camp to have a look at the barracks situation. A Lieutenant Scott accompanied him. The two Canadians met an enemy patrol on a desolate path. The Japanese charged, throwing grenades. Bishop stood his ground, opening up with the Tommy gun. When the survivors fled, Bishop and Scott counted seven bodies. Bishop's action that night won him the Distinguished Service Order.

Characteristically, Bishop exhorted Fortress Headquarters to let his men dig in and fight the invaders on the peninsula, but he was persuaded that it would be wiser to withdraw a mile and a half south to a better-fortified position, Mount Parker. All Rifle units retreated, trailed by scattered detachments of Rajputs and Volunteers.

By this time Maltby's staff had accepted the fact that the

Japanese had landed on the island. Yet they did not think the enemy would be staying long. The theory went that the defenders would regroup and counterattack, pushing the Japanese into the strait. Maltby fully supported the counterattack plan. Serving with the Indian Army, he had turned apparent defeats at the hands of the rebellious Pathans into victories by mounting lightning offensives. If it worked in the hills of northern India, it would work in hilly Hong Kong.

For two units on Lye Mun peninsula there was no question of regrouping and attacking—or even retreating. A small fort occupied by Volunteers, an anti-aircraft battery, and the first-aid post under Captain Martin Banfill were all surrounded before the inhabitants realized the Japanese had landed. Hideous massacres took place. Out of fifty-six people, only five lived to testify at a postwar trial that resulted in a twenty-year sentence for Colonel Tanaka Ryosaburo, the 229th Regiment's commander-in-chief.

At 10:30 P.M. several hundred Japanese encircled the artillery post on Sai Wan Hill. Most of the men inside the compound were relaxing and the sentries did not see the enemy until they loomed up near the walls. The Volunteers ran outside the compound and a desperate but short-lived battle ensued. The Volunteer commander, knowing they were hopelessly outnumbered, gave permission for his men to make a run for it. Thirty British and Chinese Volunteers jumped the walls and fought their way out of the trap. Twenty-six stayed inside the fort until a Japanese officer called for their surrender, saying, "No harm will come to you. We know you are not regular soldiers."

The twenty-six men walked outside, unarmed. Six officers were culled from their ranks, taken aside, and bayoneted. The others, hands tied behind their backs, were marched into the fort. For two hours the Japanese held them captive in a cramped, unlit room. Then they were led into the yard, one by one, and Japanese soldiers used their bodies for bayonet practice. Some died instantly. Others lay on the damp earth, writhing and bleeding. When all twenty had been stabbed, the soldiers threw them over a wall into an abandoned gravel pit. Other soldiers ringed the pit, shoveling and tossing rocks onto the dead and dying. Most of those men who did not perish in the initial bayoneting succumbed in the pit.

Two men survived, Martin Tso Hin-chi and Chan Yam-Kwong. Wounded in the thigh, Hin-chi fell prostrate and, his heart thumping, he forced himself to be perfectly still. A soldier aiming for Yam-Kwong's stomach shoved the blade through his wrist; there was so much blood that the soldier failed to notice his mistake and, like Hin-chi, Yam-Kwong feigned death.

Both men remained in the pit for three days and nights, unable to flee because of the constantly patrolling guards at the wall. When the guards finally disappeared for a few minutes, Hin-chi and Yam-Kwong kicked off the loose gravel partially covering their bodies and managed to leave the hole and crawl through two miles of enemy territory together.

Banfill was in the courtyard, pouring water into a leaky ambulance radiator when the Japanese reached the first-aid station. A couple of bullets whizzed over his head, and he assumed they were the handiwork of a fifth-columnist sniper in the surrounding hills. Governor Young had made an inspection tour the previous day and assured the short, wiry Montrealer that the post was not endangered.

"You needn't fret over the women on your staff," Young said confidently. "They are as safe here as anywhere else."

The radiator filled, Banfill quickly stepped inside the two-story building, robbing the marksman of a target. The ambulance departed, heading for Bowen Road Hospital carrying two injured Rajputs. Two minutes later the ambulance roared back into the yard, its body punctured with bullet holes. The driver, Kelly, and an orderly, Oakley, jumped out.

"The Japs machine-gunned us!" Oakley yelled, running into the building, clutching his bleeding thigh. "They've blocked the highway in both directions!"

Banfill found a pair of binoculars and ran upstairs. There was no smoke in the area and he could see hordes of Japanese soldiers coming from all directions, converging on the medical post. Returning to the ground floor, Banfill declared: "They're all around us. Get the women and try to escape."

Before anyone had a chance to leave, a Japanese patrol suddenly kicked open the front door and soldiers flooded the building. No one resisted. The twenty-five-member staff (most of the Chinese helpers had already fled) were rounded up and marched into the courtyard. The Rajputs in the ambulance were bayoneted and patients unable to walk were killed. Banfill dreaded the moment when the Japanese turned their attention to the women—two English volunteers, the Eurasian art student, and a dozen Chinese and St. John Ambulance workers. But, unlike later incidents in which nurses were raped and killed, the soldiers capturing the first-aid post treated them kindly. The women were separated from the others and held in captivity until their eventual internment in a POW camp.

Instead, the men were to be the victims.

A Japanese officer ordered them to remove their boots and shirts and to hand over all personal effects. Watches, rings, and wallets disappeared into soldiers' pockets. They were then marched two hundred yards down the highway to an embankment where several enemy officers stood discussing battle strategy. An officer approached the prisoners and asked who was in command. When Banfill said he was, soldiers tied his hands and placed a rope around his neck.

"We are medical personnel," the Canadian doctor said. "Noncombatants."

"I'm sorry," the officer said politely. "We have instructions from our commander-in-chief. You all must die."

The other men were led to the crest of the embankment. Two doctors, Orloff and Harrison, were shot at close range. Their bodies toppled into a hollow. Three more shots rang out and three more doctors fell. The Japanese officer turned to Banfill, who thought he was next. "I will kill you later. First you are to be questioned."

Banfill was led away on the rope. After he was gone, a bloodletting orgy erupted. As though it were a harmless game, the soldiers fixed bayonets and, laughing and joking, took turns stabbing the medical team. Two officers joined in; forcing captives to kneel, they decapitated them with swords.

Two men cheated death. Corporal Norman Leath of the Royal Army Medical Corps was struck on the back of the neck by a blunt instrument, probably a rifle butt, and collapsed into the hollow. Blood gushed from his nose and mouth and he pretended he was dead. After the frenzied slaughter, soldiers inspected the bodies, shooting anyone who moved or moaned. Leath did not twitch a muscle or cry out, even when a soldier trod on his hand. A volunteer medical officer, Dr. Osler Thomas, was wounded during the first shooting outburst. He lay beneath two corpses until the Japanese departed. Both Leath and Dr. Thomas later gave testimony that helped send Colonel Tanaka to prison.

Banfill, meanwhile, was taken over the hills to a Japanese encampment. En route the Japanese officer disclosed that he had been educated at a Church of England mission, St. Paul's College, in Tokyo.

"Are you a Christian?" he asked the doctor.

"More or less," Banfill replied.

"When I shoot you, what do you think will happen? Will you be resurrected or be dead forever?"

"I don't know. I suppose I'll be dead for a very long time."

The officer shook his head. "My mother and sisters are good Christians but there are certain tenets of Christianity I cannot accept. Yet I do think Christian morality is a positive force in the world."

Taking a small geography book from his pocket, the officer pointed to Quebec on a map of Canada and said he knew a French word: *"Oui.* That is French, isn't it?" He then said his name was Honda. "Remember the movie, *Wings of the Morning?* With Henry Fonda? Well, my name is the same but with an 'H.' "

A short while afterward, the platoon escorting Banfill came across a wounded Rajput lieutenant crawling along the path. The two soldiers leading the platoon bayoneted him. Farther along the track, four more wounded Rajputs were discovered and immediately put to death.

Banfill was not killed. At the Japanese camp a senior officer questioned him about the location of land mines and, finding the doctor knew nothing, he told a fresh platoon to march him to a post deeper in the hills. Several times the soldiers acted as though they were going to shoot him, but for a reason that still baffles him, he was always reprieved at the last minute. Ultimately Banfill wound up in a POW camp.

While the 229th Regiment was sweeping Lye Mun peninsula, the 228th and 230th were making headway to the west. The 228th created an opening and pressed straight inland, leaving the 230th to mop up coastal defenses around North Point. The latter was not an easy task. The troops quickly occupied a sugar factory and, wearing gas masks, the smoke-blanketed grounds of the Anglo-Persian oil refinery. But there were spots along the coast where resistance was so stubborn that Colonel Shoji Toshishige, the 230th commander, could not get his men off the shore front. The two positions giving the regiment the most trouble were a power station manned by Volunteers and a row of pillboxes filled with Rajputs.

All aged fifty-five and over, the Volunteers had insisted upon reporting for active duty, although they were outside the provisions of the Compulsory Service Act. Their commanding officer, Major J. J. Paterson, was an extraordinary man. This ruddy-faced six-footer was a member of the Legislative Council whose inflammatory statements had often made headlines. Something of a social lion, he had entertained lavishly at his surfside bungalow and his private box at Happy Valley Race Track. Yet he was also a war hero. In 1916–17 Paterson had been mentioned six times in official dispatches while serving with the African Camel Corps. "It had been said of J. J. Paterson," Tim Carew wrote in *The Fall of Hong Kong*, "that if he had not existed, then Somerset Maugham would have to invent him."

The sixty-one-year-old Paterson's companions at the North Point power station included T. A. Pearce, sixty-seven, the secretary of the Hong Kong Jockey Club; Edward des Voeux, seventy, the secretary of the Hong Kong Club; R. G. Burch, sixty, the chairman of an export-import firm; and "Pop" Hingston, fifty-eight, head chef at the Hong Kong Hotel. They had been joined two days earlier by seven French Volunteers, led by Jacques Egal, a prosperous wine merchant. Egal had a suave, aristocratic bearing: he sported long, white hair and a bushy white mustache, wore a cravat and carried a walking stick. This decidedly elegant gathering was supported by a smattering of powerhouse employees, armed with rifles, and other less socially prominent Volunteers.

The Volunteer detachment was, Maltby said, "assigned to prevent sabotage to the electrical plant." No one on the island thought the unit would ever see action and, in fact, the Old Boys were a local joke. "If a Jap knocked on the door, they'd all keel over from heart attacks," was a typical comment. The Old Boys' stand at North Point that night changed the laughter to praise and respect.

After reporting twice that enemy troops were landing—and being disdainfully rebuked by Fortress Headquarters—the Old Boys waited until the Japanese actually threatened their position before calling the brass again. Scouts revealed that enemy soldiers controlled a ridge overlooking the plant and had set up machine-gun nests on the adjacent highway, King's Road. Moreover, powerhouse employees patrolling the grounds were being knifed.

Paterson got headquarters on the phone at midnight. This time he was believed: the fighting was so fierce in other sectors that the landing could no longer be denied. "We'll send you help," an officer told Paterson. "There's a Middlesex camp down the road. We'll have them there in five minutes."

An armored car and two trucks carrying members of a machine-gun platoon left the Middlesex camp at 12:10 A.M., taking the fastest route, King's Road. Five hundred yards west of the powerhouse gate, Japanese machine-gunners poured bullets into the trucks, killing all but six men. The armored car sustained a direct hit from a mobile antitank gun; a Second Lieutenant Carruthers was the only person to escape the flaming wreck. All seven survivors ran to the plant, lugging two machine guns and ammunition belts.

The powerhouse employees had fled at the outbreak of shooting; only twenty-two Volunteers and the seven Middlesex were left to defend the plant. All took positions at windows and the front door. Throughout the night the Japanese attacked in waves; the small band repeatedly drove the enemy back. The two Lewis guns, the Lee-Enfield rifles, and a box of grenades were barely enough to stymie the Japanese, who outnumbered the Old Boys twenty to one. Around 2 A.M. Paterson informed Fortress Headquarters that the Japanese completely surrounded the building and the defenders were hard-pressed to keep them out. "Hold on at all costs," he was ordered. "We'll try to have a Rajput platoon relieve you." The Rajputs, however, were too busy retaining their own pillboxes to spare men for the plant.

At dawn the Japanese appeared to have retreated. The rain let up, the smoke was blowing in another direction, and the powerhouse grounds looked deserted. Surveying the body-littered yard, Middlesex Corporal Bob Dunlop was amazed at the enormous number of Japanese soldiers they had shot. R. G. Burch spoke of the Boer War, in which many of the Old Boys had served. "The Boers had a nasty trick," he said. "They'd pretend they were gone and then come at you with everything they had. These chaps could be doing the same thing."

Des Voeux nodded. "It's quite possible, all right. But I'll tell you one thing. Whatever the Japs are up to, I'd sooner die here fighting than rot in a lousy prison camp."

The respite did not last long. From the ridge the Japanese laid a five-minute mortar barrage on the building, smashing holes in the concrete walls and killing Des Voeux. Soldiers then rushed the powerhouse, flinging grenades through the windows. Three Middlesex soldiers died. Looking at the ceiling as the enemy drew back, T. A. Pearce saw that it was on fire. "If it's all right with you," he said to Paterson, pointing to a burned-out double-decker bus parked on the side of King's Road, "I'd prefer dying there than being roasted alive."

To which Paterson answered, "My dear fellow, there's a great deal to what you say."

Pearce and five Old Boys abandoned the station and, bullets flying around them, streaked to the derelict bus. Paterson and the others moved across the yard and into the main office building. Off and on for two hours the Japanese stormed the bus. On one occasion they got so close that Dunlop was mortally wounded by a slashing sword. Finally despairing of capturing the bus with infantry runs, the Japanese shifted three machine guns from another position, and all three riddled the double-decker simultaneously. One man, a red-headed Irishman named Geoghan, survived the bullets. A Japanese platoon approached the bus, assuming everyone was dead. Leaping off, Geoghan charged at the platoon, swearing and shooting. He killed an officer and three men before a machine-gun blast ended his life.

Inside the office building the remnants of the Old Boys and Middlesex units staged a remarkable battle. Twelve men—some wounded, some exhausted, all expecting to die— withstood mortars, machine guns, and incessant infantry thrusts until late Friday morning. Even when they were forced out of the shattered building they kept on fighting. Dispersing into other buildings, the twelve surrendered only when their ammunition was gone.

The aristocratic Egal, Paterson, and chef Hingston were among the survivors. A veteran Middlesex soldier wept as the Japanese tied the Old Boys' hands and dragged them off to imprisonment. His tears were not caused by despair; he was filled with pride at the valiant showing the old-timers had put on.

The Rajputs held out less than five hours at North Point but the fact that they held out at all was highly commendable. Company D, occupying a thin line of damaged pillboxes stretching across the waterfront, comprised one hundred men. The opposing Japanese force was estimated at one thousand. Fifth columnists had cut the barbed wire to help the invasion parties gain beachheads, and most of the invaders surged inland, overrunning other Rajput units and two Middlesex positions. Company D would not let them pass.

The Japanese disembarking in front of the Company D pillboxes got an immediate impression of what they were in for. The East Indians heard the boats coming and, as they touched shore, walloped them with mortar and machine-gun barrages. Pinned down and sustaining mounting casualties, the enemy unloaded mobile field guns and shelled the pillboxes. When the shelling ended, the infantrymen plunged forward. Rajputs went to meet them. Emerging from the smoke and rain, soldiers grappled in hand-to-hand combat; the visibility was so limited the two sides could not see one another until they were within touching distance (or, as a Rajput later said, "I couldn't see the enemy until I had my hands around his throat"). One group of Rajputs fought like enraged demons, leaping onto Japanese soldiers, cutting their throats, and releasing victory whoops.

To the proud Rajputs the North Point engagement was a means of achieving revenge. Company D was the same outfit that had lost comrades at Shing Mun Valley and during the mainland retreat. Captain Bob Newton, who had vowed he would die before he ever surrendered, was in charge. With only one full night's sleep since leaving the mainland, the East Indians were posted to the north shore and, still weary, they nevertheless displayed awesome zeal in combating the well-rested enemy troops.

Two hours after landing, the Japanese finally started toppling the obdurate pillboxes one by one. If the Rajputs did not run outside to fight, the enemy rolled grenades down the ventilation shafts and, if a man lived through the blasts, he was shot as he left the ruins. The last pillbox fell at approximately 2:30 A.M. Newton was dead. He had dashed from a pillbox, emptying his revolver and killing four Japanese soldiers before a volley of bullets downed him. Thirty-five Rajputs escaped; the company was, in effect, wiped out and Wallis ordered its surviving members to join Company B at Leighton Hill, to the northeast of Happy Valley Race Track.

As the Company D remnants shifted out of the combat zone, Royal Scot and Middlesex detachments were prowling the Victoria waterfront, looking for soldiers. Their own, not Japanese. Thoroughly fed up after four years' duty in Hong Kong—and concluding the colony was not worthy of personal sacrifice—nearly one hundred men had deserted coastal installations and, breaking into bars, gone on a drinking spree. Maltby failed to mention the incident in his dispatches nor is it referred to in the best-known books dealing with Hong Kong's fall. But a document in the National Defense files at Ottawa quotes a Royal Navy commodore named Douglas as saying he was present when sixty-five Scots and Middlesex deserters—all drunk—were rounded up and shot. (His story is corroborated by low-ranking soldiers, but upper-echelon officers, perhaps embarrassed by the shameful specter of a mass execution, deny knowledge of its having occurred.) Douglas added that the deserters were mostly recruits from slum districts who were known to be an undisciplined lot.

Other desertion tales abound. A police magistrate serving with the Volunteers turned up at a first-aid post with his head bandaged. When a doctor removed the swathing and discovered no wound, the magistrate pleaded to be sent to Bowen Road for further examination. The doctor refused. The magistrate was later arrested on the Peak, dressed in female clothing. Rajput units east of the Company D entrenchments, breaking and running at the initial thrust of the Japanese onslaught, were eventually found scattered in the hills. And two British soldiers, loading a stolen car with rations, hid in a cave in the little-occupied southeastern sector of the island until they were flushed out and shot by the Japanese a month after the colony fell.

CHAPTER THIRTEEN

Mount Butler, December 19

Corporal Sam Kravinchuk had enlisted because he wanted a rifle. His father, a Ukraine-born boilermaker, could ill afford to buy him one, and, dropping out of school at sixteen, the husky, slow-talking youth had needed every penny he earned as a laborer to put himself through night school. He had taken carpentry, toolmaking, and three other courses at the Dominion-Provincial Trade School; he figured a man had to be a jack-of-all-trades to land a good job during the Depression.

Hunting had been his passion. He had liked to pitch a tent in the thick woods around Norway House and spend cool autumn weekends tracking deer and moose. His friends had owned beautiful weapons, Winchester and Remington .303's, and he had longed to swap his puny .22 for something with a stronger punch. The Army had answered his prayers. By joining the army reserve in 1937, Kravinchuk had got a gleaming new Lee-Enfield .303 and, by talking nicely to an officer, had finagled permission to keep it at home. Tuesday nights he would drill at the Minto Armories; whenever he could he would be in the Manitoba bush, felling deer and moose.

It had never occurred to him that a war would erupt and he would be asked to join the Grenadiers. Hitler's machinations had seemed remote and unimportant, and anyway, if an armed conflict did flare up, the British could be counted upon to take care of it.

At 10 A.M. Friday, Kravinchuk was on the northern slopes of Mount Butler, two miles below Lye Mun peninsula. A war that neither the British nor anybody else had taken care of was about to come to him. The 229th Regiment, plowing south, was intent on capturing Tai Tam reservoir, a quarter of a mile beyond the Grenadiers' position. Following eight days of staring listlessly at a southern bay, Kravinchuk's platoon had been herded onto an open truck at 2 A.M. and driven through pouring rain into the hills. By the time they arrived at Mount Butler, they were drenched. Kravinchuk stopped saying how you would never catch an officer out on a night like this when he noticed Major "Granny" Gresham standing on the slope, his uniform soaking wet. A Winnipeg wildlife photographer, Gresham commanded Company A: he was dubbed "Granny" because he was a kind, mild-mannered soul.

Rajput Captain R. S. Cole had been alone on a track leading from the north shore to Mount Butler around 2 A.M. when a Japanese patrol materialized. He shot three armed fifth-columnist guides and the patrol fled. Learning of the episode, Brigadier Lawson ordered Gresham to take two platoons to Mount Butler, which was then undefended. Fortress Headquarters scoffed at Cole's report, claiming that the enemy could not possibly penetrate that far south in the dark and over unfamiliar landscape. Lawson sent the platoons anyway.

The Grenadiers waited on the mountain slopes for eight hours. The rain gradually diminished, but there were no trenches or pillboxes and they had to sit in the open. Kravinchuk set up his Vickers machine gun amongst a pile of boulders. All was serene in the ravine below.

"We're catching colds for nothing," a private grumbled.

The sign nailed onto the cross tells the story of what took place at that lonely spot. (National Photography Collection, Public Archives Canada Z-5202-3)

Above: Lye Mun Passage and Battery, with Devil's Peak looming to the left. Below: the Silesian Mission near San Ki Wan, scene of bloody atrocities. (National Photography Collection, Public Archives Canada PK-611 and PR-609)

Above: The Ridge, between Wong Nei Chong Gap and Repulse Bay, saw heavy fighting and a massacre. Below: St. Stephen's College, site of more Japanese atrocities. (National Photography Collection, Public Archives Canada PR-643 and PR-628)

Above: Narrow roads like this one at Windy Gap cut through the largely uninhabited hills in the middle of the island.
Below: During the fighting, soldiers took shelter in concrete bunkers half buried like this one in the rocky hillside. (National Photography Collection, Public Archives Canada PR-623 and PR-621)

Civilians and nurses tending the wounded were under siege for three days in the elegant Repulse Bay Hotel, above. (National Photography Collection, Public Archives Canada PR-641 and PR-642)

Above: News of the Japanese surrender was broadcast to the prisoners of war in Sham Shui Po barracks. Below: Lieutenant General Tanaka signed the surrender papers in September, 1945, as Vice-Admiral Fugita, at right, waited his turn. (National Photography Collection, Public Archives Canada PR-480 and PR-551)

Released POWs with a war trophy. (National Photography Collection, Public Archives Canada P-146-5)

Private Mitchel Soroka of the Winnipeg Grenadiers, left, and CQMS Harold C. Scott of the Royal Rifles, with nurse Emily King, returning home after the war. (National Photography Collection, Public Archives Canada P-127-7)

Families and friends gathered outside the British Columbia Legislature in Victoria to welcome the Hong Kong war veterans. (National Photography Collection, Public Archives Canada P-165-21)

"The Japs will never get past the coast. If the Rifles don't wipe them out, the Rajputs will."

Ten minutes later the ground exploded around them. Alarmed Grenadiers looked down to see at least a hundred Japanese soldiers running up the slope. Some had small mortars strapped to their legs; they were kneeling, firing, charging again. The mortar barrage was designed to keep the Canadians pinned down until the soldiers got close enough for a bayonet attack. Defying the bursting shells, Kravinchuk and other machine-gunners delivered a torrid stream of bullets into the Japanese front line. When a second attack wave appeared to be forming in the ravine, the machine-gunners briefly switched targets, firing over the heads of the charging soldiers to disperse their compatriots. The Grenadiers fixed bayonets and raced down the slope to meet the enemy in a chaotic battle that, in less than three minutes, resulted in a Japanese retreat.

After a short lull, enemy snipers began shooting at anything that moved. Sometimes the rifle fire was so intensive that it sounded like a chattering machine gun. A particularly loud barrage caused Gresham to call Kravinchuk from twenty-five yards away. "Kravinchuk, is that you firing?" "No, sir," the corporal shouted. "It's the enemy. The sound must be echoing." Hearing a second round, Gresham leaped to his feet. "Kravinchuk, I told you to quit firing!" he exclaimed. "Can't you obey a simple order?" A Japanese marksman saw the major and with a single shot killed him instantly.

Gresham's death cast a pall over both platoons. An intelligent, sensitive person, he was liked by everyone, from Lawson to the lowest private. The spark went out of the Grenadiers' fight; nonetheless, they held the slope against successive enemy jabs until late that afternoon. When it became apparent they were on the verge of being overrun, the Grenadiers moved south, eventually rejoining the main body of Company A.

Kravinchuk left the unit before it reached its destination. Two friends, privates Granger and Acherback, were hurt fighting a rear-guard action and at nightfall he volunteered to take them to a first-aid station half a mile to the east. Granger had a head wound, Acherback was hit in the thigh. The unarmed trio crawled most of the way: their hobnail boots made too much noise on the rocky terrain and they did not want to risk having Japanese patrols hear them. The Red Cross post was located in a pillbox. No sentries challenged the three men as they crossed a clearing to approach it. Granger and Acherback sat leaning against the outside wall, and Kravinchuk rapped on the door. "Hello, anybody home?" The door swung open and two Japanese soldiers faced him, leveling bayonets at his midsection.

He thought he was doomed. But the soldiers pushed him aside and, gesturing for Granger and Acherback to rise, marched the trio across the clearing to a shack. Canadian and British prisoners huddled inside, many of them wounded. In the morning Kravinchuk learned he was to be imprisoned for the remainder of the war. In rendering his verdict, the Japanese officer revealed an attitude prevalent among the more humane enemy leaders: he showed disgust for his prisoners but he did not interpret the Bushido Code as a license to commit wholesale butchery. The officer had deliberately allowed Kravinchuk and his friends to crawl through enemy lines—and there were roughly five hundred soldiers surrounding the first-aid post—because he knew they would be captured at the pillbox. As a result of this puzzling inconsistency in the ranks of the Japanese officers, Canadian and British soldiers never knew what to expect when they were taken prisoner.

Visiting Hong Kong with a group of naval officers in March 1921, Emperor Hirohito had made an unusual request to the colonial government. He had asked that he and his party be shown the reservoirs that provided the colony's fresh water. The government, seeing no harm in it, had consented, and the Japanese delegation had spent two hours inspecting the catchments and reservoirs.

There is no evidence that the enemy's knowledge of Hong Kong's water system was obtained during that seemingly innocent tour. Whatever the source of information, the reservoirs played a vital part in Sakai's conquest plan. The three regiments striking the north coast attempted to forge inland —rather than going west immediately to attack Victoria—in a bid to achieve two goals: (1) drive a wedge down the center of the island, cutting half of the defending troops off from physical contact with Victoria, and (2) capture the island's four principal reservoirs. The stranded troops would be denied ammunition and food supplies, and the densely populated city would have its fresh water reduced to an insignificant trickle.

By dawn Friday the Japanese were nearly halfway across the five-mile-wide island. They had all but eliminated the Rajput regiment and were within a few hours of taking two reservoirs, Tai Tam and Wong Nei Chong. Isolated Rifle and Grenadier platoons blocked their route, but the Canadians lacked the manpower to hold on much longer.

The strategy employed by the advancing Japanese was extracted from the pages of a German training manual. A French soldier, Captain Lafarge, suggested in a 1915 military magazine article that a small core of infiltration troops should focus on a particular enemy position and attack it until they effected a breakthrough. This core would be composed of specially trained, experienced men. After smashing a hole in the enemy line, the infiltrators would press ahead to the next obstacle; a large follow-up force would then assault the line, widening the hole.

The Germans experimented with the Lafarge method during World War I and, pleased with the results, they wrote it into a standard training book. Impressed with the German High Command's grasp of modern warfare techniques, Sakai and Takeo decided to try the infiltration system on the island. Seasoned storm troopers, carrying detailed maps supplied by fifth columnists, streaked for specific areas the moment they touched shore. The infiltrators made astonishing progress. Only ten hours after the landing they were so close to West Brigade Headquarters at Wong Nei Chong Gap that Lawson destroyed cipher books and equipment and cabled Ottawa: "Situation very grave. Deep penetration made by enemy."

Maltby, on the other hand, remained optimistic. "Japanese will undoubtedly try to ferry more men over tonight and continue infiltration," he advised London, "but I hope to be in a position to launch a general counter-attack tomorrow at dawn."

Besides a few hundred Rajputs, the East Brigade now comprised a Rifle battalion, two Volunteer companies, and several machine-gun units on loan from the Middlesex. Wallis and Maltby conferred at 9:30 A.M. Friday and agreed that East Brigade should withdraw to the south coast. The brigade would occupy six different positions near the village of Stanley and on Tai Tam Bay. After regrouping and acquiring additional mobile artillery from the coastal defenses, East Brigade would have the muscle to rout the Japanese from the high ground on Saturday and begin their drive back to the north coast. At least, that was how the theory went.

Victoria, December 19

Early Friday morning Corporal Lionel Speller walked into a hectic staff room at Fortress Headquarters' underground bunker. He was in a testy mood. A dispatch rider for the Royal Canadian Signal Corps, Speller was returning from delivering a package to a British colonel in a hillside pillbox.

"This has to go right away," he had been told at 3 A.M. "The colonel's desperate for it."

Two of the eight riders attached to Maltby's command had already been slain by snipers and, toting the package in a shoulder bag, the cocky, five-foot-four British Columbian was shot at several times. Fifth columnists would hear the motorcycle coming and, as he could not travel more than twenty miles an hour at night on the winding mountain roads, they would fire slightly ahead of the sound. Arriving at the pillbox intact, Speller was incensed when the colonel tore the parcel open and removed the contents, two tins of dog food for his pet Scotties.

"I don't care if you throw me in jail," Speller exploded. "I'm not risking my neck to bring you any more crummy dog food!"

The colonel said nothing, thereby affirming Speller's contention that many officers leading Hong Kong units were gutless wonders—World War I vets too old and too timid to be in the front lines. Speller slept for a couple of hours, then went back to Fortress Headquarters. As he entered the staff room, a Grenadier captain gave him a sealed envelope. "Take this to Wong Nei Chong Gap, Speller. To Brigadier Lawson."

"I trust it's important," the rider said icily, intending to balk if it was another trivial assignment. "The snipers are itching to get more riders."

"Very important. Between you and me, things are pretty hot at the Gap. Lawson has to pull out."

Probably an evacuation notice. Some officers did not consider an order official unless it was in writing and, Speller thought, Lawson might be one of them. Hurrying outside, he fired up his BSA 500 and started on the five-mile journey that was to earn him the Military Medal.

The tension that always gripped him during a dangerous ride was there now: his mouth was dry, his body taut. But he was not scared. He had made his peace with God, sing-

ing and praying with other servicemen at the Plymouth
Brethren's Duddell Street Gospel Hall. Anyway, the odds of
being killed by a sniper's bullet were no worse than being
clobbered by an artillery shell.

Speller was a fine athlete. A shoemaker's apprentice, he
had played soccer (left halfback with the Victoria, British
Columbia, titlists, the Saanich Thistles) and boxed (he lost
to Vancouver's Mickey Rogan in a Canadian amateur cham-
pionship semi-final match). But it was biking that he loved
most. Astride a blue Douglas Twin, he had competed in
cross-Canada hill climbs, often beating the husky riders
who laughed when he placed his small body on the huge
bike, and he had ridden with the Victoria Motorcycle Club
drill team in May 24 parades.

If only he had the Douglas now; it barely whispered
along. The BSA was so bloody loud the snipers had plenty
of time to prepare themselves for his arrival.

Half a mile from Fortress Headquarters, Speller's ordeal
began in earnest. A rooftop sniper on a quiet residential
street got off two shots that missed his head. Accelerating,
Speller turned a corner and left the pavement, roaring up
into the hills. The road between Fortress Headquarters and
the semiburied pillbox housing West Brigade command was
a narrow, snaking dirt track. The powerful BSA, capable of
going ninety miles an hour, was forced to maintain a thirty-
mile-an-hour crawl, even under Speller's expert driving.

The snipers were worse than usual. Every few hundred
yards bullets pinged off rocks around him. Out of sheer frustration, Speller took out his .38 Smith-Wesson and, steering
with one hand, fired at the hidden riflemen behind him.
Two miles along the road he climbed a steep hill and
rounded a curve to find a burned-out armored car blocking
the way. Speller braked fast, skidding to a stop a foot from
the radiator. Sitting there, his heart thumping, he presented
a lovely target but, fortunately, no one saw him. Starting up
again, he steered around the wreck and went unmolested

until he came to the last mile. This was the most treacherous spot on the road: a veritable sniper's lair that Grenadier patrols were constantly trying to clean out. A young dispatch rider, Ernie Thomas, had died there three hours earlier. Speller uttered a silent prayer and headed into the danger zone.

A torrent of sniper fire suddenly ripped into the rear wheel, knocking the spokes out. Speller whipped around a curve and stopped. That settled it. The bloody BSA was attracting too much fire. Pushing the bike in a ditch, he climbed a hillside and walked toward West Brigade Headquarters. Lieutenant Dick Maze and a Grenadier platoon appeared.

"We've got more than just fifth columnists bothering us," Maze said. "This area's thick with Japanese patrols."

The Grenadiers accompanied Speller the rest of the way.

Inside the pillbox, the rider was surprised to see Lawson treat the message without any great concern. Given a cup of hot cocoa, Speller sat in a corner and listened as two officers, Staff Sergeant Tom Barton and Sergeant Tony Phillips, tried to persuade the C/O to pull out immediately. "In a little while," Lawson said briskly. "I'm not finished here yet."

Speller left at 9 A.M. with a platoon going to Victoria. When he last had laid eyes on Lawson, the slim, compactly built Military Cross holder was feeding top-secret documents into a wastepaper-basket fire. Lawson's pipe was emitting smoke at a furious pace, but otherwise, he showed no external signs of being overly alarmed by the proximity of enemy soldiers.

An hour after Speller's departure, Japanese storm troopers sliced through a thin Grenadier line to the north. The infiltrators knew West Brigade Headquarters' exact location and, moving swiftly to it, they assailed the concrete structure with grenades and machine-gun bullets. Only Lawson and eight aides were inside. A Grenadier unit was trapped in a ditch two hundred yards in front of the pillbox by a vicious machine-gun barrage. Two truckloads of naval personnel, rushing from Victoria to reinforce the endangered post, were ambushed on the notorious last mile, and lost twenty-four men.

At 9:30 A.M. Barton and Phillips left the shelter, slithering on their stomachs up the hill behind the building. A hail of bullets struck them. Phillips died instantly. Seriously wounded, Barton lay in the open, feigning death, until nightfall, when he crawled to safety.

Lawson phoned Maltby at ten o'clock, stating that he still hoped to withdraw to a Grenadier holding on nearby Mount Nicholson, although the enemy was now lambasting the pillbox at close range. "They're all around us. I'm going outside to fight it out," the brigadier said.

There are three versions of what happened next. Two books and two magazine articles claimed that Lawson dashed outside, a blazing revolver in each hand, and killed eight Japanese before he died. Military historian C. P. Stacey omitted details of the brigadier's final moments from *Six Years of War*, stating only that "no witness survived to tell the story."

Sergeant Bob Manchester disputes both reports. The ex-Winnipeg welfare official says he was in the machine-gun-raked ditch opposite the beleaguered pillbox. Raising his head slightly, he saw Lawson and six staff officers emerge on the run. According to Manchester, the seven men sprinted onto a path leading up a hill beside the pillbox. As they passed a wall of granite, the machine-gunners changed targets, shooting over the heads of the Grenadiers in the ditch. "They were perfectly outlined against the granite cliffside," Manchester states. "The Japanese must have recognized the red bands on their caps as meaning they were officers. They hit the seven with a terrible barrage of machine-gun fire. The brigadier did not have a chance to shoot one gun, let alone two."

Lionel Speller, who believes Manchester's account is the most accurate, offers an explanation for the two-gun story: "Some Far East 'old hands' said they thought the Japanese started the story. By magnifying an enemy's stature, the Japanese made themselves appear larger, more powerful, because they had conquered him."

The manner in which Lawson actually perished is not of primary importance. What does matter is that he conducted himself heroically, staying in the front lines despite the heightening peril.

The shelling grew worse in Victoria. During the heaviest barrages the Japanese lobbed explosives across the harbor every twenty-two seconds. The Hong Kong and Shanghai Bank, the colony's tallest, most modern edifice, was pocked with shell holes; the elevators quit and many windows were shattered, but people still worked inside. A portion of the roof collapsed at the *South China Morning Post;* again, employees carried on as if nothing untoward had occurred. The harbor was a tangle of fractured and partially sunken sampans, ferries, and junks; flames and smoke licked the sky in Chinese sections; Peak villas were pulverized, private swimming pools and expensive cars smashed to bits. Homeless whites slept in office buildings and hotel lobbies, and the shopping arcade connecting the fashionable Gloucester and Hong Kong hotels was crammed with so many Chinese refugees that a disinfectant squad, fearing a cholera outbreak, sprayed the passageway every morning.

The colony's principal hospitals, Bowen Road, War Memorial, and Queen Mary, operated at full tilt, defying the bombardments. All three flew Red Cross flags, but that meant nothing to the Japanese: they were attempting to destroy gun emplacements that, in a classic example of misbegotten planning, were embedded directly behind hospital buildings and, in one particularly inane case, on a ground-floor terrace.

Bowen Road sustained an estimated 111 hits during the siege. Yet the shelling did not fill Kay Christie with as much dread as did the prospect of Japanese soldiers invading the premises. After word of the enemy landing spread through the hospital, almost everyone in the building realized it was only a matter of time before the island fell. This gloomy prognosis, contradicting the optimistic Fortress Headquarters viewpoint, was formed after listening to the stories told by wounded soldiers. Stories of how the Japanese fought fanatically, showing little regard for their lives; of how, vastly outnumbering the defenders, they raced inland to come up behind positions that still faced south, anticipating a sea attack; of how they ruthlessly bayoneted injured men.

The hospital was now a pulsing madhouse. The wounded were wheeled into surgery one after another in assembly-line fashion. Many staff members went thirty-six hours without sleep. The wards were packed and patients lay on mattresses strewn along corridors. Dr. Gordon Grey was stationed at the main entrance, dressing wounds and deciding which casualties required immediate attention. The traffic was so heavy at times he felt like he was working in a bus terminal.

Whenever she heard a muffled sound outside in the middle of the night—a voice, footsteps, a vehicle pulling up— Kay Christie listened intently, wondering if the Japanese had arrived. On Friday night she heard voices and the door swung open. Two ambulance men carried in an unconscious soldier on a stretcher. Bud Sweet, a Rifle from New Brunswick. His left arm was missing. The Japanese had bayoneted him repeatedly in the arm and shoulder and left him for dead. He was sixteen or seventeen but, to Kay, his freckles and curly hair made him look twelve. He should not be here, she thought. He should be home playing marbles. Gazing at the prostrate youth, she had a distressing thought: if the Japanese could savagely bayonet such a baby-faced boy, what would they do when they entered a hospital filled with helpless young nurses and incapacitated patients?

On Friday night Private Dennis Murphy awakened in a crowded hospital ward. He was lying under a wool blanket, wearing shorts and socks. His head and right leg were bandaged, and it took him several moments before the grogginess lifted and his surroundings fully registered.

"How are you feeling?" an attractive blonde nurse asked, looking at him from the foot of the bed. "A headache? Any dizziness?"

"I'm feeling terrific now that I've seen you," the former announcer said flirtatiously. "What place is this?"

"Bowen Road Hospital. You've been unconscious for hours. We'll have to make sure you don't have a concussion."

"What's wrong with my leg?"

"Nothing serious. A couple of nasty cuts."

"Oh, good." Murphy grinned as the nurse walked away. "I'll be able to take you dancing Saturday night."

The light banter disguised Murphy's true emotions. He had seen awesome things at Wong Nei Chong Gap. The Japs were determined to roll straight on to the south coast and, by God, the Grenadiers were just as determined to hold them back. Captain Allan Bowman had died rushing a Japanese patrol with a blasting Tommy gun. Captain Bob Phillips, one eye knocked out, had fought until his ammunition was gone. Lieutenant Len Corrigan had seen a Japanese officer charging with an upraised sword and, wrestling him to the ground, had strangled the man to death. Awesome things that made Murphy feel ashamed. He had been inexcusably naïve in treating the war lightly. While he had been en route to the Gap, thinking only of getting a poker game going, his countrymen were dying. His strongest desire now was to regain his health and return to the front. He had to pour everything he had into the war; he owed it to the heroes, dead and alive.

"What happened to you?" a bearded Rajput in the next bed inquired.

"Grenade. I guess the impact floored me. We were on night patrol and, I swear, the Nips have cats' eyes, for they spotted us in pitch darkness. I didn't even get off a shot."

As the Rajput went into a lengthy description of his experience at Lye Mun, Murphy's mind drifted. He had heard that a Grenadier detachment was preparing to storm the high ground at Mount Butler, a mile northeast of the spot where Lawson had been killed. Murphy had friends in the unit and he was curious about how they were doing.

Scrambling down the steep hillside, banging into boulders and shrubbery, those same Grenadiers were in rapid retreat. They had achieved their objective, taking Mount Butler in a bloody battle in which thirty-five comrades died. Now, three hours later, the platoon was on the run, trying to escape several hundred dogged pursuers.

Private Stanley Baty's leg and shoulder throbbed with pain from collisions with the granite rocks, but he did not dare stop to examine them. The enemy was too close.

"Don't panic," Sergeant Major John Osborn loudly cautioned. "Stay together and keep calm. We'll get out of this okay."

Baty thought Osborn was an incredible man. Very strict, all rules-and-regulations—but nerves of steel. Leading his men up the mountain, he had felled six Japanese with his bayonet and, afterward, he had repelled Japanese attacks by scooping up live grenades and flinging them back. Now, hurtling down the western slope of Mount Butler in broad daylight, fleeing an overwhelmingly superior enemy force, Osborn retained his cool, efficient demeanor.

The twenty-two-year-old Baty was anything but cool. He had quit a good-paying job cutting firewood for a Winnipeg

fuel supply company to join his three brothers in the Grenadiers. At Camp Shilo, he had met Charlie Smith, a Regina
smelter worker, and the two had become such fast friends
that Baty called him "my fourth brother." Now Charlie was
dead. On Mount Butler he had stood up to draw a bead on a
Japanese soldier carrying a flag and had been struck in the
forehead by a sniper's bullet. Charlie's death and the wild
rush toward the Grenadier line near the Gap had Baty's
mind in a turmoil.

At the bottom of the slope the platoon quickly reassembled. Baty noted the terror in some of his companions'
eyes: yet no one bolted. Osborn's strength somehow glued
them into a tight unit. Taking a Bren gun from a profusely
sweating soldier, Baty said he would guard the rear.

The platoon moved swiftly up the ravine. The only noise
was the heavy breathing of the more exhausted soldiers and
the scraping of their boots on the hard ground. "I think
we've lost 'em," someone said. "There aren't any Japs comin'
down the hill."

The platoon had eluded the hunters from the summit, but
other Japanese units were in the area. As the platoon approached the end of the ravine, a hidden Japanese soldier
tossed a grenade from somewhere above. The explosive
thudded to earth three feet from Osborn and six or seven
soldiers.

"Clear out!" the sergeant major shouted. In an extraordinary act of self-sacrifice Osborn flung himself on the
ground, covering the grenade with his body. The blast was
instantly fatal. (Osborn was posthumously awarded the most
prestigious medal in the Commonwealth for bravery, the
Victoria Cross.)

The platoon was stunned speechless. But the fear of more
grenades suddenly tearing into their ranks prodded the men
onward, half running, half walking. The ravine opened onto
a narrow, dry slough. Ten feet into the clearing, Baty
tripped and pitched onto his face. The fall probably saved

his life. From hidden vantage points in the surrounding hills the Japanese directed machine-gun and rifle fire into the slough. Everyone near Baty was cut down. Forsaking the Bren gun, Baty crawled to the side of the clearing to where the other fourteen survivors gathered, hugging large rocks for protection. For twenty minutes the two adversaries exchanged bullets. When the ammunition was almost depleted, the Grenadiers decided to surrender. One man rose, waving a white handkerchief. He was shot dead. "We've had it, boys," Baty muttered. "Those buggers are aching to do us in."

Ten minutes later the ammunition ran out. The thirteen men removed their rifle breeches and threw them as far as they could. Then, believing it was the last move they would ever make, they stood together, their hands over their heads. Popping up everywhere, dozens of Japanese soldiers walked slowly toward them, pointing rifles.

They did not shoot. Reaching the platoon, a Japanese officer pointed a sword at a man standing beside Baty. Two soldiers grabbed the man and hustled him off to one side, where he was bayoneted. His death was, Baty assumed, a graphic warning that if the others did not behave they would suffer an identical fate. The soldiers stripped them of watches, rings, and wallets, then the prisoners were marched north.

At twilight the platoon was placed inside a one-room building. Two hundred Canadians, Britons, and East Indians were packed into a poorly ventilated space so small that no one dared to sit, lest he be trampled. Many prisoners, wounded and moaning, were pressed upright against the walls. During the night a stray British mortar shell banged through the roof, killing several men. With no food, sleep, or water, the prisoners endured "The Black Hole of Hong Kong" for twenty hours. Some were held up by the crush of bodies long after they died.

When the Japanese finally ordered the captives outside—

one at a time and coming through the doorway on their knees—they were told they would be interned at North Point, a camp the colonial government had originally built to house refugees. A young Grenadier lieutenant, Mitchell, said he did not want to go: his brother was too badly wounded to make the long walk. He asked a Japanese officer if his brother could have medical aid. The officer barked a command and two soldiers accompanied Mitchell back into the building. The soldiers' grim expressions as they emerged moments later disclosed that they had slain the brothers.

The cruelty Baty witnessed did not prepare him for the kindness shown by a Japanese soldier en route to North Point. The prisoners marched single file, their hands linked by a long piece of telephone wire. An unusually tall Japanese soldier looped his canvas pack around Baty's neck. It was jammed with stolen food and jewelry, and the strap frequently slipped up Baty's throat, causing choking spasms. The soldier untied his hands and permitted him to tote the pack on his back. That unexpected bit of kindness was followed by an even more surprising deed. When they arrived at North Point, the soldier removed the pack, effusively thanked Baty for bearing it, and gave him a gift—a small tin of asparagus tips.

CHAPTER FOURTEEN

Wong Nei Chong Gap, December 20

On Saturday, Colonel Shoji Toshishige dispatched a communiqué to infantry commander Takeo apologizing for having incurred so many casualties at Wong Nei Chong Gap. His 230th Regiment had lost eight hundred men in mass, near-suicidal rushes at Grenadier encampments. Furthermore, Shoji said, "the terrain in this area is so rugged and separated by interlocking ravines that our contact with forward units was at one time entirely broken."

He could have added that the young, raw Grenadiers giving his seasoned troops such a hard time were not only low on manpower and ammunition but, his forward observation posts had reported, were running out of food and water. In many cases Grenadier platoons were encircled by enemy forces, and, lacking aircraft, there was no way for Fortress Headquarters to send them supplies. The Japanese had dislodged the Canadians from the core of Wong Nei Chong and seized control of the reservoir before daybreak on the twentieth; the isolated platoons were clinging to positions in the hills and on stretches of the north-south road that twisted through the Gap.

The Grenadiers' strong showing bolstered Maltby's opinion that the enemy could be ejected from the island. On Saturday morning Governor Young dropped by Fortress Headquarters to, as Maltby noted in his dispatch, "stress the importance of fighting it out to the end, however bad the military outlook might be. Every day gained was a direct help to the Empire war effort."

In return, Maltby had mixed news for the governor. The Grenadiers had not been entirely routed from the Gap and the Japanese infantry was not attacking Victoria. But the planned counteroffensive had to be postponed. Storm troopers had swept around the Grenadiers' right flank and were hitting southern defenses. He could not think of mounting a full-scale northern drive until the enemy penetration was nipped in the bud. A military transport pool, Aberdeen dockyards and the Repulse Bay Hotel, a tourist mecca, were reporting steadily increasing Japanese infantry fire.

The worst situation was at Repulse Bay where enemy soldiers, occupying a service station and the high ground in front, were shooting at soldiers and civilians inside the hotel. Maltby ordered his troops to immediately alleviate the pressure on the besieged southern positions. Shortly after, he appointed Colonel H. B. Rose, a retired British officer serving with the Volunteers, to replace Lawson as West Brigade commanding officer. He also issued a confident message to units throughout the island. Based on a radio communiqué from a Chinese general, stating that he had 60,000 men marching on the border for an imminent attack, the message said: "There are indications that Chinese forces are advancing towards the frontier to our aid. All ranks must therefore hold their positions at all costs and look forward to only a few more days of strain."

Lacking efficient intelligence sources, Maltby had no way of knowing that the 60,000-man force was, lamentably, just another phantom army.

Repulse Bay, December 20

Beyond a doubt, Ralph Ingram was leading a charmed life. How else could he explain his two narrow escapes from death in the past week? The bespectacled Hong Kong accountant had been shifted all over the island by the Volunteers' Armored Car Corps and both incidents transpired while he was riding in a motorcycle sidecar, manning a Bren gun. A fifth-columnist grenade landing beside the front wheel had failed to explode. And a sudden burst of Japanese bullets on a lonely north coast road had killed Egan, the other fellow crammed into the sidecar with him: Egan had been crouched down in the corner and Ingram had been standing erect when the bullets came.

His luck was now guiding him toward what promised to be a most pleasant assignment. He was in a Bren carrier, going to the Repulse Bay Hotel. "Take a run over there and see if everything's all right," he had been ordered. Well, everything should definitely be all right. In peacetime the hotel offered exquisite five-course meals, champagne and caviar snacks, or tea and crumpets on the front terrace. He and his mates assumed that the usual eight-page menu had been shelved but, they reasoned, whatever they had for lunch at the hotel that afternoon would be a vast improvement over canned bully beef, their normal fare.

Like travelers the world over, Ingram rated the Repulse Bay Hotel as an earthly manifestation of the Garden of Eden. Situated six miles from central Victoria, the low, white, colonial-style building was perched on the edge of a cliff and at the foot of a mountain slope. Sandy beaches below the cliff rimmed a blue, crescent-shaped bay that was ideal for swimming and boating. The sprawling hotel garden was bright with colors—the reds of poinsettias, the magentas of bougainvilleas, the deep blues of hydrangeas—

and people driving out to partake of the traditional Sunday buffet on the terrace were treated to fragrant scents carried by gentle winds. The Chinese called Hong Kong "The Place of Sweet Lagoons"; to the white Hong Kongers, Repulse Bay was the sweetest lagoon of all.

Ingram's thoughts were of a more personal nature as the Bren carrier followed the winding road south. His missionary parents had organized beach parties and, escaping the stifling heat of Victoria, a steam launch weighted down with Methodist families would descend on Repulse Bay. They had had delightful times swimming off the launch in the sheltered waters. For Ingram it was a wrenching experience to have Repulse Bay and other places he loved tainted by the evil and misery of war.

The carrier turned into the driveway and drew up in front of the hotel. A light rain was falling, and Ingram assumed that was the reason the grounds seemed deserted. Climbing from the carrier, the three Volunteers walked toward the steps. Snipers crouched inside the nearby service station opened fire and a piece of a bullet ricocheted off the carrier and burrowed into Ingram's hand. The Volunteers darted up the stairs and into a lobby crowded with soldiers and civilians.

A British medical orderly attended to Ingram's wound. "I'd better get you to St. Stephen's," he said. "That metal has to come out."

The two men ran through sniper fire to a field ambulance and drove to an emergency hospital established at St. Stephen's College, about two miles to the south. Ingram was certain he had exhausted whatever quota of good fortune the gods had allotted him. He was wrong. The next day, with the metal removed and his hand bandaged, he returned to his unit. The day after he left St. Stephen's, Japanese soldiers raided the hospital and bayoneted patients in the room where he had slept overnight. Ingram fought in the hills until he was captured and interned for the rest of the war in a camp four miles from the house in which he grew up.

The three-day battle for the Repulse Bay Hotel had had a bizarre beginning. At 7:30 Saturday morning a ragged Chinese coolie knocked on the service entrance door and asked a Filipino waiter if he could buy beer and cigarettes. Japanese soldiers had stopped him on a nearby mountain trail, he said, and sent him to the hotel. Concluding the coolie was either lying or insane, the waiter shooed him away. Ten minutes later—while guests eating breakfast on the terrace gaped in stunned disbelief—four Japanese officers, wearing white gloves and smartly pressed uniforms, appeared at the end of the driveway. For a full minute they stood calmly in the open, reconnoitering the grounds. When the officers vanished into the shrubbery, twenty-five soldiers came over a hill and occupied the gas station; six Royal Navy men, out for a morning stroll in the garden, were taken captive as they passed the station. Subsequent sniper fire from the garage and the hills cleared the terrace and brought terrified guests from their rooms to the lobby. Most of the two hundred guests were white women and children who had gone to Repulse Bay, believing it to be the safest spot on the island.

There were also two hundred soldiers on the premises. Bone-tired, unshaven, their uniforms filthy, they had been transferred from combat zones for a much-needed rest. Forty white Volunteers camped on the floor in the Ping-Pong room; one hundred Chinese and East Indians inhabited an upstairs lounge usually rented for private parties; fifty Rifles and a handful of Grenadiers and other personnel were bedded down on the dining room floor.

American writer Gwen Dew was among the guests. So were retired jockey Victor Needa (for decades the Number One rider at Happy Valley), Baron and Baroness Guillame, eighty-three-year-old American author L. C. Arlington, and a large contingent of Peak society matrons. Wealthy Swiss, French, Russian, German, and Chinese families were also there.

Some of the socialites did not take kindly to sharing their dinner tables with the Chinese. "What are these people doing here?" a haughty dowager exclaimed when a Chinese family joined her. "The only Orientals in my dining room at home are carrying trays!" The same gray-haired lady was livid again when she encountered a group of East Indians lounging in the corridor outside her room. "What is the matter with you?" she protested to manager Marjorie Matheson. "Can't you keep those creatures in the basement?"

As fate would have it, the dowager and most of the guests wound up in the basement themselves. An aged tunnel, built to drain off overflow water in the monsoon season, ran from beneath the hotel to the beach. Volunteers hung kerosene lamps on the damp walls, sandbagged the entrance, and covered the floor with boards. During the daylight hours, as the Japanese and the soldiers in the hotel blasted away at one another, women and children huddled in the tunnel. The dowager led a chorus of complaints about the cold, babies cried, and adults tensed whenever a mortar shell smashed into the basement, causing the tunnel to crack and reverberate. The fear of having the walls collapse, burying them alive, was surpassed only by the fear of having Japanese soldiers on the beach below find the dark, sloping tunnel and crawl up to slaughter them.

At night Gwen Dew was posted in the kitchen, guarding the fast-diminishing food stores. Most of the Chinese and Filipino staff had fled and there were rumors that fifth columnists among those remaining were eager to set fire to the kitchen. When Gwen returned to her room for a few hours' sleep, she found fresh bullet holes in the walls and spent cartridges on the floor, mute evidence that the British soldiers were still using the room for sniping at Japanese troops on the slopes.

From the start, the hotel defenders realized they were outnumbered. Shortly after Ingram was wounded, a Middlesex platoon stormed the gas station and cleared the building. Platoon leader Second Lieutenant Peter Grounds and twenty Japanese died in the attack. Recapturing the station was a minor triumph. The six navy prisoners were found tied up but unhurt. Scouts reported that the Japanese advance party had swollen to between five hundred and six hundred men. Three machine guns were trained on the terrace, the main road was covered in either direction by more machine guns, and enemy patrols infested the beach. In other words, the hotel was surrounded.

On Maltby's orders, Major Robert Templer of the 8th Coast Artillery Regiment went to the hotel Sunday morning. "There's one helluva mess down there, Templer," Maltby told him. "Try and clean it up, will you." Taking two Rifle platoons, Templer barged past the machine-gun nests in speeding trucks and an armored car. His presence at the hotel was electrifying. The highest-ranking officer on the premises rarely left the cocktail bar and the soldiers sorely needed a strong, authoritative leader. Striding about, barking orders, Templer insisted that every soldier wash his body and shave off unsightly facial stubble. The main core of the defensive operation would, he said, center on the lobby. And, he asserted, he had no desire to sit around and wait for the enemy to close in.

That afternoon Templer and two truckloads of Rifles left the hotel and raced up the north-south road, under persistent machine-gun fire, to attack a Japanese encampment near the Gap. He had hoped his surprise raid would break the enemy stranglehold on the Grenadier positions at Wong Nei Chong, but, as he reported to Maltby afterward, there were too many Japanese for it to have any effect. Other Templer-organized raiding parties crept from the hotel at night to flay enemy positions in the hills above Repulse Bay.

At one point during the hotel siege a Japanese patrol

slithered across the garden and got into the West Wing. This was the hotel's most exclusive section, and many Peakites had protested when Templer forced them to move into less opulent rooms, closer to the lobby. The Japanese stationed a machine gun at the end of a long, red-carpeted corridor. At 4 A.M. Templer and his men rolled grenades along the corridor blowing the gun to bits. ("More exciting than a bowling alley," Templer later remarked.) The rest of the infiltrators, who had occupied West Wing suites, fled through the windows.

Templer was strong in his judgments but not inflexible. When twenty guests sought permission to have an active role in the hotel's defense, he said no, but he was talked into it. Gray-haired Elizabeth Mosey, a retired World War I nurse, donned her old white uniform and attended to wounded men in the cocktail bar off the lobby. Gwen Dew forsook the tunnel to help her. Marjorie Matheson and a group of volunteers established a kitchen canteen, serving the soldiers tea and scones. Millionaire Henry Marsman put on a metal helmet and along with two Chinese bellboys in Philip Morris outfits (red caps, gold-buttoned jackets) climbed out a rear window not covered by Japanese snipers and dug in the garden to fill sandbags.

One of the bravest acts during the battle involved three guests in their sixties, former jockey Needa, Canadian-born oil executive W. M. Wilson, and British businessman D. A. Baker-Carr. The trio sprinted to a bullet-riddled car parked in the driveway and drove half a mile to the Lido Beach Club, where the British had hidden an ammunition cache. From the instant they left the hotel until the moment they returned, they drew heavy sniper fire; a single bullet hitting the ammunition boxes would have killed them.

Toward the end of the siege the once immaculate hotel was a filthy shambles. Mortars punched holes in the roof and walls; pieces of broken glass, shredded wood, and ceiling plaster littered the floor and bullet-scarred furniture; the mahogany dining tables were splintered and the kitchen strewn with smashed crockery. By day, soldiers sat at more than one hundred windows, shooting at movements and gun flashes on the cliffs. By night, with blackout curtains drawn, they posted sentries and slept on the hardwood floors, their packs substituting for pillows.

When the Japanese cut off the water and electricity, flickering candles cast eerie shadows in the corridors and, owing to the low reserves in the hotel storage tanks, the tea canteen was discontinued and water limited to a daily cupful per person. Mosey and Dew washed bandages in bathtubs, using the same water over and over again.

Informed by telephone of the appalling state of affairs—the ammunition and food were nearly gone—Maltby made an agonizing decision. The soldiers were to withdraw, leaving the guests and wounded men to surrender. Templer balked. "We can't desert these people, sir. Why don't we take them to Fort Stanley in lorries?"

"They'd never get through," Maltby replied. "The road's too well covered. And if they did make it, what then? The enemy's going to attack Stanley any time."

With a mixture of shame and alarm, Templer obeyed the order. He felt positive that the withdrawal was literally condemning the guests and wounded soldiers to death. Departing in groups of twenty, the soldiers quit the hotel in the middle of the night. Japanese patrols plagued Templer's rear-guard platoon throughout the two-mile hike, but no one was killed.

Only a handful of guests knew the troops were going and they said nothing in order to avoid creating a panic. Many guests awakened at dawn and, peering outside, were shocked to see that a white pillowcase had replaced the Union Jack on a garden flagpole. The Japanese came around 7 A.M. Suspecting a trap, the first batch entered through back windows. When the guests congregating in the lobby saw them they raised their hands. "There are no soldiers here," businessman Andrew Shields said in faulty Japanese. "Soldiers gone." The intruders called to their comrades in the garden and the hotel was soon crowded with enemy soldiers.

Six men wielding bayonet-mounted rifles tried to enter the cocktail bar where forty men lay wounded. Frail, gray-haired Elizabeth Mosey blocked their path. "Go away," she said sternly. "These are sick men. If you want to kill them, you'll have to kill me first." The six hesitated, then retreated.

The guests were held in the lobby and on the terrace until a general arrived. Walking over to a group of British and American merchants, he asked why they were not in uniform. A Briton answered that in his country some men stayed out of military service in order to attend to commercial interests. "It is different in Japan," the general said disgustedly. "Every man fights in wartime, no matter what his occupation is." He then pronounced his verdict on the guests and wounded soldiers' future: "Your soldiers have run and left women and children unprotected. Never mind. We will protect you."

In ordering Templer to evacuate his troops, Maltby reasoned that the enemy would be less likely to harm civilians and injured men if there were no able-bodied troops around. As there were no killings at the Repulse Bay Hotel, his decision proved to be a good one.

While the Japanese were launching their seventy-two hour struggle for possession of the Repulse Bay Hotel on Saturday, a flotilla of motor torpedo boats was chugging north, out of Aberdeen dockyards. Captain George Collinson headed the Royal Navy and Volunteer force that had taken upon itself a Herculean mission: to disrupt the stream of shallow-bottom boats ferrying soldiers from Kowloon to North Point.

It was a gray, rainy morning. Patches of fog clung to the shoreline on the island but the one-mile stretch between the mainland and North Point was clear. By dawn that day the Japanese holdings included most of Jardin's Lookout and Wong Nei Chong Gap and patches of high ground on Mount Butler and Mount Parker. Some of the enemy soldiers disembarking at North Point immediately forged south toward the Gap and Stanley peninsula while others headed west to attack allied positions lying between them and Victoria. The West Brigade was protecting the city with a jagged and confused line running from the shoreline to the west of North Point to the Aberdeen area: the Middlesex and the Rajput survivors were at Leighton Hill, the Royal Scots at Mount Nicholson and the Grenadiers near the Gap.

As the destroyer *Thracian* had done on her mainland raid, the six MTBs were banking on the element of surprise. The enemy doubtless knew there were MTBs still in service, but they would never expect the little boats to have the audacity to attack them. Not with the imposing artillery lining Kowloon and North Point waterfronts, overseeing the landing operation.

The sixty-foot torpedo boats had as many faults as virtues. They were leaky, cramped, and, in lieu of torpedoes (a promised shipment never arrived), armed with .303 machine guns, fore and aft, and grenades. Their chief assets were speed (32 knots from three 500hp Napier engines) and maneuverability. That, and the remarkable degree of derring-do that infected all of the crews.

The MTBs struck in pairs. A junk and two large sampans were crossing the harbor when the first two British boats attacked, their guns chattering. The junk caught fire and sank. The MTBs circled the spot where the junk went under and machine-gunned most of the forty-odd soldiers thrashing about in the water. Japanese artillerymen on both shores pelted the channel with shells. Lobbing grenades, the torpedo boats set a second craft ablaze and forced the third to scurry back to Kowloon. As she returned to the rendezvous point, a shell hit the engine room of MTB 07. The other boat tossed her a line and towed her away from the battle area. For this role in the daring assault, Royal Navy Lieutenant R. W. Ashby was awarded the Distinguished Service Cross.

The second pair of MTBs moved into the channel. The Japanese had stopped ferrying troops and, before she could reverse her course, MTB 18 took a direct hit in the conning tower that killed her captain and a sublieutenant. A second shell wrecked her propeller and, racing out of control, flames licking the deck, MTB 18 headed straight for Kowloon. She struck a seawall on the waterfront and exploded, killing everyone on board. MTB 11 was also devastated by shells. Five crewmen were dead and four others severely burned. There was a fire aft and the hull was taking water in three places. Two Zeroes from Kai Tak splintered her deck with machine-gun bullets as Royal Navy Lieutenant A. C. Collingwood stood in the shattered conning tower, trying desperately to guide her back to Aberdeen. Miraculously, MTB 11 limped into the naval yard and, once the fire was extinguished, she was berthed in a drydock.

Captain Collinson radioed the last two boats, stating it would be futile to continue the raid. The commander of MTB 26, Lieutenant W. D. Wagstaff, either did not hear the message or decided to take a crack at the Japanese regardless of the return-to-port order. Wagstaff's boat dashed along the North Point coastline, her guns rattling. The torpedo boat was no match for the artillerymen. Shells ripped into her engine room and conning tower, stopping her cold. The Zeroes strafed the crippled vessel, then dropped light bombs on her. Wagstaff and all hands perished before the boat sank.

More than half of the personnel engaged in the raid were killed and only one of the MTBs remained seaworthy. Within an hour the Japanese resumed ferrying troops and weaponry to the island. If the mission failed to seriously affect the landing operation, it did succeed in giving the

Royal Navy and Volunteer forces a tremendous feeling of pride in the gallantry their comrades had displayed.

Victoria, December 20

On Saturday afternoon Emily Hahn was at the War Memorial Hospital, waiting in a lineup to have breakfast in the noisy, crowded kitchen. Three members of the Hong Kong Food Control Committee were seated off to one side, wolfing sausages, eggs and toast, and the spunky American writer glared with all the loathing she could muster. She had been given nothing except cereal or rice since leaving the Selwyn-Clarke villa to become a volunteer nursing aide. It took an enormous effort to stop herself from tongue-lashing the neatly dressed bureaucrats who openly stuffed themselves while telling others in the colony to eat sparingly.

Food was only one of Emily's problems. The older British nurses acted like crosses between police matrons and queen bees. They resented volunteers trespassing on their private territory and behaved coldly, brusquely, toward all of them. Emily was treated worse than the others because she was Hilda Selwyn-Clarke's friend and, in the nurses' ill-conceived opinion, Hilda was a snob, for she was a Peak socialite married to a VIP.

Fortunately the senior nurses did not have the authority to fire the volunteers, so Emily and her baby shared a tiny ground-floor room with Hilda and, while Carola slept, the writer boiled instruments, changed bandages, and performed an endless succession of menial chores. It was far from a pleasant situation, but keeping busy was a lot better than sitting in a cellar listening to popping shells.

"Oh, Emily, there you are."

Entering the kitchen, her face pallid, Hilda had the look

of a person bearing grave news. Instinctively Emily felt that someone she knew was involved.

"Charles has been wounded," Hilda explained. "He's at the Queen Mary."

"Is he all right?"

"I don't know. I just heard he was shot."

Emily moved to the door, her mind in a turmoil.

"Don't go there," Hilda implored. "Your duty is to your baby."

For one awful moment Emily thought her friend was like all the others, the oh-so-proper Peakites who would not let her in their homes because they disapproved of her affair with a married man. She was called "the scarlet woman." That did not bother her, but the fact that many community pillars shunned Carola as though she had leprosy (a bank vice-president refused to have the baby sleep in his villa overnight) was infuriating. Looking into Hilda's troubled eyes, Emily realized she had a different motive for keeping her and Charles apart. Hilda was frightened and did not want to be at the hospital without her if the Japanese came.

"I have to go," Emily said. "I'll phone someone to take care of Carola."

After a friend promised to be right over, Emily donned a steel helmet and left the hospital. It was five miles from the Peakside War Memorial to the Queen Mary in the south. Five miles of debris-blocked streets, begging refugees, and sudden encounters with enemy aircraft: three times Emily crouched in doorways as bombers bashed holes in surrounding buildings. Walking and hitching rides on military vehicles, she finally reached the hospital at 3 P.M. When she got there, the elevators were not working and she had to climb the marble stairs. For twenty minutes she searched the wards, her thoughts bedeviled by images of a dead or badly mangled Charles Boxer. When she saw him, he was lying on a cot in a small, pleasant room; a young soldier on the next cot, his leg amputated, was cursing everyone in sight.

Charles looked pale and weak, yet his face broke into a grin as Emily removed her helmet and sat beside his cot.

"You shouldn't have come," he said. "The streets are too dangerous."

"I wanted to come. And what on earth have you been doing, Charles Boxer? You told me staff officers never fight."

"I must revise that. Staff officers *hardly ever* fight."

He had taken a bullet between his left shoulder and chest, barely missing his lung. After lying all night in a rice paddy, losing blood, he was brought to the hospital in a delirious condition. Blood transfusions saved his life and, he said, all he needed now was a bit of rest.

"I really didn't think I'd ever fight, you know. I was on the road to Repulse Bay when a bunch of soldiers came along. They had lost their officers and were retreating. Well, we couldn't have that, could we? I turned them around and led them back to the Shouson Hill. Some sod put a bullet in me as I was climbing from a ravine. I didn't even see the swine."

Delighted that he was alive and basically intact, Emily relaxed.

"I'll have to wash your face and comb your hair," she said lightly. "You're a terrible mess. If you want to go around pretending you're Errol Flynn, you can't look grubby. Heroes don't have dirty faces."

CHAPTER FIFTEEN

Wong Nei Chong Gap, December 21

Major Ernie Hodkinson's men adored him. Whereas Lawson had been reserved and gentlemanly, and Osborn strict and authoritarian, Hodkinson deftly blended firmness, respect for rules, and a good-guy quality that made him easy to approach. During the battle for Wong Nei Chong Gap his men learned he had another side to him: awesome tenacity.

Hodkinson was in command of Company D, a Grenadier detachment struggling to retain its steadily loosening grip on the center of the island. With the Repulse Bay Hotel and other southern holdings under fire, Fortress Headquarters was loath to mount an all-out counterattack; nevertheless, Colonel Rose, the new West Brigade commanding officer, organized some semblance of an offensive aimed at pushing the Japanese northward. The Grenadiers' Company B, under Major H. W. Hook, was shifted from the south to help bolster Hodkinson's battered unit. Royal Scots, Punjabis, sappers, Volunteers, and Royal Navy seamen joined the strike force. All told, about five hundred men were allotted the unenviable job of clearing the Gap and perpetrating an enemy retreat. Unenviable, and well-nigh impossible, for the enemy had seventy-five hundred troops on the island and was landing hundreds more every hour.

To the small, slight Hodkinson fell the gigantic task of

recapturing the Wong Nei Chong police station. Sitting on a knoll overlooking the north-south road, the station was a command post from which enemy storm troopers were making infiltration forays. Hodkinson accepted Fortress Headquarters' order to take the nerve center without protesting that it was a near-suicidal mission. That, he knew, would be a waste of time, for if anything characterized the senior officers at Fortress Headquarters it was obstinacy. Inwardly, he had deep qualms. His platoon comprised forty men and two Bren guns. Five hundred Japanese had been counted having breakfast on a Wong Nei Chong slope and, the thirty-one-year-old major surmised that, with so many troops around, the police station was bound to be protected with superior weaponry. But he had his orders.

Starting out from Company D headquarters at 7 A.M. Sunday, the Hodkinson platoon took ten hours to cover half a mile. After capturing West Brigade headquarters and killing Lawson, the Japanese had sent infiltration patrols into the Gap and, moving along the road and slopes, Hodkinson and his men encountered enemy soldiers practically every yard. The major's determination to reach the knoll was amazing. Running in front, he threw grenades, fired his revolver, and shouted encouraging words. When the platoon reached the base of the knoll, Hodkinson radioed for reinforcements. Two armored cars drove up and the major in command said they would support the platoon's uphill attack. However, the Japanese spoiled their plan: a volley of mortar and machine-gun fire from the summit disabled both vehicles. At twilight, drizzling rain soaking their uniforms, the Grenadiers followed Hodkinson toward the post. The slope was so steep they could not see the station as they climbed.

The platoon was halfway up when the Japanese attacked. Forty or fifty soldiers lined the crest, shooting rifles and flinging grenades. Seconds before he felt his body lifting, Hodkinson heard explosions and agonizing screams. When he thudded back down, his left side torn by a grenade blast, he blacked out.

An hour later the major regained consciousness. It was dark and strangely quiet. Dead Grenadiers were spread all over the slope. His side hurting and bleeding, he crawled down the slope, praying that the obscure figures moving on the road were Canadians, not Japanese. As his strength ebbed, he uttered a feeble cry for help. Then he passed out. When he opened his eyes again, he was in a Queen Mary hospital bed. His wound would heal, a nurse said, and he would be hospitalized for a few weeks. Hodkinson did not have to ask how the attack on the police station turned out. The number of bodies on the slope was silent evidence that the mission had failed.

The ill-fated assault on the police station preceded other abortive bids in and around Wong Nei Chong to recapture newly fallen positions. Grenadier attacks on Mount Nicholson and the Wong Nei Chong reservoir and Grenadier Royal Scot assaults on Jardin's Lookout resulted in hundreds of casualties.

The Canadians fought so ferociously that the Japanese overestimated their strength. Colonel Doi stated in a dispatch that the Grenadier force attacking one of his positions comprised four hundred men, whereas fewer than one hundred actually participated. In that particular fight, Doi reported the Japanese suffered 40 per cent casualties and, when they depleted their ammunition supply, his men resorted to throwing rocks at Canadians climbing a precipitous cliff.

The rock-throwing incident may have been unique for the well-equipped Japanese but concocting makeshift weaponry was nothing new for the Canadians. Several times Grenadier units were forced to throw rocks, empty rifles, and pieces of packing crates and machinery at advancing Japanese; they also fired smoke bombs from mortars and charged swinging bare fists when ammunition ran out.

Other heroic, and often bizarre, incidents occurred during the fight for Wong Nei Chong. Lieutenant Hugh MacKecnie bumped into a Japanese patrol in pitch blackness and, jumping to one side to assume a firing position, he inadvertently leaped off a cliff. The two-hundred-foot fall broke his tail-bone.

Reverend U. Lait, a Newfoundland-raised army chaplain, refused to leave a windowless concrete shelter housing thirty-seven wounded men. The enemy encircled the building as the padre dressed wounds and rationed water and cigarettes. Lieutenant T. A. Blackwood and a Private Morris crawled out under enemy fire to bring in a wounded Volunteer lying on the roadside. When the ammunition was gone, the post surrendered; the enemy spared the lives of those who could walk.

One dark night Private George Meredith was with a platoon that slept behind an enormous boulder. In the morning a Grenadier rose to stretch his legs and, glancing behind the rock, saw twenty-five Japanese sitting there, eating breakfast. "Jesus Christ!" he yelled, alerting both encampments. "There's friggin' Japs here!" The adversaries clashed with fixed bayonets, then both sides pulled back.

Private Ted Schultz saw a corporal drop to his knees and freeze as a Japanese platoon rushed his unit. The corporal was a skilled instructor who trained recruits in how to handle machine guns. He could take a Vickers apart and reassemble it blindfolded. At his first taste of real warfare, he gaped dumbly ahead, immobilized by fear: a grenade blasted the earth beside him and he toppled over, dead.

Major Harry Hook and a ninety-eight-man unit, soaked and miserable after spending all night in drenching rain and a high, cold wind, engaged the enemy in repeated forays that reduced the detachment by one third.

Sergeant Bob Manchester was on a path when he came

across two men wrestling in the dirt for possession of a knife. One was a Grenadier, the other Japanese. He raised his Bren gun and released a round over their heads. Startled, the pair dropped the knife and rolled off the trail, down a slope. Manchester's blast alarmed an enemy patrol and, driven back by sniper fire, he did not see who won the deadly struggle.

Corporal Walter Birch and two companions spotted an enemy platoon advancing along a ravine. Out of ammunition, the trio hid under a shell-tattered tent discarded in a ditch. As the platoon passed, a Japanese machine-gunner sprayed the tent, not knowing anyone was beneath the lumpy canvas. Hit in the leg, Birch did not utter a sound. When he emerged, he discovered both of his friends were dead.

Private Art Lyons walked over a hill with six buddies and met eight Japanese standing in the open. Caught off guard, the enemy soldiers raised their hands. As the Grenadiers approached, seven of the men broke and, hurling themselves in a dry creek bed, escaped. The stranded man dropped his hands but stood perfectly still, looking bewildered. A Grenadier shot him in the arm; he still remained motionless. Another Grenadier with a Bren gun poured bullets into him. So many bullets punctured his body that he twisted around and around, trapped in a bizarre dance of death.

Private Art Lousier, a young recruit who had never seen a rifle range or handled a grenade, went to a forward observation post and asked a Lieutenant Davis how he was doing as a spotter for mortars. As Davis turned to answer he was shot in the head. Lousier ran back and told a Lieutenant Hooper what had happened. "I'll kill every one of those swines," Hooper said, jumping up. A sniper got him in the chest. The two veteran officers died, and Lousier, with only seven weeks' army experience, lived.

Despite the Grenadiers' gritty efforts to turn the tide, the situation worsened hourly. The Japanese not only declined to retreat but were gradually gaining more territory. Late Saturday afternoon, Colonel Rose sent word that the Grenadiers and the assorted units supporting them were to withdraw from the Gap area. Most would go to Mount Cameron, the next mountain to the west, while the others would buttress defensive entrenchments between the Gap and the southern beaches. A twelve-man Volunteer outfit, commanded by public school headmaster Evan Stewart, stayed behind, defending a tiny Jardin's Lookout foothold. This largely Eurasian unit held out for sixteen hours after the Canadians departed. A Royal Scots company, joining the Grenadiers at Mount Cameron, retained the north and west slopes in the face of brutal shelling and incessant infantry attacks that began the minute the Allied troops arrived.

With Lawson dead, the Grenadiers needed an expert top-level officer at the front to direct minute-by-minute operations. Colonel Rose was at Fortress Headquarters and depended upon regular telephones, field phones, and foot runners to get his orders into combat zones. The Japanese soon wrecked the communications system. Some above-ground cables were chopped, others tapped to listen in on messages. At one stage a Japanese officer used a captured field phone and, speaking English, issued orders that resulted in two Canadian platoons' firing at each other across a valley.

The runners were equally unreliable. Many were shot by Japanese patrols and their communiqués fell into enemy hands. Unable to receive up-to-date instructions, isolated Grenadier platoons remained in the vicinity of Wong Nei Chong Gap after the main body pulled out. Men wandered aimlessly in the hills, their food and ammunition gone, ducking Japanese, vainly seeking a friendly camp. Enemy sentries were jumped at night by lone Canadians who rummaged their packs for food. Hardtack, the dry, hard biscuit normally despised by enlisted men, was treasured like a luxury item, and lost platoons rationed it accordingly. Yet no one surrendered just to be fed. Countless Grenadiers endured two, three, even four days of not eating and gave up only when they were surrounded and had no ammunition.

Steve Kashton was among the stranded Grenadiers. He and another private sat in a dugout atop a desolate knoll north of the Gap for forty-eight hours, manning a machine gun. They had plenty of ammunition but no food. Every now and then the Japanese attempted to rush up the slope and the two Canadians staved them off. After going two days without eating, Kashton's buddy volunteered to walk to the Gap for rations. He never returned. Kashton waited thirty-four hours, expecting him any second, not daring to sleep in case the Japanese attacked. When he could stand it no longer, he carried his machine gun toward the Gap. En route he met isolated platoons, disorganized, leaderless, confused. "I haven't a clue what's happening," a sergeant told him. "As far as I'm concerned, it's every man for himself." Gulping bully beef and a chocolate bar the sergeant gave him, Kashton joined the platoon and, marching west, ended up stationed on Mount Davis.

The confusion was not confined to Wong Nei Chong or the island.

The Canadian Government was aware that the defenders were in dire straits but had a blurred, puzzling picture of what was actually transpiring. Defense Minister Ralston sent Lawson a message requesting more information. "The anxious hearts and hopes and confidence of the Canadian people are with you all in the magnificent fight you are putting up against heavy odds," Ralston stated.

By the time the Minister dispatched his cablegram, Lawson and one of his best aides, Colonel Pat Hennessey, were dead. Hennessey, a fifty-six-year-old Military Cross winner, and paymaster Captain Davis were killed when a shell devastated a Canadian command post in a Peak villa. The message did not reach Hong Kong until Monday, December 22. In the absence of Lieutenant Colonel W. J. Home, the most senior Canadian officer who was fighting in the south, Lieutenant Colonel J. L. R. Sutcliffe composed what turned out to be the final communiqué from the Canadians at Hong Kong. Sutcliffe explained about Lawson and Hennessey and then said:

"Situation critical. Canadian troops part prisoners. Residue engaged. Casualties heavy. Troops have done excellent work. Spirit excellent."

That last sentence conveyed an inaccurate impression. Spirits were far from excellent. Tired, hungry, and disorganized, the two battalions were in the throes of a deep despair. Still they would not give up.

CHAPTER SIXTEEN

Churchill was aboard the H.M.S. *Duke of York,* sailing across the gray Atlantic for conferences and speeches in Washington and Ottawa. Freed from the crush of day-to-day business, the Prime Minister was using the week-long voyage to reflect on the total war picture and, at a leisurely pace, to prepare papers based on his conclusions. He was dictating a policy statement to a secretary when Field Marshal Sir John Dill entered the cabin.

"More bad news, I'm afraid," Dill announced. "I doubt we'll be able to hold onto Hong Kong. The enemy's pushing across the island."

Churchill sighed. "That's all we need. Another blasted setback."

In the past week England's wobbly military posture had been dealt several jarring blows. Italian frogmen had blown up two Royal Navy battleships, the *Valiant* and the *Queen Elizabeth,* in Alexandria Harbor. The Japanese had captured Penang, a west coast Malayan city, and were pressing toward Singapore. Three British destroyers and four cruisers had been wrecked in a Mediterranean minefield. The German Air Corps was pounding Malta, and Rommel was gearing for a new desert offensive. Now this. The "Gibraltar of the Orient," as the tourist pamphlets called it, was likely to crumble much sooner than his Hong Kong advisers had anticipated.

"What about the Chinese Army?" the Prime Minister asked.

"A dark horse at best. They keep promising to relieve the garrison but, according to our latest information, they can't possibly get there until January. By the looks of it, that will be too late."

After Dill left, Churchill took the only course he felt was open to him. Instead of troops or armaments, he sent a message to Governor Young that was to become the most widely quoted of all the communiqués associated with the fall of Hong Kong. It read:

"We are greatly concerned to hear of the landings on Hong Kong island which have been effected by the Japanese. We cannot judge from here the conditions which rendered these landings possible or prevented effective counterattacks upon the intruders. There must however be no thought of surrender. Every part of the island must be fought and the enemy resisted with the utmost stubbornness.

"The enemy should be compelled to expend the utmost life and equipment. There must be vigorous fighting in the inner defenses and, if need be, from house to house. Every day that you are able to maintain your resistance you help the Allied cause all over the world, and by a prolonged resistance you and your men can win the lasting honor which we are sure will be your due."

Stirring words, but in Hong Kong's case the sword was considerably mightier than the pen. On Sunday, December 21, as the Churchill message was cabled to Hong Kong, the Japanese were swelling their ranks in the south. Two areas near Repulse Bay saw blistering action. Twenty Punjabis and five naval men formed a unit that battled the enemy on Shouson Hill, an exclusive residential enclave atop a precipitous cliff. The Japanese had chased the wealthy occupants out, and the East Indians' commander, Lieutenant Colonel Gerald Kidd, swore he would regain the houses for them. The attackers made it to the summit, but the enemy was too solidly embedded. Only three Punjabis and one Royal Navy man survived the bitter, house-to-house fighting; Kidd was among those killed.

North of the Repulse Bay Hotel, the bald hill known as The Ridge experienced a series of savage clashes. As the Japanese were inflicting heavy casualties, Maltby ordered the one hundred British soldiers and fifty Royal Rifles to withdraw. One party did not get away in time. At dusk Sunday the enemy swooped down to capture Lieutenant Colonel Macpherson and thirty members of the Royal Army Ordnance Corps. Normally stationed at supply depots, dispensing uniforms and the like, the ordnance men were mostly misfits—too short, too chubby, too old—for regular army duties. This band of misfits fought surprisingly well at The Ridge, and those caught by the Japanese were, almost to a man, wounded and unable to make a speedy exit. The Japanese tied their hands, clubbed them with rifles, and then executed the entire unit.

Another massacre, even worse in proportion, occurred the same day. Fifty-three Rifles and British prisoners were marched to a seaside cliff to the west of the Repulse Bay Hotel. Binding their hands, the Japanese shot, bayoneted, or beheaded them in groups, then rolled their bodies off the cliff. One man, a Middlesex sergeant, survived. He and three Canadians were forced to kneel on the blood-soaked ground and to look at the bodies heaped on the sea-washed rocks below. The sergeant turned his head as a firing squad unleashed its volley; a bullet pierced his neck and cheek; the impact knocked him over the edge but he fell short of the rocks, landing on a paved path where he lay motionless until the Japanese were gone.

Meanwhile, on the north shore, fifteen Middlesex pillboxes lying between downtown Victoria and Japanese-held North Point were being hammered unmercifully by the Kowloon artillery. A Middlesex sergeant reported that his position took thirty hits; whenever the shelling got particu-

larly nasty, he and his eight companions temporarily evacuated the box, which resembled a pile of rubble more than
anything else.

Skirting the heavily shelled waterfront, Japanese storm
troopers stole into the outskirts of Victoria and congregated
in the region of Happy Valley Race Track. A sizable contingent of fifth columnists melded with the infiltrators and
helped them take over commercial buildings and private
homes. A ragtag collection of fifty men—signalers, gunners,
Scots, Volunteers, and civilian police—assembled at Fortress
Headquarters and hurried to Happy Valley. Many had just
returned from hospital and were still in a weak condition.
All the same, they occupied the Lee Theatre and adjacent
houses and exchanged sniper fire, keeping the enemy at bay.

To the east of the race track, thirty-five Middlesex and
seven Volunteers defended Leighton Hill with rifles and six
Vickers machine guns. The Japanese wanted the hill badly:
it would give them a wide route from North Point to Happy
Valley. The forty-two men endured everything that the Japanese could muster—shells, aerial bombs, round-the-clock infantry thrusts—and did not abandon the hill until they were
surrounded and had to fight their way off on Christmas Eve.

Although the bogged-down Japanese attack picked up
steam again Sunday, showing advances in several sectors,
most Fortress Headquarters officers maintained that a dra-
matic turnabout was still possible. The strategists reasoned
that the over-all resistance was holding firm and, to prove
their case, they reminded skeptics that not a single Japanese
had set foot past Happy Valley.

Around midnight the strategists received a rude jolt.
Small groups of Japanese snipers were prowling streets and
gardens on the Peak. They had crept through British and
Canadian lines and penetrated the haunt of the very rich
from behind, coming over uninhabited hills on a fifteen-mile
network of foot paths Peakites had created for weekend nature walks. More soldiers would obviously follow, and For-

tress Headquarters had no reserves capable of plugging the defensive leak. Even the most optimistic senior officer had to admit, if only to himself, that unless a massive Chinese Army suddenly materialized, the colony needed a revitalized, superhuman effort to trounce the invaders.

The Peak, December 22

Sergeant Howard Donnelly walked into the kitchen of a luxurious villa Monday morning, intending to cook breakfast. When he turned on a tap, nothing came out. He tried the second tap and found it was dry too. "The dirty buggers," he muttered. "They've cut off our water."

The Japanese had captured three reservoirs and divebombed the fourth, reducing its output to a pathetic trickle. Many Hong Kongers now had to drastically ration water from small rooftop tanks or carry it from reopened wells, but most houses and office buildings had neither source. "The city of Victoria is helpless," the waterworks director informed Maltby in a memo on Monday. "Close to 1,700,000 civilians have no water whatsoever."

Donnelly, a former *Family Herald* subscription salesman, was cooking for the Grenadier supply post because the Chinese cooks and orderlies had bolted at the first sign of fighting. Between kitchen sessions, he helped load a truck and deliver rations to troops.

Donnelly, anticipating the water emergency, had arranged for a commandeered gasoline tanker to haul water from a well to the Peak depot. While Hong Kongers fixed meals without water, while toilets in the swankiest hotels plugged and stank, while some people paid enterprising Chinese as much as ten dollars for a jug of brackish water, the unit Donnelly cooked for did not have to change its dietary habits. The food had a distinct gasoline taste to it, but Donnelly gathered it was not enough to be harmful. He had

touched a match to a plateful of eggs and they did not catch
fire.

Fourteen days after the Japanese first crossed the frontier,
Victoria, the garden spot of the Pacific, was a bleak, sullen
wasteland. Refugees emerged from the rubble every morning to line up at food-distribution centers. Around them lay
the bodies of looters, shot by police and left in the streets all
day as a grim warning. Black-market salesmen demanded
high prices for flashlights, blankets, and other scarce commodities. Women guarded their homes with guns, fearful
that looters might try to steal their vegetables, meat, to-
bacco, or coffee. Grief-stricken white civilians carried deceased relatives or friends up the slopes, looking for suitable
burial grounds.

On Monday the War Office issued orders to blow up three
more oil refineries lest they fall into enemy hands, and the
thick dark smoke billowed over the north shore. In the clear
patches white puffs of anti-aircraft flak appeared whenever
Japanese planes returned for another raid. Here and there,
houses and office buildings burned out of control.

Late Monday night a huge, bluish flame snaked skyward
in central Victoria. Concerned that the Japanese might take
the city and consume vast amounts of alcohol, precipitating
a killing binge, Fortress Headquarters ordered the destruction of a liquor warehouse. Howard Donnelly was among
the Canadians who set the warehouse afire, in the process
stuffing his tunic with bottles.

As Victoria was collapsing, the defenders lost more
ground on the south coast and in the hills. Colonel Doi
unleashed an all-out artillery and infantry assault on Mount
Cameron. Around midnight his thousand-man force grabbed
the summit from one hundred Grenadiers. The Canadians
scattered in disorder but quickly reassembled in two locales
to the west, Wan Chai Gap and Mount Gough. In tena-
ciously retaining two slopes at Mount Cameron, the Royal

Scots again vindicated themselves for their reputedly poor mainland performance. Before hostilities ended, the Scots lost 390 of the 500 soldiers fighting in the center of the island.

The most serious threat to the island's defense was taking shape in the Repulse Bay area. By capturing the hotel and bringing in heavy weapons to establish an impregnable roadblock on the coastal highway, the enemy succeeded in splitting the island in half. A British gunboat, the H.M.S. *Cicala* and MTB 09 skirted the blockade and, weaving past offshore mines, took ammunition to the twenty-five hundred soldiers and Volunteers cut off from Victoria and boxed in on Stanley peninsula. The *Cicala*, a flat-bottomed river boat, had been sinking deserted freighters anchored in Victoria Harbor so the Japanese could never use them. On Monday a gunboat darted into Repulse Bay and turned her two six-inch guns on a Japanese fortification. The enemy responded by summoning six aircraft that bombed and strafed the *Cicala* into a partially sunken wreck. Lieutenant Commander John Boldero detonated depth charges to give her a proper burial.

The fighting in the Stanley region sealed Hong Kong's doom.

In its official record of the colony's defeat, the Hong Kong Volunteer Defence Corps veterans organization described the situation on Monday:

"Our troops were beginning to feel the strain. The Volunteers who had fought on the mainland had been on the move for fourteen days with practically no rest. The past three days had been days of continuous fighting without pause for sleep or opportunity to eat. The Japanese with their vast superiority in numbers could afford to rest their men; we could not. They had the initiative; we were compelled to try and anticipate their attacks.

"There was a growing feeling among the rank and file that further resistance merely postponed the inevitable, and was not worth the waste of life, though among the higher ranks it was well understood that every day, every hour, was of vital importance to the Empire war effort and that we should fight it out until the bitter end."

The majority of the Rifles trapped at Stanley subscribed to the same views as the Volunteer rank and file. Three hundred and fifty men were dead, wounded, or missing. Like the Grenadiers around Wong Nei Chong Gap, isolated Rifles were stranded in the southern hills, very low on food and ammunition and without a communications link with Brigade Headquarters, which was located in the staff dining room at Stanley Prison. They and the main body of the Quebec battalion fought tooth and nail, despite a widespread desire for the battle to end, and despite a widespread ignorance of the weapons they handled. A small unit under Major Jack Price was defending a mountain road when a column of armored cars appeared. "Take an antitank rifle and try to knock them out," Price told Rifleman Leslie Shore. The young soldier apologetically admitted he had never fired one. Price, who had shot a round once at Camp Borden, showed him how. When he was finished, Lieutenant Don Ross asked for a mortar demonstration. He wanted to shell a Japanese machine-gun nest but had never seen a mortar fired. Both novices did well, and Ross was even mentioned in the Rifles' war diary for performing "extremely good work in preventing an advance."

The Rifles lost positions at Sugar Loaf Hill, Stanley Mound, Stone Hill, and Palm Villa. They counterattacked, regained the ground, then were pushed back again. Rifleman Sidney Skelton, married ten months and with his wife in Ontario expecting a baby, summed up the Rifles' nightmarish existence in this diary notation:

"Death and blood all around me. They just got Jack next to me. We were talking when suddenly a shell made a mess of him. Today's Mother's birthday. I wonder if she's thinking of me. Noise all around. They are coming closer. Oh, God, it doesn't seem that I can stand it any longer."

Shortly afterward Skelton and two friends walked into a hidden machine-gun nest. His friends were killed. Skelton, hit in an arm and a leg, rolled down an embankment and crawled to the Rifles' line. He was taken to St. Stephen's twenty-four hours before the Japanese raided the hospital.

The Japanese were swarming south by the hundreds. Tough, shaggy ponies carted bulky weapons over hills, and, bypassing the pockets on the north-shore road that were still occupied by defenders, infantrymen moved up and down cliffs with ropes and mountaineering boots. Brigadier Wallis ascertained on Tuesday that the seesaw struggle for the inland hills—Stanley Mound had changed hands three times—was costing too many lives. He ordered Rifles, Volunteers, and other units to retreat farther south, joining the troops bottled up on a flatter, narrower front, Stanley peninsula. The Japanese spent most of the daylight hours staking claims to abandoned positions and reconnoitering. By nightfall the enemy had expanded their territory to the extent that they now possessed almost two thirds of the island.

North Point, December 23

The behavior of the Chinese peasants baffled Bill Laidlaw. Stationed in a six-story waterfront apartment building near North Point, the former Eaton's debt collector witnessed large families locking themselves in their rooms when the Japanese attacked. They did not have much to lose—a couple of sticks of furniture, a kerosene camp stove, and a bunch of chipped crockery—yet the people would not come out, even when shelling set the premises on fire. Whole families died behind locked doors rather than leave their homes.

Laidlaw had no illusions about what he would do if his building caught fire. He'd go down the stairs three at a time or head first out the window, regardless of the consequences. The Grenadier sergeant and five comrades were in their third day of manning a machine gun in a third-floor flat overlooking a deserted canal. Grenadiers, Middlesex, and Volunteers occupied apartment blocks on the residential street and, between shellings, the enemy went from building to building, taking them one at a time. The canal had no strategic value: the six Grenadiers were there to delay the Japanese advance.

Laidlaw doubted that he and his men would survive another day. Their ammunition was almost exhausted and soldiers in other buildings were so low on shells that they were lobbing smoke bombs from mortars.

"Let's look at the bright side," Private Ross McGavin said humorously. "If we live and we're taken prisoner, we'll have something different to eat."

Laidlaw grinned. "Sure, instead of hardtack, it'll be hardtack with boiled rice."

"On the contrary," McGavin retorted, "I have it on good authority that the Peninsula Hotel caters all Japanese POW camps. Seven-course meals. And that's only for breakfast."

Most of the men in that room never discovered what the POW camp menu actually was. A mortar shell came through the open balcony doorway and, passing between Laidlaw's legs, exploded on the floor behind him. Laidlaw did not see any of his companions again, although he was later told that McGavin and one other man survived the blast. The concussion knocked him out. When he regained his senses, he was lying on the floor of a hotel ballroom, surrounded by hundreds of civilian prisoners.

Fort Stanley, December 23–24

To a man, the Rifles were thoroughly exhausted. Soldiers stumbled out of marching formations and collapsed on roadsides; officers dozed in trenches; men attacked enemy positions recklessly; some officers had trouble uttering coherent sentences. Sickened at the likelihood of having his battalion annihilated, Lieutenant Colonel Home telephoned Fortress Headquarters at ten o'clock on Christmas Eve and requested a forty-eight hour respite. Getting Maltby on the line, Home said he would not be responsible for what might occur unless the Rifles were relieved. Maltby consented. The main Rifle contingent filed into Fort Stanley and the soldiers immediately bedded down in the barracks and garage; the officers occupied the vacant married officers quarters. Scot, Volunteer, and Middlesex units replaced them at the front.

For three Rifle platoons the respite was all too short. At 2:30 A.M. Wallis called Home at Stanley Prison and ordered him to occupy the high ground overlooking Stanley village. Home protested, but complied when the brigadier explained that there was a grave danger of a Japanese breakthrough. Soldiers who had logged the most sleep—three or four hours —were shaken awake and sent to the threatened hill. They arrived less than one hour after the enemy barreled down the north-south road going right past the feeble Canadian and British defenses in armored vehicles and light tanks.

A thickly populated isthmus, seven hundred feet wide at the narrowest point, joined Stanley peninsula to the island. The fishing village and prison were on the isthmus; Fort Stanley was a mile south. Three tanks spearheaded the enemy's bid to cross the isthmus. A Volunteer unit lay in their path. Placing an antitank gun on the road, the unit scored hits on the first two tanks, which burst into flames, and damaged the third, which retreated at full speed.

The enemy then attacked the isthmus with a reserve infantry detachment, and the brunt of the assault fell on Stanley village. All night long the two sides struggled for control of a police station, a post office, a soccer field, a tennis court. Two Scottish platoons were wiped out, fourteen members of a twenty-eight-man Volunteer unit were killed or wounded, and the Rifles lost one half of their peninsula detachment. By sunrise the village was in Japanese hands and the enemy was pressing a bungalow-studded ridge on Prison Road to the south. Sixty-eight Volunteers and twenty-nine Middlesex held the ridge. Striking in massive waves, Colonel Tanaka's 229th Regiment sustained hundreds of casualties before using flame-throwers to force the defenders into the open. Seven Middlesex and thirty-eight Volunteers survived a ghastly hand-to-hand confrontation, and, every one of them wounded, they joined the remnants of other units flocking to Fort Stanley for a last stand.

CHAPTER SEVENTEEN

Dawn, Christmas Day

Rising red and warm in an empty sky, the sun was bringing scorching-hot weather to the thirsty, festering island. Inside St. Stephen's College, the thirty-year-old boys' school nestled on a rocky hill near Stanley village, most of the ninety-five Canadian and British patients were awake. The ominous sounds of the approaching battle had meant a night of fitful rest for soldiers lying in the hallway and adjoining classrooms.

Nurses moved among the patients, passing out food and reminding all that Dr. George Black had a case of whiskey in the headmaster's office that he planned to break open for a noon-hour Christmas party. Black, a white-haired, soft-spoken general practitioner who had worked in Hong Kong for fifty years, was in charge of a medical staff that included a British nurse from Bowen Road, six English nursing aides, four Chinese nurses and four British orderlies. His second-in-command was a Royal Army Medical Corps officer, Captain John Whitney.

Around 6:30 A.M. Black was in the packed hallway, telling a wounded Canadian officer that he could see no point in evacuating the hospital. "Where else can we go?" the doctor said. "Frankly, I'd sooner be here than with the soldiers at Fort Stanley. The people at the Repulse Bay Hotel weren't harmed because they had no able-bodied soldiers on the premises. I'm sure that's what will happen to us."

As he finished talking, Black glanced out a window. More than two hundred Japanese soldiers, spread in a wide arc, were heading toward the building. Many had broken into a Stanley bar and were treacherously drunk. Black swiftly stepped into a classroom and, tearing a white sheet from a bed, proceeded to the front entrance.

"Don't be alarmed," he said to the soldiers on the floor. "The Japanese are here. There's a Red Cross flag on the roof, and I'll tell them to leave us alone."

Captain Whitney ran down the hall and got to the door as Black pulled it open. Placing an arm across the doorway, the elderly doctor declared to the first group of Japanese soldiers, "This is a hospital. You mustn't come in. Leave us in peace."

A soldier raised his rifle and shot Black in the forehead. Whitney recoiled in horror, then fell as a second bullet struck him. The advance party lunged forward, trampling the sheet and bayoneting both bodies repeatedly. Then they darted into the emergency hospital, followed by a swarming mass of charging comrades. Fifty-six defenseless soldiers lying in the hallway were bayoneted to death.

Rifleman Sidney Skelton was reclining on a cot, naked beneath a thin blanket, when he heard screams from the hallway. He and twenty-odd soldiers were in a classroom; the desks were piled against the blackboard. A nurse had administered a pre-operative anesthetic and he was losing consciousness. Suddenly a dozen Japanese soldiers burst into the room, shouting, "Banzai!" Skelton's groggy mind registered images of Orientals in khaki jackets, breeches, and puttees thrusting bayonets into wounded men. With a tremendous surge he flung himself on the floor and rolled under a cot. A moment later a Japanese grabbed his arm and dragged him out. Skelton feigned death. The soldier kicked his face and ripped off his bandages. Although in excruciating pain, he did not blink an eye. Assuming Skelton was dead, his tormentor rejoined his comrades and they dashed from the room, seeking more victims.

Fighting the anesthetic, Skelton bandaged his arm and leg and lay among corpses until half an hour later when he heard a British voice loudly proclaim, "They say anyone who can get to the front door will be spared." Skelton crawled to the door, pulling his blanket. When he arrived, he saw a Japanese soldier select a Volunteer from a row of prisoners and, pointing to the knife in the man's belt, bayonet him for having it. A Japanese officer took Skelton's wristwatch, slapped him across the face with the flat of his sword, and then ordered him to go upstairs.

Forty male captives were locked inside a windowless ten-by-twenty-foot storeroom on the second floor. All morning they lived in terror. The Japanese opened the door every half hour and picked two or three men at random. They were taken to another room and, forcibly held down beside corpses, mutilated before they were killed. Listening to their chilling screams, Skelton and the other prisoners in the dark, hot storeroom dreaded the instant when the door swung open and the Japanese selection committee resumed its ghastly task. Four Rifles taken prisoner at Stanley village were chosen for what they believed was a torturous death, only to be released. The Japanese made the four stand by while soldiers cut out one man's tongue and chopped off another man's ears. "Go to Fort Stanley and tell your officers what you have seen," the Japanese commander told the four. "Hong Kong must surrender or else all prisoners will be killed in this manner."

Early that afternoon Japanese soldiers went to the small room where the women were confined. The three youngest Britons and four Chinese nurses were dragged, crying and writhing, into the torture room. With soldiers holding their arms and legs, they were placed on top of corpses, gang-raped, and bayoneted to death. The other female captives were not slain but many wished they had been. Individually, or in pairs, the Japanese forced them into the torture room every few hours: they were gang-raped, locked up, then gang-raped again. When a British lieutenant in the storeroom asked a Japanese captain if he could see his wife, the enemy officer agreed. He was led outside to a stack of bodies lying in the bushes. His wife, a pretty English nurse, was among those raped and killed. The lieutenant had to be physically restrained from attacking his captors and, back in the storeroom, he babbled incoherently. His subsequent erratic behavior in a POW camp convinced his friends that he would never fully recover from the shock of the St. Stephen's experience.

Eight miles north of the boys' school, three Grenadiers were having a Christmas party. Cut off from their unit, Private Earl Mawson, David Tuck, and Archie Clements sought cover from the shelling in a deserted villa owned by the Dutch consul. To their delight the house possessed a well-stocked kitchen and wine cellar. The trio feasted on smoked oysters, crabmeat, and other canned delicacies. Mawson decided to make the celebration complete by taking his first bath in three weeks. No water flowed from the taps but that did not deter him. He filled the tub with gin and climbed right in.

The three Grenadiers fared better than Maltby. For his Yuletide treat, he shared a tin of asparagus and a half-empty bottle of wine with an aide. The depressing situation they were enmeshed in did not stop other soldiers and civilians from trying to celebrate Christmas either. Dr. Gordon Grey distributed pieces of the fruitcake his mother had given him before he left Toronto to staff and patients at Bowen Road. Grenadier Bob Lyttle's platoon caught a pig in the hills and, although an attempt to cook it failed miserably, they ate the partially raw animal. A Volunteer played Yuletide favorites on a Parisian Grill piano surrounded by singing soldiers. Drs.

John Crawford and Jack Reid were eating dinner when a shell crashed into the room; no one was hurt, but Crawford got a piece of metal in his posterior. Temporarily held at an old paint factory, Gwen Dew and the Repulse Bay Hotel captives were handed three cans of beer and a box of soda crackers by a Japanese officer who smiled and said, "Merry Christmas." Captured Grenadier Bill Laidlaw was taken to a former British military compound on Christmas Day and told to wait until he could be transferred to Kowloon. He snooped around the empty canteen and found two bottles of beer: he drank one and used the other for shaving. Less fortunate was the Middlesex platoon whose cookhouse filled with roasting chickens was demolished by an enemy shell minutes before the birds were ready for the table.

To help mark the holiday, the *South China Morning Post* issued a one-page special, headlined Day of Good Cheer. Considering the glowering specter looming over the colony —and the dearth of food and water—the article was remarkably up-beat in tone:

"Hong Kong is observing the strangest and most sombre Christmas in its century-old history. Such modest celebrations as are arranged today will be subdued, with an eye to Japanese opportunism, but they will be nonetheless high-hearted on that account.

"For the first time in years the streets lack stocks of ready-to-erect Christmas trees; when people thrust at shop doors or stood in lines yesterday they were not seeking gift trinkets but bread or rice. However, if yesterday's shopping was confined to necessities, friends remembered to toast one another, in moderation, and at city hotels, which were crowded. Beards were budding and salvaged suits were looking a bit scrubby, but all were cheerful in the knowledge that, for all their present hardships, they would not go either hungry or thirsty this Christmas."

The paper also ran a Christmas message from Governor Young:

"In pride and admiration I send my greetings this Christmas Day to all those who are working so nobly and so well to sustain Hong Kong against the assault of the enemy. Fight on. Hold fast for King and Empire. God bless you all in this your finest hour."

Most of the islanders had sworn to fight on, but Maltby was wavering. Two civilians captured at the Repulse Bay Hotel, Andrew Shields and Charles Manners, arrived at Fortress Headquarters around 9 A.M. on Christmas Day. The Japanese sent them on a peace mission. There would be a three-hour cease-fire while the English pondered whether or not to surrender. The two men described the vast number of troops and guns they had seen during a forced march up the middle of the island to North Point. It was, they said, useless to continue fighting.

Maltby called a staff meeting and heard the latest distressing news: Japanese advance parties now occupied many Peak mansions. The Aberdeen naval yard defenders had only sixty rounds of ammunition left. The enemy had butchered a group of St. John's Ambulance stretcher-bearers when they surrendered at Happy Valley medical post. Only six mobile guns still functioned and each possessed roughly one hundred and sixty rounds. Enemy storm troopers had circumvented Grenadier and Scottish positions and taken over air raid tunnels in the Wan Chai district. And southern phone lines had been severed, terminating all communication with soldiers trapped on Stanley peninsula.

Nevertheless, Maltby's advisers urged him not to quit. They wanted to fight until the last building fell—as Churchill had called upon them to do. Shields and Manners returned to North Point to report that the surrender proposal was rejected. For hours after the pair departed, Maltby wondered if he had made the right decision. At 2 P.M. he telephoned the Middlesex commander, Lieutenant Colonel Stewart, and inquired how much longer his men could retain the north-shore pillboxes. "They're in a bad way," Stewart told him. "I'd say an hour at the most." His answer was the final determining factor for the commander-in-chief. At 3 P.M. Maltby traveled to Government House and advised Young that his troops would be surrendering. "It's a hopeless situation, Mark. Once the pillboxes are gone, the enemy will flood into Victoria. We haven't the strength to stop them."

Young vehemently opposed the surrender—as did countless senior officers who to this day speak of Maltby's decision contemptuously—but he went along with it. At 3:15 P.M. Maltby ordered his men to lay down their arms and to give themselves up at the closest Japanese position. In his official dispatch Maltby explained that he capitulated because "further fighting meant the useless slaughter of the remainder of the garrison, risked severe retaliation on the large civilian population and could not affect the final outcome."

Unaware that the colony had surrendered, wandering platoons in the hills and Rifles at Fort Stanley continued to attack the Japanese, in many instances until late on Boxing Day. The impending enemy occupation caused a frenzy in Victoria. Mothers created hiding places for young daughters in cellars and upstairs closets; the prices of black-market Japanese flags sky-rocketed; embassies and colonial government staffs darted from room to room, burning documents in wastepaper baskets; Chinese lawyers, doctors, and other professionals put on coolie outfits and disappeared into slum areas. The guests at the Hong Kong and other luxury hotels worried about the Japanese getting hold of liquor. Hundreds of bottles were smashed in the streets, and champagne and Johnnie Walker used to flush toilets. So many bottles were emptied on bar floors that alcoholic rivers ran through some lobbies.

The atrocity stories had not prepared Kay Christie for what occurred when the Japanese came to Bowen Road Hospital. She had yet to hear of the St. Stephen's bloodbath, but she had heard of other massacres. Especially Nanking, where Japanese soldiers had raped twenty thousand women and murdered two hundred thousand men. She knew, too, that many generals encouraged mass rape as a method to humiliate and thus subdue conquered people. The Canadian nurse did not mention the depth of her fear to Dr. Gordon Grey, but he somehow understood. When she snatched a few minutes' sleep on a floor mattress, he tried to stay in the room so she would not be alone if the enemy appeared.

In her imagination Kay envisioned a pack of Japanese soldiers, stampeding into the hospital in the black of night, bent upon an orgy of death and destruction. When the enemy did arrive, it was on a hot, dry afternoon. A handful of Japanese officers simply drove up to the main entrance, talked briefly with hospital officials, and declared Bowen Road a POW camp. Enemy soldiers erected a barbed-wire fence around the brick building, and Kay, the Holy Terror, and other nurses were confined to the premises.

The St. Stephen's College bestiality ended around four o'clock Christmas Day. Learning that the colony had capitulated, the Japanese opened the storeroom door and said the survivors could come out. There were two stipulations: they had to remain on the college grounds and they had to cremate corpses. The prisoners carried bodies from the torture room on stretchers, heaping them in the yard. Quebec-born priest James Barrett tried to organize a burial party for the seventy victims but was refused. The Japanese demanded they be cremated. The seven dead women were added to the pile and a hundred bodies gathered from fields around the college. Blood-stained blankets and mattresses were used to start the huge funeral pyre. Barrett asked about the surviving women but was not allowed to see them until the next morning. They walked and talked like zombies, the padre testified at a war-crimes trial, for "they had experienced dreadful things during the night."

Late on Christmas Day Governor Young crossed the wreckage-strewn harbor on an MTB flying a white flag to sign unconditional surrender papers at General Sakai's headquarters, the Peninsula Hotel. He was taken prisoner as he left the formal ceremony in the ballroom and was confined to a hotel room, pending his transfer to a North Korean POW camp.

The full impact of the Japanese victory did not hit the colony until December 27. That afternoon Sakai instructed his battalions to join the few thousand soldiers who had Hong Kong to themselves for two days.

Astride his stallion, Sakai led a triumphant march through downtown Victoria. Sixty-two planes flew overhead, dropping leaflets proclaiming the infallibility of the new Asian empire. Thousands of Chinese lined the streets, waving banners and flags and summoning false smiles. An open limousine in the procession, occupied by a Japanese general, provided the one source of amusement for people in the crowd who understood English. Confiscated from a Dutchman, the car bore a windshield sticker stating HOLLAND SHALL RISE AGAIN.

The conquerors began a fifteen-day rampage after the parade. Soldiers looted stores and robbed civilians; watches and fountain pens were the favorite items and many Japanese were observed sporting an array of watches from their wrists to their elbows. There was no mass slaughter similar to that which transpired in Nanking in 1937, but countless white citizens were slain trying to hold onto material goods in their homes.

Hundreds of women were raped. A British businessman was having dinner with his wife and teen-age daughter when soldiers entered through the french windows. The man was tied to a chair and the women abused in his presence. For the most part, however, the soldiers seemed to prefer Chinese to white women.

As for the Allied soldiers, the majority had not been mistreated when they surrendered. Dispatch rider Lionel Speller buried his tarpaulin-wrapped revolver beneath an elm tree outside Fortress Headquarters and, accompanied by Captain Jim Billings, walked to a Japanese post bearing a white sheet. Howard Donnelly's unit smashed their rifles and placed the pieces in a neat pile. James Bertram and a Volunteer detachment marched in formation to a Japanese camp, all whistling "Tipperary." And Tony Grimston and two buddies were walking unarmed on a mountain path when three Japanese popped up and, after a thorough search, led them away.

After their commanding officers officially declared all Chinese females to be prostitutes, soldiers strode into private homes demanding *fa ku niang* (flower girls), the Cantonese euphemism for whores. Some houses were entered and the same women assaulted so often that their husbands or parents agreed to let them become personal flower girls for Japanese officers. That way, the girls got less abuse and their families were assured a steady food supply.

Volunteer John Fonseca's apprehension concerning the fate of his mother and fiancée turned out to be groundless. Because his future father-in-law was the Rice King—and therefore of potential importance to the occupying government—a large seal was placed over the door of his villa stating it was off limits to military personnel. Ignoring the sign, two soldiers marched in and began looting the house. A passing Japanese officer had the pair escorted to the street and shot.

The mass pillaging and raping was brought to an end by a military decree. British civilians were to be arrested and interned; three months' imprisonment faced any soldier found guilty of rape thereafter; looting would be restricted to car parts, industrial machinery, and other essential commodities that would be shipped to Japan. A welcome calm settled over the colony. Banks reopened, debris was cleared, ferries salvaged, tramcars ran, professional prostitutes staffed army brothels. For the civilian and military POWs, however, the ordeal was far from over. It was, in fact, only shifting to new arenas: the filthy, disease-ridden hellholes the Japanese deemed fitting environs for prisoners of war.

CHAPTER EIGHTEEN

Kowloon, January 7, 1942

Exactly two weeks after Hong Kong collapsed, General Sakai asked 180 leading Chinese citizens to a luncheon at the Peninsula Hotel. Upon receiving the printed invitations, 47 went underground, melting into the vast coolie population. Donning their best suits, 133 showed up to find the hotel ballroom ablaze with Japanese flags and banners. Clean linen, glimmering silverware, and wineglasses covered the banquet tables and, when the guests sat down, immaculately dressed waiters served ample helpings of seafood, fresh from Aberdeen. The guests enjoyed the meal but cast nervous glances at the head table where Sakai and a line of ranking subordinates were seated. There was speculation that it was all an elaborate, cruel joke, preceding their arrest and internment. There was also talk of soldiers suddenly entering the ballroom and shooting them all.

Sakai had no such plans. He had staged the luncheon to enlist their aid in the reconstruction of Hong Kong. Rising, the short, round-faced general read a prepared text, which a civilian interpreter translated into Cantonese. He was leaving the colony soon, Sakai said, and a Lieutenant General Isogai would become Governor-General of the conquered territory.

"Order must be restored. Peace must be maintained. We

know you will help us because we, the Chinese and the Japanese, are the same race. We have liberated you from one hundred years of evil white rule. The English cared nothing for you. While Chinese Volunteers and men from India died on the front lines, the British hid in the hills. An age of co-prosperity has dawned in Hong Kong. Together, we will share it."

Sakai said a four-man Representative Council would be appointed (the suspected fifth columnist leader Chim Lim-pak was among the appointees) and schools, courts, and civil service offices would reopen. "We could have levelled Hong Kong with 500-pound bombs," he concluded. "But we did not. We saved you from total destruction because we did not want the Chinese to suffer for the Englishman's sins."

Lukewarm applause followed the speech. Worried that the general might interpret the unenthusiastic response to mean that the Chinese opposed the occupation blueprint, several businessmen rose and pledged their wholehearted support. One merchant actually thanked the Imperial Japanese Army for coming to Hong Kong. His eloquent outburst astounded those in the gathering who knew that his factory had been destroyed, his villa taken over by troops, and his daughter was a Japanese major's "flower girl."

A desire to please the conquerors—and to placate the Japanese's dreaded wrath—permeated the Chinese community. People who had cheered the Canadians when they disembarked in November now treated them despicably. During the three-month period after the colony fell, Rifles and Grenadiers were transferred from a North Point camp next to a stinking garbage dump to Sham Shui Po barracks on the mainland. Crowds gathered on Kowloon streets, jeering, spitting and throwing rocks at the "foreign devils" who had risked their lives defending them.

Their behavior surprised the Canadians, but not as much

as the situation at Sham Shui Po. The Japanese forced them to sleep on flea-infested rattan mats in stucco and tarpaper huts that had been stripped of windows and doors by looters. Buckets were used for toilets, the food was strictly rationed, and the medical facilities were appalling. Moreover, the officers on Commandant Tokunaga's staff included Japanese nationals who had infiltrated Sham Shui Po working as newsboys, barbers, and cooks when it was under British control. The biggest surprise of all, however, was the conduct of a Canadian-born interpreter, Sergeant Inouye Kanao. Raised in Kamloops, British Columbia, Inouye had gone to Tokyo in 1938 and, enlisting in the Army, became Commandant Tokunaga's official translator. His father had served with the Canadian Army in World War I—and was awarded the Military Medal for bravery.

Sergeant Bob Manchester discovered precisely what being a Canadian meant to Inouye when he arrived at Sham Shui Po early in 1942. Smiling broadly, the thin, twenty-seven-year-old interpreter walked up to a line of Grenadiers at the front gate and asked, "Anybody here from Kamloops?" Thinking he had met a kindred soul, a young soldier replied briskly, "Yes, I am." Inouye punched him in the face and, as the youth collapsed, the interpreter lashed out with his other hand, striking Manchester on the cheek with a clipboard. It hurt like hell, but Manchester knew better than to protest.

All Sham Shui Po captives learned never to trust Inouye, even if he was grinning, talking gently, or making outrageous promises. ("You behave yourself here," he told Major Ernie Hodkinson seriously, "and when the war's over, I'll get you a good job on the CPR.") His favorite form of punishment was to have two soldiers hold a prisoner while he punched and kicked him. Others were physically tortured in solitary-confinement rooms or starved until they begged and cried.

Inouye attributed his vendetta against the Canadian soldiers to racial prejudice in Kamloops. He recalled not being invited to a birthday party when he was ten years old because his friend's mother did not want "a Jap face" in her snapshots. And, on a trip to Vancouver, he was denied entry to a public swimming pool by a cashier pointing to a wall sign, NO COLOREDS, JAPS OR CHINESE. "You called me a yellow bastard in Canada and now you people are going to suffer," he told Private Tony Grimston.

The Kamloops Kid, as he was secretly labeled, hinted that he belonged to the Kempei Tai, the Japanese equivalent of the Gestapo. Whether he actually did or not, he was the most sadistic and treacherous of all the Japanese officers at Sham Shui Po camp.

In all of her world-wide travels, Gwen Dew had never met anyone like Emily Hahn. She was a law unto herself, a charming daredevil who always laughed when told what society matrons thought of her brash language and the Charles Boxer affair. And now Emily had taken another step that had the old girls bristling—while they were locked away in a Stanley camp, Emily was free as a breeze.

She accomplished this incredible feat by boldly striding into a Japanese police station and persuading suspicious officials that she was married to a Chinese merchant living in Shanghai. As the Japanese had said that Asiatics or their spouses did not have to be interned, Emily was granted a special permit allowing her to live in a vacant villa, visit Charles at the hospital, and shop for friends in the Stanley camp.

One chilly February morning Emily called on Gwen at the Kowloon Hotel. The latter was fighting her transfer to Stanley on the grounds that she was a journalist, but the Japanese had just informed her Tokyo was ignoring her pleas and she would be sent to the camp any day. During their conversation Gwen mentioned that she needed a wrap for her strolls around the city and, true to form, Emily returned that afternoon with a new khaki overcoat. *A Japanese officer's overcoat.* "Somebody left it at the house I moved into," Emily explained. "Don't be shy about wearing it. I'm sure nobody will mind."

Gwen was more than shy. She was terribly nervous. What if the Japanese considered it an insult for a civilian to wear officer's clothing? Or if anyone caught in officer's clothing was liable to severe punishment? After Emily was gone, Gwen tried the coat on. Exquisitely tailored, it seemed specially made for her slim body. It would, she concluded, be rather foolish to go around shivering while a lovely coat hung in her closet.

The next morning Gwen wore the coat on the street. Merchants, coolies, children, all stared. With curiosity, puzzlement, and, yes, respect. They obviously assumed that whoever was in the coat, male or female, was someone to be handled with kid gloves. Gwen's baptism under fire came when two Japanese soldiers approached on a bustling street. The pair stepped aside, awkwardly, as though they were trying to decide whether they should salute, bow, or shout banzais.

Gwen spent her last yen notes, worth roughly twenty American dollars, to buy things she could use in the camp. An electric iron, laundry soap, silk stockings, a needle and thread. She had no trouble getting what she wanted. The streets were lined with long tables containing every item imaginable, selling at rock-bottom prices. The booty from looted mansions. Swedish blown glass, rare scrolls, Dunhill pipes, finely crafted silverware, electrical appliances. Rummaging through the bargain piles Gwen added a tin of California plums and a John Bunyan book (PROPERTY OF YALE UNIVERSITY was stamped inside) to her supplies.

Before going to the hotel, she dropped in at Domei, the Japanese news bureau, to see a journalist she had known in prewar days, a Mr. Ogura. His eyes glittered at the sight of the overcoat.

"How lovely," he said. "New, isn't it?"

"Oh, this old rag," Gwen said casually. "It's an English riding coat. Very popular with the horsey set."

"I don't think so," Ogura replied laughing. "It's a Japanese officer's coat and I happen to know who it belongs to."

Smiling to herself, Gwen left the office. Tell the original owner I'll make him a deal, she thought. He can have his coat back if he gives us back our island!

When Sakai announced that British residents would be interned, Chief Justice Sir Athol MacGregor suggested that certain Peak streets be designated as POW camp sites. The general deplored the idea. The English should be stripped of their elegant homes, he said, and, besides, his troops would feel uncomfortable having whites gaze down upon them, physically and psychologically, from a lofty enclave. Sakai chose what he felt was a more suitable venue—seven drab apartment blocks that originally housed East Indian laborers. The buildings were huddled together on Stanley peninsula and were too low to catch cooling sea breezes. Whereas 290 East Indians once inhabited the sparsely furnished rooms, thousands of whites were jammed inside: up to 90 people took turns using a single toilet. "I think that they (the Japanese) took particular glee in putting those who lived in the best surroundings in the worst now," Gwen Dew wrote in *Prisoner of the Japs*.

Indeed they did. Visiting Japanese reporters or government officials toured Camp Stanley to enjoy the amusing spectacle of Sir So-and-So peeling potatoes, Lady So-and-So wearing rags, or a one-time millionaire diligently scrubbing a latrine.

Apart from the miserly meals, the stifling heat, and the communicable disease toll, the worst aspect of life at the camp was the crushing boredom. Cleaning rooms, preparing food, and playing bridge were the main daily activities. And, of course, gossip. When not talking about each other, the captives discussed stories published in an English-language propaganda sheet, the *Hong Kong News*. Sir Robert Kotewell's conduct appalled everyone. A civil politician knighted by the King for his pro-Empire speeches and articles before Pearl Harbor, Kotewell was the most prominent Hong Konger to fully cooperate with the conquerors. The *News* reported his addresses at Japanese rallies and stated that when Governor-General Isogai assumed office, Kotewell rose in the audience to shout three banzais. Other leading white and Chinese citizens switched their allegiance to the Japanese—including ex-jockey Victor Needa, who made the heroic ammunition run at the Repulse Bay Hotel—but none embraced their role with the passion Kotewell exhibited.

The conditions at Camp Stanley prompted a prisoners' committee to send Commandant Tokunaga a protest letter. "The sanitation, the food, the cramped quarters are quite unbearable. We urge you, sir, on humanitarian grounds to undertake immediate improvements. Otherwise, deteriorating conditions will undoubtedly lead to much suffering and death." Tokunaga did not bother answering. Perhaps because he knew that, compared to Sham Shui Po and other concentration camps, Stanley was a Florida resort.

The Sham Shui Po prisoners never gave up hope. Even when they were used as beasts of burden to dig and carry baskets of earth fill for a new airport at Kai Tak. Even when their bodies shrank from malnutrition and illness to such skeletons that Canadian Private Nelson Galbraith wrote in his diary, "This would be a good place for some fat dame who wants to get thin. They're sure doing a fine job on me." Even after savage floggings killed three Riflemen, the captives reassured one another that the Japanese would ultimately be defeated.

The ball game helped. On July 1, 1942, the Canadians challenged the guards to nine innings on the parade ground

—and trounced them soundly. The Japanese refused to play baseball again.

By the fall of 1942, almost every prisoner suffered from dysentery, vitamin-deficiency diseases, or diphtheria. In one five-week period alone 130 men, 41 of whom were Canadians, died from diphtheria, and the Japanese, realizing it could spread to their own ranks, finally provided a supply of serum. Beri-beri, malaria, tapeworms, and other intestinal parasites were commonplace. Lacking sufficient medicine and equipment, chief medical officer Dr. John Crawford did the best he could.

Attempting to reduce the death toll, the prisoners' commanding officer, Maltby, repeatedly urged Tokunaga to increase the food rations. How, he argued, could sickly, starved men be expected to work for ten months building an airport? To Maltby's disbelief, the Japanese did not only refuse to increase the rations, they cut them in half. A communiqué from Prime Minister Tojo ordered all commandants to provide no more than a handful of rice or barley daily for prisoners.

Tojo also sanctioned corporal punishment for the slightest disciplinary offenses, and he cautioned, "It is necessary to take care not to be obsessed with the mistaken idea of humanitarianism or be swayed by personal feelings towards those prisoners of war, which may grow in the long time of their imprisonment." For the more bloodthirsty commandants, the Tojo communiqué was, in effect, a license to kill. Throughout occupied territories prisoners were drowned, beheaded, mutilated, set on fire, and, in the case of a New Guinea camp, picked at random and bayoneted for an afternoon's "entertainment." In Hong Kong, captives were tied to yard posts and starved to death for trying to escape or beaten for very little reason. Captain Jack Norris was punched, breaking his glasses, because he was a few seconds late for a roll call.

Possessing a secret radio and listening to Allied newscasts

was an act that, next to plotting escape, infuriated Tokunaga and his henchmen more than anything.

Dennis Murphy's first thought when two guards entered
the barracks late one night and ordered him outside was
that Cecil Boone must have reported on him. Around noon,
the Grenadier private had seen the British major leaving
Tokunaga's office and, passing him, remarked acidly, "Trai-
tors never prosper—or do they, Boone?" It was a stupid thing
to do. Boone, a surly individual who emulated the Japanese
officers—shaving his head, wearing his shirt outside his
pants, bowing—had the pull with the commandant to have
Murphy flogged. But the sight of the strutting artillery
officer returning from yet another hearty meal—and, no
doubt, assuring his place at future sittings by informing
once more on his fellow prisoners—was too much for
Murphy to bear.

Inouye was waiting in the yard as the soldiers brought
Murphy from the barracks. The interpreter sat in the front
seat of a Japanese staff car, a burly driver beside him.

"Boone's turned me in, has he?" Murphy said quietly,
hoping not to arouse Inouye's hair-trigger temper.

"This has nothing to do with Boone," he said annoyed.
"Get in."

A transfer, then. To North Point or Argyle Street. Tokunaga sometimes sent prisoners to either camp for no apparent reason. Well, that was all right with Murphy. There were
Canadians in both camps and he would soon make friends.

Again, Murphy was wrong. Seated in the back, a soldier
on each side, the Canadian was surprised to see the car
wind through Kowloon's bustling streets and halt in front of
a military police station. Inouye was silent all the way. Now
he turned to Murphy and, taking a book from his pocket,
said coldly: "I want you to think about this while you are
inside. This is the Kempei Tai training manual. On page
seven, it says, 'Torture can include kicking, beating and any-

thing else connected with physical suffering.' The Kempei Tai are superb torturers, my friend. They have taken the phrase 'anything else' and made it an art form. Tell them what they want to know. That is my advice to you."

"Tell them what? I don't know anything."

Inouye said a few words in Japanese and the soldiers prodded Murphy out of the car. Inouye was peering through the window, grinning at some unspoken joke, as the vehicle left. Inside the building, the soldiers turned Murphy over to three men—two Kempei Tai officers and a black-suited civilian. He recognized one officer, Sergeant Saigo, who staged raids at Sham Shui Po looking for clandestine radios and escape tools. The trio took him to a cell and, handcuffing his hands behind his back, wordlessly began hitting and kicking him. When he was on the floor, writhing in pain, Saigo asked, "Where is the radio?"

"I don't know anything about a radio," Murphy told him.

Saigo kicked him. "We know the men in your barracks have a small radio. They listen to lies on British broadcasts and tell others what they hear. We must know where it is hidden."

"You can beat me to death, and I still won't know. Believe me, I'm telling the truth."

For the next nine hours, Murphy underwent harrowing torture: electric shocks, water immersion, vicious beatings. Toward dawn, he was bundled into a car and driven back to Sham Shui Po. He was barely alive, yet he felt peace of mind. He had not gotten out of the hospital before the battle ended and, consequently, he had never lost the guilt he had harbored about having regarded the war so lightly. Defying the Kempei Tai—and not telling them the British had a radio stashed behind a latrine wall panel—was the bravest thing he ever did. Murphy, the poker-playing ex-announcer, had finally done something he was proud of and in doing it became worthy in his own eyes of calling himself a soldier.

CHAPTER NINETEEN

Hong Kong's rapid fall and the uncertain fate of the surviving soldiers stunned the Canadian populace. What had gone wrong? news editorialists asked. Why had the Canadians failed to put up a longer fight? Ontario Conservative leader George Drew supplied answers. A World War I battery commander who held the rank of lieutenant colonel, Drew said in a 1942 speech:

"At the very last moment a large number of untrained men were attached to the forces. Many gallant young Canadians went into one of the bitterest battles in all history with little knowledge of the weapons they were called upon to use."

His statement sparked a nationwide furor. Private organizations, editorial writers, and Opposition MPs demanded an inquiry, and Mackenzie King, stressing the need for wartime secrecy, agreed to a closed-door investigation. Supreme Court Chief Justice Sir Lyman Duff, a former Liberal party executive, conducted the probe. Questioning Drew and a procession of military officers, Duff released his findings on June 4, 1942. He said "some lack of energy" had regrettably delayed the transporting of vehicles to Vancouver in time for the *Awatea*'s sailing but, in sending the battalions to the Orient, there had been "no dereliction of duty on the part of the Government of Canada or its military advisors." The Chief Justice added that he was privy to top-secret papers and he was certain "nothing emerged before the departure of the expeditionary force which could have been considered to be a justification for the withdrawal by Canada from the responsibilities she had undertaken."

With the dogged obstinacy befitting an old soldier, Drew would not give up his fight. He termed the Duff inquiry a whitewash. Interviewed by reporters, Drew said: "It is almost impossible to believe the summary of the report I have read in the press has any reference whatever to the evidence given before the inquiry that I attended. I am asking the government to make a full disclosure of all inquiry evidence."

Defense Minister Ralston was outraged. Drew, he said, would be prosecuted under a Defense of Canada regulation forbidding utterances liable to prejudice recruiting. If the threatened charge (which never did materialize) was designed to muzzle the Tory leader, it failed. On July 11, 1942, Drew sent King a thirty-two-page letter criticizing Duff's conclusions. King and Drew disagreed on whether or not the letter should be tabled in the Commons. Drew said its contents would show the Canadian people that the military required a drastic overhaul; King said the tabling of information relating to the expedition would aid the enemy.

The Canadian Press news agency acquired a copy of the letter and wired a seventy-five hundred-word partial text across the country. Newspapers were advised not to print it unless it reached the floor of Parliament. All but one paper, the Winnipeg *Tribune*, complied. Publisher Wes McCurdy and editor John Bird deleted material they felt might contravene the secrecy regulations and, on July 17, 1942, the *Tribune* filled nine columns with excerpts. The heavily edited text included these comments:

"The war committee and the general staff knew that an early attack by Japan was possible. They knew that these men might be called upon to fight a desperate enemy at any time. Nevertheless, Canadian units were sent which never had any firing practice with any weapons. And in a war in which vehicles to move weapons are an absolute necessity, they went into action before a single one of their vehicles had arrived in Hong Kong. If that could happen to a small force, what may happen if hundreds of thousands of men are involved unless steps are taken immediately to reorganize the Department of National Defense and the headquarters' staff?"

The King government resolutely rode out the political storm. Neither the *Tribune*, nor the *Toronto Telegram*, which later published the partial text, were prosecuted and, by the winter of 1942, the press and public were more concerned about another military setback involving Canadian troops, the Dieppe fiasco.

Even if they had known of the Drew-Duff controversy, the prisoners would not have cared. Attaching blame would have seemed a futile exercise to starving men. Sergeant Howard Donnelly, cooking for seven hundred Canadians, enhanced the daily rice menu by brewing occasional batches of what the captives called Green Horror Soup—potato peelings, buttercups, carrot tops, and whatever he could scrounge. Sidney Skelton watched the 900-calorie-a-month diet shrink his body from 145 to 89 pounds. And whenever a group of prisoners could bribe a guard into giving them a piece of bread, they used a ruler to ensure everyone got an equal share.

The disease and work-injury toll remained high. Dr. Crawford and others performed surgery on a wooden bench; the few instruments were boiled in the kitchen pots. Chloroform was the only anesthetic, sulfa drugs the principal antiseptic for wounds. One surgeon operated on Rifleman Jimmy Fleming's infected finger with a razor blade; the chloroform was poured on cotton batting in a tomato can with punched holes. On cold nights, rags were stuffed in broken windows to help ease the discomfort of patients who didn't have blankets.

Dr. Crawford eventually learned how to talk his captors into giving him more medicine. "A direct request, however reasonable, was automatically rejected," he said in a postwar debriefing. "Then I discovered that by taking a different tack, and making a personal request, a Japanese officer could be placed in a position where a refusal would result in a 'loss of face.' After I made that intriguing discovery, I conducted all my dealings with the Japanese along those lines."

He learned, too, how to capitalize on the Japanese guards' reluctance to go to their own medical officer, who had them punished for contacting venereal disease. The four-man Canadian medical team treated VD cases in exchange for black-market medicine. A Japanese sergeant eager to improve his English was another source: in return for drugs, Crawford corrected his pronunciation—while the sergeant read aloud scenes from *Romeo and Juliet*.

As for equipment, ordnance corps mechanics stole bits of metal, nuts and bolts, and pieces of wood to manufacture ingenious devices. Their finest creation was a surgical table adjustable to three positions; it had a built-in tiltometer for spinal anesthetics. The mechanics also presented Crawford with an optical perimeter, a sterilizer, a surgical lamp that burned peanut oil, and, for testing vibratory sensations, a tuning fork. The latter was much larger than necessary. It was, in fact, a monstrosity that needed two men to hold it and, when in action, it nearly shook the legs off patients.

In the midst of all the suffering, a crude form of humor blossomed. The antics of a scholarly, absent-minded doctor provided a great deal of amusement. "I've been terribly constipated lately," a soldier told the physician. "My stool is like wood."

"Oh, really?" the doctor said with genuine interest. "What kind of wood?"

That story was told and retold but it did not get half as much mileage as the pin tale. A patient complained of numbness below the waist and the doctor was mapping out the anesthetic area with a pin when he was called away. Returning the next day, the soldier undressed. "I'll be with you momentarily," the doctor said, fumbling in his clothing. "As soon as I find my pin."

"Is this what you're looking for?" the patient said, turning his rear toward him. "You left it in my ass yesterday!"

When work on the Kai Tak airstrip neared completion early in 1943, 650 Canadians were sent to Japan to labor in coal mines, factories, and shipyards. Although some of the jobs involved moving extremely heavy loads by hand, their diets remained the same, a bowl of rice and a cup of water a day. A Canadian sergeant, Charles Clark, won the Distinguished Conduct Medal for risking certain execution and setting fire to a shipyard building: the destruction of equipment and materials reduced production at the site by 60 per cent for eight months.

Four hundred more Canadians were shipped to Japan during 1943. None wanted to go. As harsh as conditions were in Hong Kong, they at least had the hope of escaping overland and finding refuge with friendly Chinese. Then, too, there was the radio. How would they know what was really happening at the front without the BBC broadcasts? The Japanese-controlled *Hong Kong News* had lost what little credibility it may have had when it published a front-page item claiming that Japanese bombers had wiped out the bridge between Vancouver Island and Vancouver.

Grenadier Major Ernie Hodkinson was involved in the dangerous operation of a camp radio. Smuggled into Sham Shui Po piece by piece, the radio was assembled and hidden with another contraband item, a battered typewriter. Hodkinson took shorthand notes of the newscasts' highlights and typed them on a sheet of paper. The paper was surreptitiously passed from hand to hand. The major continued his furtive nocturnal activities even after three other Canadians were implicated in the radio conspiracy and executed without trial.

Their deaths, and the execution of four Canadians captured after escaping from Sham Shui Po, depressed the prisoners. But their spirits rose every time word-of-mouth brought reports of a successful escape. Four Royal Navy officers went over the barbed wire at North Point and, stealing a sampan, paddled to safety on the mainland. Two other North Point prisoners slipped into a manhole and, crawling along a wide concrete drain, emerged on a hill outside the camp; they, too, made it to China in a stolen boat.

Rumor had it that Governor Young had fled the Peninsula Hotel, dressed in a coolie outfit, and was being wined and dined by a rich, beautiful Eurasian lady in a Repulse Bay villa. The truth was less glamorous. Young was transferred to a North Korean camp reserved for top-level military and government officials. As they had at Stanley, the Japanese took delight in placing the once-powerful men in squalid surroundings. Young, two American generals, and the former governor of Malaya were in charge of the camp goat herd and, if an animal went missing or failed to give its milk quota, severe punishment was meted out.

The number of escape stories greatly exceeded the number of actual escapes. Altogether, less than a dozen men broke out of Hong Kong camps and found sanctuary in mainland China. The biggest mass exodus occurred in 1943—and it was through a repatriation agreement, not successful escapes.

Two hundred and fifty people, primarily civilians, were handed over to the Allies in a prisoner exchange. Canadian nurses Kay Christie and May Waters were among those repatriated; so were Gwen Dew and Emily Hahn. Typically, Emily balked at going because she did not want to leave Charles Boxer. But the Japanese convinced her that it would be best for her child. Boxer obtained a divorce after the war and married Emily.

The bulk of the prisoners was released in 1945. Because most of the official records were destroyed during the battle, authorities conducted interviews with participants to get a clearer picture of what had happened. Maltby estimated his over-all casualties, excluding civilians, at 2,000 killed or missing and 2,300 wounded, and he set the Japanese figures at approximately 3,000 killed and 9,000 wounded. Of the 1,975 Canadians who sailed on the *Awatea* and *Prince Robert*, 557 died: 254 deaths occurred in POW camps.

Crossing the Pacific on the *Prince Robert*, the first batch of survivors was greeted by an emotional crowd on a Vancouver pier. Wives embraced husbands; mothers, sons; children, fathers. Hundreds of faces were wet with tears of joy. The Canadians were home, only to find the emotional reaction to their survival did not extend to the government mandarins. They were, in fact, soon to become engaged in another bitter, long-drawn-out fight.

On the morning of April 22, 1947, Sergeant Inouye Kanao faced the bench in a Hong Kong courtroom to hear Chief Justice Sir Henry Blackall pronounce sentence. He was originally charged under a war-crimes statute that had produced a twenty-year sentence for Commandant Tokunaga, but his lawyer argued that the statute did not apply because he was a Canadian citizen. The lawyer's maneuver backfired. The prosecution laid a high-treason charge and, as Inouye stood in the box, fiddling nervously with his tie, Blackall issued a death sentence. Three days afterward, at 7:03 A.M., Inouye was hanged at Stanley Prison.

Like other war veterans, Hong Kong survivors blended into the Canadian mosaic. George Meredith opened an Edmonton barber shop. Ernie Hodkinson joined the staff of a Winnipeg auto parts plant. Kay Christie worked as a nurse for a Toronto psychiatrist. John Fonseca moved to Vancouver and took up journalism. Sidney Skelton found em-

ployment with a Scarborough, Ontario, utilities commission.
Dr. John Crawford became director of medical services with
the Department of Veterans' Affairs in Ottawa. Unlike other
veterans, the Hong Kong survivors had to form their own organization and battle the federal government for medical
and pension rights.

The struggle began practically the day they returned
home. Department of Veterans' Affairs hospitals rejected
many Hong Kongers: doctors had never heard of the rare
tropical diseases some soldiers had contracted and, loath to
admit their own ignorance, the doctors accused men of fak-
ing symptoms and "malingering." Mental problems result-
ing from prolonged captivity elicited a similar response, and
one survivor says a Toronto doctor told him, "You guys are
crybabies. Why don't you act like real men and forget about
the war?"

The Department of National Defense showed the same
degree of compassion. Applying for Pacific Campaign
benefits, the Hong Kongers were awarded fifty dollars
apiece. The department said only the last six months of their
imprisonment counted because the payment system was not
adopted until mid-1945.

In 1947 the Hong Kong Veterans' Association learned
from a sympathetic Member of Parliament that the government was sitting on $15 million in assets seized from Japa-
nese and German sources. As the United States Government
was using similar funds to pay imprisoned American servicemen lump sums, the HKVA asked Ottawa to do the same.
Four years of bitter wrangling followed. The Americans
were paid $1.50 for every day of forced labor, plus an extra
$1 a day for ill treatment. In 1951 the Canadian Govern-
ment agreed to a miserly $1 a day and checks totaling $1,300
were mailed to each survivor. Another eight years of negotiations resulted in Ottawa's hiking the payments by fifty cents
a day.

What the Hong Kongers wanted most of all was 100 per

cent disability pensions. (As of 1978, fifty-one different briefs and submissions over a twenty-eight-year period increased their pensions to 50 per cent, or slightly over $200 a month; only 177 survivors qualify for a full 100 per cent pension, worth roughly $372 a month.) At the core of the Ottawa-veteran dispute was the regulation passed in 1945 requiring a Hong Konger to prove that his disabilities stemmed from wartime experiences. That was an almost impossible task, particularly in cases of emotional stress or late-developing ailments caused by vitamin deficiencies.

Various nonpartisan research projects have supported the veterans' fight. One study disclosed that 25 per cent more deafness and blindness occurred among Hong Kongers than any other group of ex-soldiers. Another survey revealed that Hong Kong veterans have an abnormally high death rate from heart disease and suffer unusually high instances of chronic depression and fatigue. Yet another study, carried out on one hundred sets of brothers, showed that the brother who had been in Hong Kong suffered a significantly greater number of psychological and physical problems than the brother who served somewhere else and was not imprisoned.

Premature aging, muscular defects in the hands and feet, stomach ulcers, and bad dental health are also peculiar to Hong Kong veterans. So are alcoholism, early retirement, and broken marriages.

"There is a direct link between extended physical suffering and bodily malfunctions that occur as much as thirty-five years later," says HKVA executive Howard Donnelly. "What about stress? If a man drinks himself to sleep every night, or has recurring nightmares in which he's back in a prison camp, surely he deserves a better break from the country he served. There are less than a thousand of us left. Every month somebody dies, or I hear he's blind, or he's unable to function in his job. By the time Ottawa recognizes our plight, we'll all be dead."

On a warm spring morning ten years ago, twenty-two Hong Kong veterans gathered in a hillside cemetery overlooking the Crown colony where their comrades fought and perished. A bugler played "The Last Post" and solemnly, reverently, the veterans bowed their heads for two minutes of silence.

When the remembrance ceremony ended, the twenty-two marched down Sai Wan Hill, past rows of squatters' shacks, to a chartered bus taking them to a Canadian consulate reception. Wine and hors d'oeuvres were served and a Canadian government official made a brief speech, praising the colony's heroic defenders. Then came the bitter pill. The Canadian embassy in Tokyo had bowed to Japanese requests regarding the forthcoming appearance of the twenty-two at a war cemetery in Yokohama. They must not wear their uniforms. The firing party must leave its rifles at the airport. And if they wanted to play "The Last Post," the bugle must be taken to and from the ceremony in a bag.

"I'm sure you can appreciate the necessity for these restrictions," the official said. "After all, gentlemen, we don't want to risk offending Japanese sensibilities, do we?"

BIBLIOGRAPHY

Adams, Ian. "For King and Country." *Maclean's Magazine*, July 1968.

Allen, Ralph. *Ordeal By Fire*. Doubleday, Toronto, 1961.

Allister, William. *A Handful of Rice*. Secker & Warburg, London, 1961.

Bateson, Charles. *The War with Japan*. Cresset Press, London, 1968.

Bergamini, David. *Japan's Imperial Conspiracy*. William Morrow, New York, 1971.

Bertram, James. *Beneath the Shadow*. John Day, New York, 1947.

Bloodsworth, Dennis. *The Chinese Looking Glass*. Farrar, Straus & Giroux, New York, 1967.

Bruce, Charles. *News and the Southams*. Macmillan, Toronto, 1968.

Bryant, Arthur. *The Turn of the Tide*. Collins, London, 1957.

———. *Triumph in the West*. Collins, London, 1959.

Butow, Robert. *Tojo and the Coming of the War*. Princeton University Press, Princeton, New Jersey, 1961.

Carew, Tim. *The Fall of Hong Kong*. Anthony Blond, London, 1960.

Carmichael, David. "The Men Who Remember What Hell Was Like." *The Canadian*, January 28, 1967.

Chadderton, Cliff. "The Hong Kong Veterans Story." *The Fragment*, June 1966.

Churchill, Winston S. *The Grand Alliance*. Houghton Mifflin, New York, 1950.

Collins, Robert. "Canada's Most Tragic Christmas." *Star Weekly*, December 23, 1961.

Crawford, John, Dr. "Barbed-wire Humor." *Canadian Medical Association Journal*, Fall 1947.

Dew, Gwen. *Prisoner of the Japs*. Alfred A. Knopf, New York, 1943.

Dobbs, Kildare. "The Canadians Who Came Back from Hell." *Star Weekly*, August 28, 1965.

Elliot, J. G., Major. *A Roll of Honor: The Story of the Indian Army.* Cassell, London, 1965.

Feasby, W. R. *The Canadian Medical Services: Vol. 1.* Department of National Defense, Ottawa, 1956.

Goodspeed, D. J., Lieutenant-Colonel. *The Armed Forces of Canada: 1867–1967.* Canadian Forces Headquarters, Ottawa, 1967.

Goodwin, Ralph. *Passport to Eternity.* Arthur Barker, London, 1956.

Hahn, Emily. *China to Me.* Blakiston, New York, 1944.

Hannon, Leslie. *Canada at War.* McClelland & Stewart, Toronto, 1968.

Howard, Michael. *The Continental Commitment.* Temple Smith, London, 1972.

Hughes, Barry Con. "Still Fighting, Still Losing." *The Canadian,* December 9, 1972.

Ika, Nobutaka. *Japan's Decision for War.* Stanford University Press, Stanford, California, 1967.

Ismay, Lord. *The Memoirs of General Lord Ismay.* Viking, New York, 1960.

Kato, Masuo. *The Lost War.* Alfred A. Knopf, New York, 1946.

Kirby, S. Woodburn, Major General. *Singapore: A Chain of Disaster.* Macmillan, London, 1971.

Leasor, James. *War at the Top.* Michael Joseph, London, 1959.

Lindsay, Oliver. *The Lasting Honour.* Hamish Hamilton, London, 1978.

Lowe, Frank. "Hong Kong 1941: Christmas of Defeat." *Weekend,* December 23, 1961.

Maltby, C. M., Major General. "Operations in Hong Kong, December 8–25, 1941." *London Gazette Supplement,* January 27, 1948.

Okada, Minoru. *After the Violent Storm.* Suzuki and Sata, Tokyo, 1954.

Ommanney, F. D. *Fragrant Harbor.* Hutchinson, London, 1962.

O'Neill, Herbert T. *The War Moves East.* Faber and Faber, London, 1942.

Rivett, Rohan D. *Behind Bamboo.* Angus and Robertson, Sydney, Australia, 1946.

Russell, Lord. *The Knights of Bushido.* Cassell, London, 1958.

Selwyn-Clarke, Sir Selwyn. *Footprints.* Sino-American Publishing Co., Hong Kong, 1975.

Seward, Jack. *The Japanese.* William Morrow, New York, 1972.

Snow, Edgar. *The Battle for Asia.* Random House, New York, 1941.

Stacey, C. P. *Arms, Men and Governments.* Queen's Printer, Ottawa, 1970.

——. *Six Years of War.* Queen's Printer, Ottawa, 1955.

Stanley, George F. G. *Canada's Soldiers.* Macmillan, Toronto, 1954.

Summerlee, Richard. *Asian Conquest.* New Dawn Press, New York, 1958.

Takeo, Ito. *Problems in Occupied Areas of China.* Institute of Pacific Relations, Tokyo, 1941.

Toland, John. *But Not in Shame.* Random House, New York, 1961.

——. *The Rising Sun.* Random House, New York, 1970.

——. *Tokyo Record.* Reynal & Hitchcock, New York, 1943.

Tuchman, Barbara W. *Stilwell and the American Experience in China.* Macmillan, New York, 1971.

Ward, Robert. *Asia for the Asiatics?* University of Chicago Press, 1945.

White, Theodore, and Annalee Jacoby. *Thunder Out of China.* William Sloane, New York, 1946.

Wigmore, Lionel. *The Japanese Thrust: Vol. IV.* Australian War Memorial Society, Canberra, Australia, 1959.

Wingate, Sir Ronald. *Lord Ismay, A Biography.* Hutchinson, London, 1970.

Woodcock, George. *The British in the Far East.* Weidenfeld & Nicolson, London, 1969.

OTHER SOURCES

The material in the Department of National Defense archives in Ottawa is too extensive to list. However, anyone undertaking research into the Hong Kong venture would be advised to study the informative reports of Captain H. A. Bush, Corp. W. R. Pierce, Corporal H. E. Mayberry, medical historian Lieutenant Colonel C. A. R. Gordon and Major G. W. L. Nicholson, as well as the interviews with Drs. John Crawford, Martin Banfill, and Jack Reid, and Lieutenant Colonel W. H. Home. Other intriguing documents include the Crerar-Ralston communiqués, the Royal Rifle and Grenadier war diaries, Colonel John Lawson's personal diary, and the postwar interrogation reports on Japanese officers, including Colonel Shoji and Colonel Tanaka.

Also recommended are the Hong Kong Volunteer Defence Corps' official record of the battle (published by Printrite Press, Hong Kong, 1953) and the 1948 Canadian Jewish Congress book, *Canadian Jews in World War Two.*

INDEX